HORSEMAN, PASS BY

THE AUSTRALIAN LIGHT HORSE
IN WORLD WAR I

by

Lindsay Baly

SPELLMOUNT
Staplehurst

British Library Cataloguing in Publication Data:
A catalogue record for this book is available
from the British Library

Copyright © Lindsay Baly 2003, 2004

ISBN 1-86227-255-7

First published in Australia in 2003 by Kangaroo Press,
an imprint of Simon & Schuster (Australia) Pty Ltd

This edition first published in the UK in 2004 by
Spellmount Limited
The Village Centre
Staplehurst
Kent TN12 0BJ

Tel: 01580 893730
Fax: 01580 893731
E-mail: enquiries@spellmount.com
Website: www.spellmount.com

1 3 5 7 9 8 6 4 2

The right of Lindsay Baly to be identified
as the author of this work has been asserted by him
in accordance with the Copyright, Designs
and Patents Act 1988

Cover photograph: 2nd Brigade, ANZAC Mounted Division (5th, 6th and
7th Regiments) march out from Esdud, Palestine, 1917.
Photo by Frank Hurley, Australian War Memorial B01556

Printed in Great Britain by
St. Edmundsbury Press
Bury St. Edmunds, Suffolk

CONTENTS

O, farewell!

Farewell the neighing steed and the shrill trump,
The spirit-stirring drum, the ear-piercing fife,
The royal banner, and all quality,
Pride, pomp, and circumstances of glorious war! …
Farewell! The colonel's occupation's gone.

John Mortimer: Horace Rumpole in
Rumpole and the Bright Seraphim,
after *Othello* Act 3, Scene 3

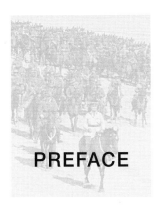

PREFACE

The last Light Horseman of World War I died on 26 July 2002, just short of his 103rd birthday. He was Trooper Albert Ernest Whitmore of the 9th Regiment. His state funeral was at Barmera, South Australia, on 3 August.

They are now beyond our ken. Only my generation knew them well and we are going too, now. I should like to put down what I can recall about one of them, and have learned of others collectively, while I can.

My mother married a Light Horseman after the war, and claimed they were prototypes that stopped with that one breed and were no more. Pressed, she said it had something to do with confidence and a capacity to engage the grand, princely gesture when others might dither. This always seemed a romantic view, but did have its resonances in war. She was a Brisbane flapper in World War I and their hearts fluttered for soldiers, not pop stars; there was no mass media then.

Without radio, our parents entertained themselves by singing and there were clues, if not keys about them, in what they sang. My father's passable baritone would thunder over the washing up:

'You'll know the call,' said the Trumpeter tall,
'When my trumpet goes a-speakin'.
I'm rousing 'em up;
I'm wakin' 'em up,
The tents are astir in the valley,
And there's no more sleep with the sun's first peep,
For I'm soundin' the old ... "Reveille!"'

Mother's untrained contralto delivered 'Drink to Me Only ...', 'The Cornish Floral Dance', 'Father O'Flynn', 'Annie Laurie'. He was all Sir Henry

Newbolt and Kipling, she was restraining, uplifting, refining, in that powerful feminine praxis that has gone out of existence. Dirt poor, we children felt happy and secure on singing nights.

They were both fourth-generation Australians, but on the big issues, fixedly British. They scorned the 'radical' Republican push of the late nineteenth century and had no political aspirations beyond the independent dominion status enjoyed since Federation. This indivisible British-ness lasted until the Korean War: I recall debating it with participants and we concluded that we really didn't know whether we were still British, then.

Yet our parents nevertheless celebrated, even sardonically sometimes, their differences from English and Scottish forebears and 'new chums', though in a cultural/social sense only.

Suddenly:

The bugles of England were blowing o'er the sea,
As they had called a thousand years, calling now to me,
They woke me from dreaming in the dawning of the day,
The bugles of England — and how could I stay?

The Australian poet J.D. Burns wrote himself out of our consciousness so categorically with this that it was last published in 1928.

In 1914 my father heard the bugles in Buenos Aires, having worked his passage there on a promise of painting the ship before he left it. That done, he got a job with the American Meat Export Company, but on the outbreak of war he hurried home to enlist. He brought with him a set of castanets and his colossal Spanish dictionary: *Nuevo Diccionario Enciclopedica Illustrado de la Lengua Castellana*. I still have it.

In the resounding recessional language of the time, now the preserve of sports commentators, the summons had come from the Hub of Empire, the Mother Country, and what Sir Henry Parkes called 'The crimson thread of kinship' that 'runs through us all' would not be severed by this Australian. Being free, white and 'British' he could live up to his own standards only by repairing gladly to his duty with the colours, as his brothers had done before him in the Boer War.

There was another, natural yet darker strand of motivation. In a nutshell, the men wanted to go to war. A male instinct, somewhat smothered in our time, had responded and like Banjo Paterson's stock-horses, they snuffed the battle with delight.

It was a time when Great Britain basked in the height of Victorian achievements, most notably the acquisition of half the globe; when Napier's message, 'Peccavi' (I have Sindh), on his conquest of that Indian province, brought the House of Commons down (it was also the golden age of the pun); and when elderly clubmen would scowl at the boisterous and skittish young members and mutter that they needed some sense knocked into them with a bit of hard campaigning on the Peninsula (Crimean). The rite of passage to be tested under fire was recognised and expected; an approving society pushed and those young men who resisted courted the anonymous white feather, cowardly in itself, indicating cowardice.

In his Official History of the Sinai and Palestine campaign, Sir Henry Gullett devotes a chapter to the Light Horseman's character. He says he was essentially a countryman and refers to a 'spirited rush' to the recruiting stations in every country district: 'Looking back on that throng of great-hearted countrymen riding in to enlist … one ceases to be astonished at [their] war deeds'.

Just fifty slowly changing years earlier, those well-publicised young Americans flocked to the Civil War. Their individual motivation, conviction and impatience to engage great causes, and immoderate naivety would be shared by these Australians — though fortunately not the cinematic cliché of companions at a fork in the road and one turning north, the other south. (They pause, aghast, and ride on.) And something the Australians ponder, but seldom voice is that they are to be measured against centuries of British battle honours, and in that hothouse ethos must not fall short. For their lives.

This story will be understood only if some acquaintance is made with army anatomy. Nowadays, journalists tend to call any army unit a 'brigade', all warships 'battleships' and lump all air force ranks together as 'airman' and without exception they commemorated the death of the last Australian soldier at Gallipoli as the 'last ANZAC'. The whole country followed suit in apparent ignorance that there were a dozen ANZACs still alive — not counting any New Zealanders. They were of course, infantrymen from the Western Front and Light Horseman Whitmore.

A brigade is not a catch-all title for any wandering gaggle of men, but three regiments. The trend needs arresting, before we sink to 'thingummies in one of the services'. Herein, a simple table suffices:

Unit	Manpower	Commander
Mounted regiment	600	Lieutenant Colonel
Brigade (3 regiments)	1800	Brigadier General
Division (3 or 4 brigades and Division's HQ, artillery, engineers, signals, medical, transport etc.)	7–8000	Major General
Mounted corps (2 or more divisions)	approx. 20,000	Lieutenant General

In recent years, an increasing interest in World War I by young people has been well documented and one of my hopes is to stimulate their imaginations with what these particular forebears did three or four generations ago, and what they were like. As time passes, things fade from collective memory, and now remembrance observances tend to centre on Gallipoli — where the Light Horse also served, dismounted.

This book covers a less familiar arena and one of such complex tactics and strategy that there is a risk of merely confusing the reader. These are the necessary scaffolding of the story, but I have constructed it lightly in order that those inner senses may better hear the drumming hooves, the shellbursts and the shouts, feel the quart pot and bayonet scabbard bouncing and banging on the saddle, smell the smoke, see the plains of Palestine rippling like a darksome wheatfield under 20,000 mounted men, and taste the warm and grudging water bottle and the gulped bully beef of a thousand rugged rides.

Imperial and Metric Measurements

All distances, weights and temperatures in this book are given in the imperial measures that were then used in Australia. A conversion chart to metric follows:

Length

1 inch = 25.4 millimetres
1 foot = 0.305 metres
1 yard = 0.91 metres
1 mile = 1.61 kilometres

Weight

1 pound (lb)   = 0.45 kilograms
1 stone (14 lbs) = 6.3 kilograms

Money

12 pence   = 1 shilling
20 shillings = £1
Temperatures of 120–30° Fahrenheit are 49–54.5° Centigrade.

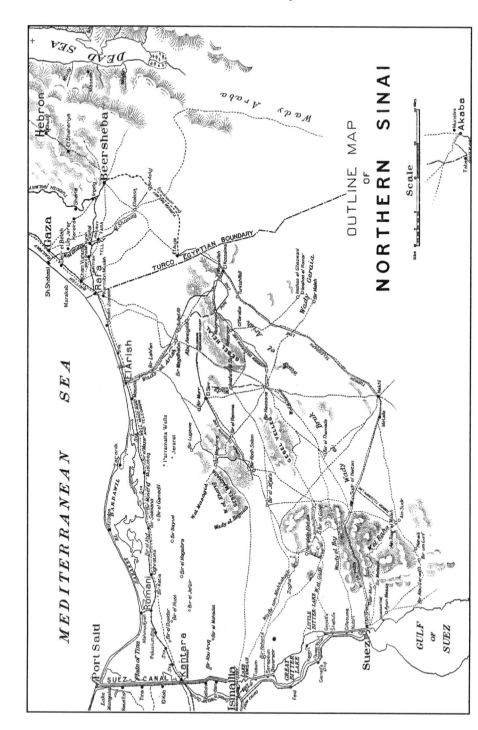

OUTLINE MAP
OF
NORTHERN SINAI

Scale

ONE

Soldier of the King: Egypt

Trooper Byron (Jack) Baly No. 1079 sailed from Sydney in June 1915 as a reinforcement for the 7th Australian Light Horse Regiment, which he seemed to think was in England and that's where he thought he was going. He wrote to his mother from the troopship HMAT *Chilka*, 'an old devil of a boat, very dirty, however am enjoying the trip in spite of a great deal of work with the horses which need attention'. Later, he said there was 'dirty work' to do with horses and later still, when he thinks he has evaded the censor, confides 'they nearly all got strangles in the cold and 7 of them died and had to be taken ashore at Fremantle'.

There was some target practice in the Bight, 'at a floating target in tow behind the ship. My eye and hand have not forgotten their cunning, as 3 bullies [bull's eyes] from a rolling ship at a floating target … out of a possible 5, goes to show.'

He tells his mother, in Colombo they were sent on a route march in heavy winter gear: flannel tunic, breeches, leggings, bandolier, rifle and pack in sweltering heat. Apparently, they had no hot weather kit. He expected

> not many would stick it out, being on the boat so long and out of condition, but only one man knocked up and he had not been well, so it shows the good material of Australians …

Do not know where we are bound, but all now feel we are doomed to Egypt and hoping it will not be so ... two men got cold feet and skipped in Fremantle ... we are better off without them, but the pity of it is there are plenty of men who would give anything to get away.

He was bound for Egypt and writes next from Maadi Camp, on the outskirts of Cairo. We don't know when he learned that his 7th Regiment had gone to Gallipoli, but he first mentions this, and that he is in line to join them, almost as an afterthought in a letter in August 1915:

We are allowed by the Egyptian Government 8½ pence per day in the way of a mess fund and so can have butter, preserved fruit and fish for meals. We are issued a thin khaki shirt, short knickerbockers, puttees and helmets to wear instead of the heavy uniforms. The fellows look like large Boy Scouts. Am glad to be even this far along the road and would not change places with the King of England.

Am glad you are keeping well, you are a brave old Mum and one to be proud of ... We are still in the dark about getting away, they keep sending little batches of men to reinforce our regiment which has been doing splendid work, it is known as the 'Fighting Seventh' ... they are under a very good Commanding Officer, Colonel Arnott, the men swear by him.

Presumably my father does not identify the place name out of security considerations.

In fact, the 7th Regiment had gone in the preceding May. In Egypt, the reinforcements filled in the waiting time with mounted and dismounted drills. They 'taught' Egyptian newsboys English and 'a boy coming along the street will call out, "Egyptian Mail, rotten rag, up to putty, all lies, very good paper, big one". We are not getting much news from the front except from the many wounded arriving every day.' On 25 September he wrote:

we are leaving here for the Dardanelles in the morning. Am very glad to be going. If this is the first you hear of my going you will know that I was not able to send a cable. Tell all the others and give them my love, have not time to write as we have only just been told … and have a lot to do.

Cheer up dear old Mum, am sure we will be all right and you know how glad I am to be here and that my duty will be done. So long Mumsy, lots of love from

Yr. very fond son

Jack.

TWO

Dismounted at Gallipoli

Winston Churchill, then First Lord of the Admiralty, has been blamed by some for the Gallipoli defeat instead of his service advisers. The failure was one of British arms, not politicians.

On 10 August 1914, Turkey, not yet a belligerent but a client state of Germany, allowed the passage of German warships through the Dardanelles into the Black Sea. The Germans made a gift to the Turkish Navy of the two ships, *Goeben* and *Breslau*; and still under German command, they bombarded Russia's Black Sea ports on 29 October, disrupting exports of war material to Britain and France. In response, Russia declared war on Turkey, and Britain and France followed suit a week later. The Russians asked their allies for help to re-establish this valuable supply line and Britain saw advantage in the opening of a successful front against Turkey, not least as relief from the casualties and emerging stalemate of the Western Front.

The Admiralty supported Churchill's idea of a fleet of British and French warships forcing the Dardanelles and bombarding Constantinople into submission with naval guns. The attempt was made in mid-March 1915 and ended in a crushing allied defeat, with shocking losses of ships and men.

There were minesweepers at Gallipoli, but they were converted trawlers, slow and encumbered and, in the face of enemy shore batteries, ineffective. The fleet's attempt to force the Dardanelles was blasted into submission by the mines, and Turkish guns on commanding heights firing down from close quarters. The navy's appreciations and preparations had been faulty. On 25 and 27 May, the battleships *Triumph* and *Majestic* were sunk at anchor by German submarines. Smaller ships patrolled underway. The loss of two capital ships *at anchor*, and only days apart, was avoidable.

If on 25 April the ANZACs had landed on the gentle slopes of their designated beachhead, the campaign would have had a more promising start. However, either a tide had swept the invaders northwards, or some of the warships and transports had anchored in the wrong place. The navy should have studied the tides above all, and to anchor so absent-mindedly was inexcusable.

In the air, the German Taubes, Rumplers and Albatros were superior to the British and French Sopwith Pups, Farmans, Short seaplanes and Nieuports. On land, the British Army sent, with exceptions, second-line and green troops to Gallipoli along with second-line generals. General Stopford's brand new 9 Corps of 25,000 men landed in Suvla Bay on 7 August with the aim of joining the ANZACs the next day for a major summer offensive. But overnight, they dug in on their ground instead, where they were contained by contemptuous Turks.

WHEN NEWS OF THE LANDINGS AT CAPE HELLES AND ANZAC COVE AND THE horrific casualties of the 1st Australian Infantry Division reached the Light Horseman in Egypt, both mounted brigades volunteered their services on Gallipoli dismounted. They were disinclined to leave the horses, but no operational use for them was anywhere in prospect.

The volunteers were snapped up. Brigadier General Harry Chauvel went with his 1st Brigade (1st, 2nd and 3rd Regiments) to Gallipoli on 12 May and the 2nd Brigade (5th, 6th and 7th Regiments) arrived on the 19th. The 3rd Light Horse Brigade (8th, 9th and 10th Regiments) were en route to Egypt, and on arrival were re-equipped as infantry and followed.

So much of the Gallipoli story is about dying well, futilely, and nothing illustrates this better or in greater numbers pro rata than Light Horse casualties during the failed summer offensive of 7 August 1915.

The plan was — still — to take the high ground of the peninsula, from which there would be nothing to stop an advance on Constantinople.

However, all the elements of it were interlinked. It needed precise coordination and luck, but had neither.

The New Zealanders had scaled the craggy heights of Chunuk Bair before, on the first day, and had looked on the gentle hinterland of the Narrows, with its fields and streams, olive groves, mulberry trees and old stone farm houses. No-one else ever saw this vista, and to those confined in burrows on the rough and scrubby headland what lay beyond acquired a grail-like attraction. The New Zealanders were driven off, but now, three months later, they were utterly determined to take Chunuk Bair again. The Australian infantry and Light Horse were to secure the adjacent high ground of the summit and the fresh British 9 Corps were to join up with them from Suvla Bay.

That advance never started and the New Zealanders' assault failed after desperate attempts and intolerable casualties. The Australian infantry divisions' attack on Lone Pine and German Officers' Trench failed to secure the latter.

Chauvel's regiments of Light Horse were required to launch frontal attacks uphill, over bare ground, in daylight, against well-defended entrenchments, in support of the attack on The Nek. The 1st Light Horse Regiment started from Pope's Hill and actually penetrated to the third line of Turkish trenches, but there was never-ending trench after trench beyond. The 1st had suffered 150 casualties out of 200 men and with Chauvel's concurrence, withdrew. At Quinn's Post, the first wave of the 2nd Light Horse Regiment was obliterated, losing 50 of its 55 men within seconds.

Chauvel's two regiments suffered 204 casualties out of 255 men engaged, and Brigadier General Hughes' 3rd Light Horse Brigade lost 362 out of 400 engaged. This was at The Nek.

This story is familiar to us from Peter Weir's film *Gallipoli*, Jack Bennett's novel based on the film script and a body of historical works. The Nek, a ridge of high ground central to the whole operation, was to be taken by the 8th and 10th Light Horse Regiments advancing from Russell's Top, a distance of 400 yards.

In the pre-dawn of 7 August, the 8th (Victoria) and 10th (Western Australia) Light Horse Regiments stood to in their trenches. The softening-up bombardments of the Turkish positions by British artillery and warships commenced on time at 4 am, but stopped inexplicably seven minutes early at 4.23. The Light Horsemen shifted about uneasily. The hitch, delay, was worrying: what did it mean?

At 4.30 am Colonel White of the 8th called 'GO' and led the first line out at a run. He was killed after ten paces. Some of his men fell back shot on the parapets, some made a few yards. In half a minute, not a man was standing. In the seven-minute lull, the Turks had scrambled from their support trenches and saps, manned their firing positions, composed themselves, set their rifle sights and waited. They knew what was coming.

After a two-minute interval, the second line of the 8th launched itself. A survivor recalled passing the clumps of sprawling dead, so they must have pushed a little further before they fell.

It was now the 10th's turn and regimental officers represented that the attack should be called off. But the men had been issued with small red and yellow flags to mark the Turkish trenches and one had been reported: somebody had got there! Perhaps more than one.

The brigade major of the 3rd Brigade, Major J.M. Antill, met the entreaties of Colonel N.M. Brazier of the 10th Regiment with only fierce reiteration of Brigadier General F.G. Hughes' original orders — the attack must go on. Hughes was 57, ailing and not up to it. As Les Carlyon put it in *Gallipoli*: 'Hughes was the brigade commander and he didn't command. Antill wasn't the brigade commander and he did.'

On Antill's orders, the first line of the 10th sprang to their deaths through the dead and wounded of the 8th. Again Colonel Brazier tried to stop the second line but his voice was lost in the uproar of gunfire. The right of the line started off, believing the order had been given — it might have seemed that the colonel, who was shouting something, gave it; no-one knows. Somebody, seeing the right move off, signalled the rest forward. They ran, colliding and stumbling over the heaped bodies, into the storm of fire and were wiped out.

In journeyman's words, the London *Daily Express* trumpeted: 'Unsurpassed in History. Deathless story of Australian Light Horse's Heroic Charge in Great Crisis.' 'Deathless' is unfortunate. The paper says what, but not why. It has been rumoured that two staff officers, one British, one Australian, failed to synchronise watches, but if so no-one was court-martialled; and why did the bombardment start on time?

We fare no better with the more searching aspects of 'why'. Like the Turks, the Australians knew what was coming. Death. In the 10th, brother said goodbye to brother, friend to friend. C.E.W. Bean, official historian and eye-witness, wrote: 'For sheer bravery, devoted loyalty and that self-discipline which seldom failed Australian soldiers, they stand alone in the annals of their country'. He concludes his dispatch with: 'During the long hours of that day, the summit of The Nek could be seen crowded with their bodies. At first, here and there, a man raised his arm to the sky, or tried to drink from his water bottle. But as the sun of that burning day climbed higher, such movement ceased. Over the whole summit, the figures lay still in the quivering heat.'

THE HISTORY OF THE 7TH LIGHT HORSE REGIMENT BY ITS LAST COMMANDING officer, Lieutenant Colonel J.D. Richardson, records my father's arrival at Gallipoli: 'Fortunately, on October 2nd Lieutenants Roberts and Brunton arrived from Maadi with 104 reinforcements'. Fortunately because the regiment was much depleted by evacuations for casualties, dysentery and jaundice.

Two days later, the newcomer wrote:

Everything is OK except cracks and screams and bursts, part of the game. Had a good wash today, the first for 90 hours. We are well fed, considering: jam, condensed milk, good stew once a day, rice, bully beef, biscuits and a little bacon for breakfast. The worst trouble is flies, the worry of our lives.

The trenches are models of cleanliness, different to what one's led to believe, you would not even see a match on the floor. Am very glad to be here, would not have missed it for the world, grim and gruesome mostly, but we make the best of it.

These trenches, around Holly Spur, were dug by the 2nd Brigade in July and August and the new complex became known as (Brigadier) Ryrie's Post. Richardson says: 'The trenches ... were now the show ones of ANZAC and parties of officers from other sections of the line were frequently taken over them'.

Compare this with the trenches at Lone Pine, fifteen feet from the Turks, described by Trooper Ion Idriess of the 5th Light Horse in his diary in September, published post-war as *The Desert Column*: 'the stench is just awful, the dead men, Turks and Australians are lying buried in the sides of the trench and built up into the parapet or half-buried in the trench bottom, maggots are falling into the trench now … the sun warms them … it is beastly … a dead man's boot on the firing possy has been dripping grease on my overcoat and the coat will stink forever. The roof of this dashed possy is intermixed with dead men who were chucked up on the parapet to give the living a chance [protection] from bullets while the trench was being dug.'

A terrified young reinforcement whose job was to smother with sandbags any Turkish bombs (grenades) thrown into the trench was violently ill watching Idriess trying to eat a biscuit and jam: 'I wrapped my overcoat over the tin and gouged out the flies, spread the biscuit, held my hand over the tin, drew the biscuit out of the coat. But the flies flew into my mouth and beat about inside. Finally I threw the tin over the parapet. I nearly howled with rage.' And a few yards from his periscope is a freeze-frame of some vile video game from Hades: 'The Australian's bayonet is sticking, rusty and black, six inches through the Turk's back. One hand is gripping the Turk's throat, while even now, you can see the Turk's teeth fastened through what was the boy's wrist. The Turk's bayonet is jammed through the boy's stomach and one hand is clenched, claw-like, across the Australian's face.'

At Lone Pine and at Quinn's Post, men went mad. Bean said a watch in these places was equivalent to being in constant action for 24 hours. After a frightful night in which Turkish mortar bombs and .75 shells razed Idriess' parapet to the ground and blew up burst sandbags, baulks of timber and odds and ends of dead men that came back 'plop, whack, plop, into the trench', during which 'we simply crouched, partly dazed and I kept firing and firing, there was nothing else to do', they are relieved. Idriess continues: 'At last the man behind me whispered "File off!" I stuttered the word on and we pressed, man against man, shivering in the hope that soon we would be under some sort of cover. Apparently some new recruits were not moving, backing up and tending to block the trench.' Then:

> we saw hissing sparks flying over the parapet — a choking cry,
> 'Bomb! Bomb! Christ!'
> I tried to jump back but the … new hands didn't know what to do. Poor old King … jumped forward but the men ahead crouched … the trench was blocked. King was on a slight incline … the hissing thing rolled horribly towards him. I threw my overcoat over it,

clenched my arms across face and stomach and pressed desperately back against the men behind. Then all was a suffocation of deathly fumes — I was on my back, quite distinctly hearing the clash of bayonets as rifles thumped across me. Then followed a strange, dull silence, ears ringing like mad. King called out, 'I'm wounded, boys.' I called out, 'So am I, Kingy' and struggled up.

No-one writes to mothers about such things, but my father refers to them in abstract: 'if one were to see at home what we see here, it would prey on the mind for a long time, but we just look and pass by, thinking nothing of it … otherwise, we could not stand it'.

In fact, he had an easier time of it than those who had fought through the summer. Richardson calls the campaign from September to December the last phase. However, the worst winter for many years was breaking. On 27 November a Turkish attack was repulsed, twenty of them killed by the 7th Regiment, and the next day, Richardson notes, 'a great rain storm and blizzard took place … the snow gently covered the bodies in front of the trenches'.

My father said it was getting horribly cold and what about sending him a new pipe, lest his only one should be commandeered for use against the Turks as gas; and what about inviting the Turks to play the next half of this match in Australia. He adds, 'Jacko is a pretty fair fighter and has a lot in his favour'. He could be exasperatingly cheerful in bad times. There was disruption to food and water supplies because lighters could not berth at the piers, there was little wood for cooking fires and none for heating. The weather remained severe right up to the evacuation.

It seems likely that the despairing reality of stalemate was now affecting at least the old hands, whose physical and mental fibre must have been fraying. All minds must have been turning to getting out, though with sad contrition at leaving the dead, somebody said, 'Do you think they will hear us?' It is well known and accepted that the secret withdrawal of all British forces on the peninsula on the nights of 18 and 19 December was brilliant of organisation and miraculous of execution: and my father's and Colonel Richardson's accounts of it reflect that, but add nothing new.

The Light Horsemen reassembled at Maadi and for the time, with the resilience of youth and resumption of mounted work, put Gallipoli behind them.

Horror Revisited

It is 1996. A thin old voice quavers on the airwaves: 'I can't sleep, I get no rest. I shot these Japanese prisoners. I was supposed to escort them to the rear, but I didn't want to go back. We got to thick jungle and I took them off the track …' and the voice breaks. The talkback host cuts in:

'Oh, that must have been terrible. We didn't want to stir up such memories. Unless it helps, you want to tell us?'

The veteran says, 'I want just to get it off my back …' The voice breaks down completely, he can't go on.

There was a small spate of such confessions, triggered by a debate over war crimes, theirs and ours. Mercifully it was short-lived.

When wars are over and the men come back, they gladly and gratefully throw themselves into work and raising families, and for most of their busy lives think they have driven out the demons. But, they are still there. They are just waiting.

Patsy Adam-Smith, in *The Anzacs*, records a woman speaking about her father revisiting trench warfare in France: 'He has begun to wake in the night crying and it seems he hasn't forgotten one sight he saw or any sound he heard. By his cries in the night, the sounds and sights must have been unendurable.' Another veteran of the Western Front told the author, 'We thought we kept the awful things out of our minds, but now I'm an old man they come out from where I hid them every night'. Those demons drove many to alcoholism (Idriess), some to suicide (my father).

The World War I and II veterans had little assistance, and counselling lay in the future. Some were beyond it anyway, such as the ex prisoner-of-war and survivor, one of six, of the Sandakan death march. In his last tragic days, he walked around outside his house at night, shouting and cursing at shadows he took to be his Japanese torturers. 'Nishimura, you bastard! Get away from me! Nagasawa, come out where I can see you. I'm going to kill you.'

In 1984, Ronald Conway described in *The End of Stupor*, 'Those boozy old World War I diggers [whose] sad, rheumy old eyes have been once bright with adventure. Even [their] arrogant alcoholic chauvinism ("When did *you* ever fight for your country, mate?") was understandable. Perhaps no company of young men in modern history endured so much in time of war with less complaint … and been rewarded by experience of comparable horror.'

We who look back on long lives serenely lived, have so many reasons to be thankful.

THREE

Mounted in Sinai

Warfare on horses was in a state of slow transition. There were still classic cavalry regiments, mostly Indian, armed with swords and lances, but since the Sudan and the Boer War it had been recognised that, with developments in the fire power of artillery and machine-guns, cavalry charges could not be expected to prevail against entrenched positions. It could still be done, notably, but not exceptionally, by the ANZACs, for example at Katia and Beersheba, but the concept of mounted infantry had been universally adopted. In this, the horse became simply a means of rapid transport for patrolling, reconnaissance and, especially, transporting the fighting man in relatively fresh condition to where he was needed to fight on foot. Such were the British Yeomanry, the Australian Light Horse and the NZ Mounted Rifles. They had the big disadvantage that, in action, one man in every four had to be out of the firing line as a horse holder, but this was the necessary price. After Gallipoli, the ANZACs concentrated on their infantry drills just as much as practising mounted dispositions for attack and defence, outpost schemes and the manoeuvring of led horses.

Camp life was safe and comfortable, yet with it came a return to the army's exasperating insistence on what some thought irrelevancies: parades, proper dress and deportment, saluting officers, polishing stirrup irons (the chlorine tablets for purifying the water were good for that). They soon grew impatient, and envious of their infantry compatriots from Gallipoli, now enjoying the fancied attractions of France and England, while they stayed in Egypt training. No-one knew that the infantry would be trapped for years in worse trench warfare than Gallipoli and that their casualties and suffering would be of a much higher order. They just knew the infantry were in action again — and going to England on leave. As volunteers, they felt entitled to grumble, if there's fighting to be done, let's do it and go home.

There was fighting to be done.

Now that a huge Turkish army was freed from the Peninsula, the British considered what it might do next. Like the Pharaohs, Alexander the Great and Napoleon, the Turks had crossed the Sinai Desert before, lured by the Nile Delta, and obviously this possibility arose again. Accordingly, the British deployed their 5th Mounted (Yeomanry) Brigade on a line of outposts 22 miles east of Suez, centred on the biggest oasis in the area, Romani. Their responsibility was to give early warning of a Turkish advance and to resist it.

At the same time, the ANZAC Mounted Division was formed under Chauvel, then a major general. It consisted of the 1st, 2nd and 3rd Light Horse Brigades, together with the New Zealand Mounted Rifle Brigade (Auckland, Wellington and Canterbury Regiments) and the supporting Royal Horse Artillery Brigade (Inverness, Ayrshire and Somerset Batteries). The division was based at Salhia, a large green oasis to the west side of the canal.

On 22 April 1916, the 5th Mounted Brigade were routed by just what they were there to prevent: a Turkish surprise attack. The survivors fell back to the canal and the next day the 2nd Light Horse Brigade were ordered to Kantara, Duedir and Romani by forced march, to retrieve the position. A long doggerel poem of my father's, much prized by his fellows and his family, says:

We knew no destination or what might come about.
But guessed there's something doin' by the way we hustled out.
We headed for Kantara and pushed on all that day
Till 9 pm, while halting, tucked some bully beef away.

We rode across the Suez by the pontoon bridge that night,
And kept on making eastwards until dark gave way to light.
And late that night, still riding, we learned what was our mission:
Wounded men on Red Cross cars explained the whole position.

Small, straggling groups of horsemen were also making back.
The Turks had caught 'em napping and they'd taken to the track.
We questioned, as we passed them, 'What's up? Abdul scooped the pot?'
Their answer, coming wearily, 'Aye, chum. We've 'ad it 'ot!'

This was it. Forget France and England, this was the big one. This was what they were for.

The Yeomanry camps told their stories. There were dead men and horses, the occasional one still dying. Stragglers and wanderers, horses stampeding in at the scent of water. Small heaps of cartridge cases beside individuals who had burrowed in the sand and fought to the death. Others were bayoneted through their blankets. Too much of a good thing in beer and wine for officers' messes. Men tortured by Bedouins, garrotted with the thin baling wire used for horse fodder. The Bedouins had hung around the camps cadging food, pretending to be friendly, spying for the Turks; then they killed and stripped the soldiers, crying 'Finish British! Turks Kantara! Turks Port Said! Turks Cairo!' ANZAC policy, made then and never relaxed, was to treat them as hostile. The 6th and 7th Regiments buried 80 Yeomanry at Katia, then eight days later another 300 corpses were found. The only outpost that had held out was at Duedir, twelve miles from the canal, the most insignificant, and the only one manned by infantry: 100 Royal Scots Fusiliers.

For nearly three months, the 2nd Brigade searched for Turks on the Sinai front by ceaseless reconnaissance from the meagre wells and scant palm hods of Romani. It was strenuous work in high summer, one day in May climbing to 126° Fahrenheit according to Gullett (my father said 128), on short rations, short water and short sleep. The Yeomanry's scattered camps at separate oases had been overrun piecemeal, and while the ANZACs evaded that trap by concentrating at Romani they paid a price in long, gruelling rides. Two were full-strength, overnight sorties to Bir el Abd, 25 miles away:

A silent march we stole that night across the moonlit sand,
Expecting that the dawn would find us fighting hand to hand,
But the Turks had smelt us coming, for when we reached the place,
We found an empty firing line, of Abdul not a trace ...

They were in the saddle for 27 almost unbroken hours.

At times, there might be just sections of four men scouting locally, and there were also night listening outposts and 'Cossack posts' —four men to resist any Turkish advance, then jump on their horses and gallop back with intelligence — to provide, and a stand-to for all ranks at 3 am each day. Then when the exhausted troopers could snatch a few hours off, many found sleep impossible because of the heat and flies. Yet there were wild swings of temperature between day and night, and men on outpost duty at night suffered from the cold.

The colonel of Idriess' 5th Light Horse Regiment introduced the Queensland spear-point pump into the desert. This pointed, perforated tube could be hammered into the sand and draw water in under a quarter hour, whereas it took two men half a day's work to reach it by digging. The water was brackish, fit only for horses, and at first they wouldn't drink it, but grew to tolerate it.

Idriess writes:

May 15. The sun rose, a ball of quivering fire, hurrying from the east, a wind straight from a furnace. The horses bent their heads and gasped ... I think this is the most hellish wind I've experienced. It sears through the oasis, through our blanket shelter and scorches our naked bodies ... some of B Squadron collapsed after yesterday's patrol. They had a terrible trip ...

I walked out in the sun ... and the burning wind seemed actually to strike me. The leather of our boots is shrinking from the blazing sand ... One of our officers has been sent away with sunstroke.

My father said the khamsin blew through the camps in fierce, burning whirlwinds, sending showers of dust, chaff and dry manure in the tents, in the food, down breeches and shirts and 'A trip to France would be quite the thing, freshen the fellows up mentally and physically. They have had too much desert, tired and losing interest in many ways, becoming irritable and fighting with one another, a bad sign, especially among Australians, who normally hit it off A1 together.'

One early morning the 6th Regiment and the Canterbury Regiment (NZ) rode south from Romani on reconnaissance, each man carrying one quart water bottle. The temperature rose to 126 degrees by 10 am. The men had already exhausted their water bottles and, together with their horses, were in extreme distress. The reconnaissance completed, the regiments withdrew out of the sun to a hod and rested under the palms, but the water there was foul and the wells had to be picketed by guards with fixed bayonets to prevent their distraught companions drinking. A disaster was averted by the forethought of medical officers at Romani who, apprehensive about the soaring temperature, had a number of ambulance camels loaded with fantasses (small copper or tin tanks) of water and accompanied them out to succour the column. En route, they met semi-conscious stragglers making towards Romani with their exhausted horses.

Some of the men lay comatose for hours. Sand carts were brought out to them and no lives were lost, but over 50 men had to be evacuated to hospital and 500 horses remained sick for some time. In Cairo the Commander-in-Chief, General Sir Archibald Murray, already appraised of the ANZACs' quality ('the only really reliable mounted troops I have'), signalled to Chauvel that he did not think any other troops could have undertaken the operation successfully 'in the present weather'.

After that, most men got hold of an extra water bottle and all possible marches were made at night. It was found that if troops still dependent on one bottle could keep it in reserve until their objectives had been reached — possibly not until noon the next day and probably including a battle — they fared better than those who drank their water early and had no more to look forward to.

According to Gullett: 'Some idea of the strain of that summer on the horsemen may be gathered from the fact that between 70 and 80 per cent of the Australians developed temporary heart trouble'.

The Turks, on the other hand, had tougher constitutions and accepted the greatest privations as a matter of course. They drank contaminated water, scavenged for the poorest of food and lived in camps of extreme squalor and offensiveness with apparent impunity. Such conditions should have been a liability, but their ability to surmount them turned to a positive advantage.

After their surprise attack on the Yeomanry, the Turks had withdrawn 20–25 miles east of the Suez Canal. Then, having sized up their new ANZAC opponents, they began to move closer. They hid from British aircraft in the palms by day and moved by night. The ANZACs demonstrated, trying to draw them into battle while denying them the Romani water. Each side was feinting, seeking favourable terms to engage the other. As time passed, the tempo gradually increased and the occasional sighting of a Turkish patrol would be accompanied by shots, then hit-and-run skirmishes. The horsemen sought to draw the dogged Turkish infantry on to Chauvel's prepared ground.

Typical of this phase, a squadron of the 7th Regiment blundered onto a superior force of enemy concealed by dunes and sparse bushes. The Turks snatched at their bridles, and opened a heavy fire as the Australians galloped away. But their shooting was inclined to be wild when they were surprised and the squadron was unscathed. On another day, another squadron of the 7th under Major Richardson (later colonel and author of the 7th Light Horse history), came across a superior force of Turks in the same way. The squadron broke away for two or three hundred yards, dismounted and fired at the Turks; then as they advanced, mounted, rode away and again dismounted to await the still oncoming enemy. This was repeated several times, at one halt the Australians boiling up their quart pots for tea as the Turks toiled up to them.

By late May, the 1st and 3rd Brigades of the ANZAC Mounted Division had joined the exhausted 2nd, and with the advance of railhead from the canal the 52nd (Lowland Scottish) Infantry Division was deployed at Romani. But Brigadier Antill's 3rd Light Horse Brigade had by then been positioned over twenty miles to the south-west of Romani at Bally Bunion — imaginatively named for just another indistinguishable speck in the waste of sand — to guard against a Turkish left-flanking movement around Romani. On the eve of battle, Chauvel made the dismaying calculation that he could put only 1600 dismounted riflemen in the firing line. The 2nd Brigade regiments were under strength and over 500 horse holders had to be found.

Then the British contingent, under General the Hon. Sir H.A. Lawrence (not to be confused with Lieutenant Colonel T.E. Lawrence of Arabia) consisted of the 52nd Scottish Division, not yet tested in Sinai but energetic and of a renowned fighting race, and two battalions of the 42nd

Division (East Lancashire) Territorials. Both these divisions had had experience at Cape Helles on Gallipoli, and on the mounted side they were augmented by the refurbished 5th Mounted (Yeomanry) Brigade, which should at least have been looking to salvage its reputation. On the eve of Romani, General Murray signalled his assessment to the War Office: 'infantry fair, cavalry good'.

The Turks were expected to deploy 12,000 to 14,000 rifles against a British 10,000, all up.

FOUR

Fighting for Romani

Romani is a large complex of wells and sand dunes clustered together. All the armies of the Pharaoh Thothmes III, Alexander, Napoleon and modern great captains have used it for staging across the desert and have fought for it. On his final reconnaissance before the battle, Chauvel renamed the big sand dunes on and around which he preferred to fight — leaving to the Turks the job of surmounting the deep and yielding sand on foot. He christened Mount Meredith (230 feet) and its ridge stretching to the north-east Wellington Ridge, and Mount Royston (220 feet). He left Katib Gannit (226 feet), the most northerly dune its original name. Between the dunes ran narrow, upward-sloping lanes to the rear and, winding in and out as they came and went, these were the paths taken by soldiers probably from the earliest times. Of course, the Turks appreciated this, but what they did not know in this instance was how these lanes were defended.

In the fortnight preceding the battle, day and night patrolling and probing, making and breaking contact with advancing Turks, had reached such a pitch that a trial of strength was the only logical outcome and indeed came to assume a predestined status. The 1st and 2nd Light Horse Brigades were taking alternate day and night watches to man the contracting ring of listening posts and Cossack posts around Romani and provide the large and small patrols and reconnaissances in force. They knew, and confirmed afresh each day, how and where the enemy was closing in, and each day the contacts were more aggressive, the exchanges of fire more intense. In this sense, there was a piecemeal commitment to the Battle of Romani, but there did come a starting point for its culminating three days.

On the night of 3 August 1916, the 2nd Brigade returned to Romani from reconnaissance and observed faintly a longer line of men following them. One shot sounded, then two more, then silence.

The 2nd Brigade was allowed to proceed to their camp at Etmaler, three miles in rear of the Light Horse and infantry lines. They were coming off duty, to be in reserve, and Chauvel knew he would need them fresh in the morning. The 1st Brigade manned their firing positions, shallow trenches in the sand commanding the inlets to the narrow gullies sloping up to Wellington Ridge. This was the essential feature to hold, because it overlooked the whole British position and if the enemy gained it, that advantage would be reversed. The 52nd Infantry Division also stood to in their line, on the Light Horse's left, running to the north a full six miles to the sea.

Where would the Turks strike? They chose dead centre of the Light Horse line.

At 1 am came the Turkish battle cry — 'Allah! Allah! Finish Australia!' — and heavy firing, but no proper targets could yet be seen by either side. The Australians returned fire at rifle flashes. In the fantastic play of flashes and jumping shadows up and down the dunes, they had no idea what the Turks were doing and with hammering hearts and straining eyes and ears, prayed for daylight. This phase was a trooper's battle of individual responses, with such command and control as could be exercised falling on troop leaders.

The Light Horse line was not continuous, but was more accurately a series of posts in close touch. It was appreciated early that the thin, scattered line must be penetrated under such ferocious attack, though no breach could be seen. At 2 am Lieutenant Colonel G.H. Bourne of the 2nd Regiment ordered his right flank squadron to go to his left and support the left flank squadron which was fighting for its life, but such movement over the yielding, sloping sand was strenuous and slow and Bourne also committed his last squadron in reserve to support the left. The line held, but the Turks increased the pressure below Mount Meredith: they took their boots off to scale the sandhills better and came on in overwhelming numbers. However, as Gullett noted, 'the old Gallipoli spirit was aflame again and every man resolved that the Turk, if he did gain ground, must pay a heavy price for it'. Each individual knew that the security of the whole British force was in his hands.

At 2.30 am, there was a terrible howl and 8000 Turks charged up the slope with fixed bayonets. The moon had set, the darkness was unrelieved, but the massed humanity gave the Australians an almost point-blank target ahead and large numbers of shot Turks just rolled back down again. Still, the Light Horse could not guard against flank attacks and by 3 am it was clear that they were being encircled and the Turks were gaining on Mount Meredith. The 1st Regiment, which had been held in reserve, was poised on the crest and fired down on them with great effect, but suffered badly itself and by 3.30 had been forced back to their led horses.

When Bourne gave the order to withdraw the Turks were even then closing on the Australians' horses with fixed bayonets and so close was the fighting that four troopers were simply engulfed by the enemy and made prisoners. A big Queenslander, thinking to hoist a wounded comrade up behind his saddle, discovered halfway up that the fellow was a Turk. The Australians broke away mounted, carrying their wounded.

Bourne had already selected a reserve position on the ridge behind. There is no more severe test of discipline and moral fibre than galloping away from such a storm of bullets crouched on a good horse (Bourne wrote the bullets were making little spurts of flame all round them, caused by phosphorus in the sand) than for an individual to obey an order to halt, dismount, hand over his very means of escape, face about and put himself through the same ordeal he had just got away from. With military understatement, Bourne said, 'the question arose in our minds as we rode, "Can we re-form?" The order "Sections about — Action front" was given as we reached the position and was splendidly carried out. This high test of discipline gave us renewed confidence.'

The 3rd Light Horse Regiment conformed to the 2nd's actions and the two regiments scraped out their holes in the sand again to re-engage the Turks. But once more, they could only delay: a machine-gun on Mount Meredith swept them and first light disclosed the enemy in such masses that, while they offered a target at close range, the Australians' slender line must be smothered. Then the outflanking recommenced: large numbers of enemy on the right half-circled the whole brigade and were enfilading the led horses: time to go again. Troop after troop of Light Horsemen backed slowly up the slope covering each other, onto Wellington Ridge. They lost more killed and wounded but dug in quickly in undulating ground that offered good protection. But the Turks opened fire with artillery, sweeping the line on the ridge with shrapnel, at once effective. Neither side had ventured to use its artillery in darkness, but now the Light Horsemen expected their own to reply, though it did not for some time. Reluctantly facing the prospect of yet another withdrawal, at 4.30 am the men were overjoyed to see the 2nd Brigade cantering to their support, led from the camp at Etmaler by no less than Chauvel himself on his little chestnut mare. The 1st Brigade held on.

Chauvel was not worried. The battle was going quite as he had foreseen and planned for. He knew he could trust his two veteran brigades, if not to hold their ground literally under the onslaught, at least to give it up grudgingly and at greater expense to the Turks. His confidence in leaving the 1st Brigade unsupported overnight so that the 2nd would be fresh for the day's work had been justified. A hot and waterless day lay ahead for the Turks, whose momentum must falter, and while the ANZACs held the wells it must in measurable time stop. In that sense, time was on the British side.

The immediate danger, however, was a new advance of the Turkish left flank, to drive in between Etmaler and Mount Royston and threaten the railhead just west of the British position. Chauvel ordered Brigadier General J.R. Royston, temporarily commanding the 2nd Brigade while its regular commander was on leave in England, to send the 6th and 7th Regiments in on the 1st Brigade's right and block this flanking movement.

The 6th and 7th dismounted a mile from the Turks and advanced in a long and vulnerable line. They were heavily enfiladed, but the enemy's machine-gun fire was awry and his shrapnel burst too high and fell behind them.

The battle swung in the balance for an hour. By that time the heat was already fierce, the Turks were thirsty and exhausted from their night of forced marching up sandhills. They were also denied the possession of Wellington Ridge, which they had expected to gain six hours earlier, and British artillery had at last opened fire on them to good effect.

But their flanking movement to the west was still making headway. Provided the Light Horse could save the railhead and the water at Etmaler, it was best that they give ground rather than risk hand-to-hand encounters, for such odds against them could destroy them; and every hundred yards the Turks advanced brought them nearer defeat.

The Turks rushed the lower slopes of Mount Meredith and found cover at the foot of Wellington Ridge, 300 yards from the Light Horse line. The 7th Regiment in particular took heavy punishment and continued to give ground under sustained shrapnel, machine-gun and rifle fire. At 7 am, the Turks took the ridge. The 1st Brigade was withdrawn to near Etmaler camp and resistance to further Turkish progress fell on the 3rd, 6th and 7th Regiments and the Wellington Mounted Rifles, all of which fell back slowly by alternate squadrons. As always, wounded were carried back with them over the heavy sand.

The Turks did not properly exploit their possession of Wellington Ridge owing to exhaustion. They were within 700 yards of Etmaler camp and water, and if they had pressed on the crisis point of the battle would have been reached. But by the time they showed themselves above the ridge line, British artillery was ranged and waiting and swept them off it, and kept them off it.

The battle no longer raged. Between 10 and 11 am the Wellington Mounted Rifles (there had been a swap: the 5th Light Horse Regiment was temporarily with the NZ Brigade, *vice* the Wellingtons with the 2nd Australian Brigade) were disposed with the Light Horse regiments across the whole front and it became stationary. It was now beyond doubt that unless the Turks attacked again with great vigour, their enterprise must fail. And the only sustained activity they seemed capable of now was artillery and machine-gun fire.

Chauvel saw a cavalry opportunity. If he could get his Light Horse Brigades out of the line and mounted, he could swing round the flank of the enemy and join up with the New Zealanders and the 5th Yeomanry Brigade (under General E.W.C. Chaytor coming in from Hill 70) in a general enveloping attack. If such a movement succeeded, and he could not envisage any factors suggesting it would not, the whole Turkish force would be 'yarded' immobile and the fighting immeasurably curtailed.

He sent a staff officer to the nearest brigade commander of the 52nd Infantry Division to explain this plan and request the brigade relieve his troops in the line so that their horses could be watered and the operation launched. The 52nd Brigade commander said he must take his orders from his own general, who was planning a counterattack eastwards himself 'when the proper moment arrived', for which the particular brigade was in reserve. No action had yet come the 52nd's way.

Chauvel had no alternative but to accept the reply, as his only avenue of appeal was to the British General Lawrence in overall command, who against advice had established himself 25 miles away at Kantara and the telephone line to him had been cut by enemy agents. But how sick at heart Chauvel must have been to see his own 'proper moment' slip away as the day advanced, and his superb troopers still bogged down as infantry while no infantryman proper had yet fired a shot. The 52nd remained at its posts right away from the Turkish attack.

This lesson on the hazards of divided command was not lost on the ANZACs, but took some time to permeate through the British hierarchy.

Soon after, the beleaguered troopers were heartened to see General Chaytor's New Zealanders and the Gloucester Regiment of British Yeomanry canter in, dismount and take Mount Royston, recently occupied by 2000 Turks.

It was 6 pm and the long hot day was closing. The Turks held not one well, and what they would eat that evening could not be imagined, whereas the ANZACs in their line were served tea by the gallant 2nd Brigade cooks from their bullet-riddled kitchens at Etmaler camp.

Whose plan it was is not recorded, but overnight the troopers prepared themselves mentally and physically for a bayonet charge in the morning.

FIVE

Moving off:
Katia and Bir el Abd

There was nothing resembling rest that night. After fighting until dark, the two ANZAC brigades stood to with particular watchfulness, aware that a long line one man deep is too easily penetrated by stealth. The horses were to be fed and watered, ammunition, water, rations and orders issued for the next day, and, highest priority of all, wounded to be evacuated. No officers closed their eyes and troopers snatched only odd minutes of unconsciousness.

Casualties had been heavy, the hospital tents were overcrowded and the wounded lay under the cold stars, with the lanterns of medical officers and orderlies moving among them. Surgeons worked in tents deep in the palm hods to the accompaniment of bursting shells, pattering shrapnel on the palm leaves and the whine of 5.9s passing over towards railhead. But it was accepted that any shells falling among the wounded were accidental: only days before, a German aircraft dropped a note right at the entrance to Chauvel's tent asking the troops to mark their ambulances more clearly in order not to be bombed. As at Gallipoli, the Turks had so far respected the Red Cross scrupulously.

ANZAC responsibility for the wounded ceased on delivery to the railhead at Etmaler and the tardiness and inefficiency of their further evacuation was unacceptable. One consignment of wounded lay under fire and under the blistering sun all morning while an empty train lay in the siding, and despite the protests of medical officers the train was eventually used to take Turkish prisoners to the rear. The Light Horsemen were taken to Kantara in trucks, the journey of twenty-three miles taking up to fifteen hours in some cases. These wounded were without attendants and a number who could have been saved, died. At Kantara hospital, there were still no attendants or food. Strong protests led eventually to an enquiry and 'some improvements'.

Orders for 5 August 1916 were to attack vigorously at first light with all forces. At 4 am, the 1st and 2nd Light Horse Brigades, with the infantry on their left cooperating, leapt from their long irregular line and advanced with the bayonet. On their right, the enemy offered little resistance, and after firing a few shots everywhere surrendered, but in the centre, opposite the 7th Light Horse Regiment and the Wellingtons, the Turks fought hard. The ANZACs rushed a hod with their bayonets and overwhelmed a party of Turks. They paused for breath, then Lieutenant Colonel G.M.M. Onslow of the 7th and three men charged forward again: all were shot down by concealed Turks almost underfoot and Onslow was severely wounded, but the two regiments were on their heels and swept over the top of Wellington Ridge and down onto the main body of Turks assembled below. 'Gaunt from prolonged sleeplessness,' wrote Gullett, 'their eyes bloodshot from glare and strain, their faces begrimed with dust and sweat and bristly with a few days' growth of beard, the Australians and Wellingtons might have unnerved troops in better condition than the unfortunate Turks opposed to them.' And they wilted facing bayonets, shot wildly, and as these apparitions reached them, surrendered.

It was the turning point: Turks began surrendering all along the line with expressions sounding like the Turkish equivalent of 'Thank God'. They were waterless and had only green dates to eat. However, some, presumably in better shape, retreated in haphazard fashion towards Katia, the nearest oasis six miles further east.

There could be no savouring of victory for the two ANZAC brigades who, having born the brunt of the whole battle, had to immediately resume their cavalry role in hot pursuit of retreating Turks. By 6.30 am they had re-assembled, but as the temperature was climbing to another day of murderous heat, it was decided to water the horses again. This took longer than usual in the disordered base and it was not until 10 o'clock that the 1st and 2nd Brigades were mounted and moving on Katia.

The 52nd Infantry Division was closest to Katia and had been ordered to march out early before the heat of the day, but it did not start until 9 am and had made little progress by 2 pm. Chauvel's chances of taking Katia with just his tired and depleted mounted brigades were thereby reduced.

What went wrong with this division is not clear, though its own General Officer Commanding said his men were 'undersized and quite incapable of sustained effort'. Since they appeared hardy enough and later won a staunch reputation in Palestine, they seem to have been nursed at Romani and not well-led.

My father missed the Battle of Romani, in which his regiment played such a prominent part. He was in hospital in Cairo with 'general debility'. 'Don't be alarmed, nothing serious,' he wrote to his mother. 'Am in off the desert for a spell, was run down and in need of rest. Left camp a week ago, stopped at Port Said in a British hospital for 2 days, came down here yesterday [to No. 3 Australian General Hospital] and I think the next move will be to England for 2 or 3 months … It is a treat to be clean again, and rid of the dirty old desert clothes I have worn continually for 7 months.'

Then on 3 August he wrote:

No doubt you will have received cable saying I was going to England for a spell. Well, while waiting for the boat, the news has arrived of the trouble with the Turk, where our boys have been keeping them back. Now things are in earnest and more exciting out there, I could not rest in hospital and have at last persuaded the doctor to let me out and rejoin the regiment. So the trip to England is off, much as I would have liked to have taken it. But I simply couldn't do it, feeling pretty fit and leaving some of my good friends who left Aust with me, fighting out there on the desert. So I will be well in amongst it in a day or two again.

Everything is OK am feeling all right, so don't worry.

He took the train to the old Etmaler camp and arrived at some time on 5 August, after his regiment had made the bayonet charge and gone in pursuit of Turks to Katia:

I found our camp deserted, in a terrible mess, blankets and mess tins and dirty dishes all over the place, the tents were full of bullet holes and bomb holes on the ground. On the horse lines there were still a few horses, some dead from shell fire, the others done from the work they'd been doing. However, I found a rifle and ammunition and a horse and went out to look for the boys. Came up with what was left of my troop, they were halted for an hour ... lying asleep, holding the horses, which didn't need much holding. They said I looked nice and clean; they were the dirtiest looking lot of scrubbers you'd ever see, and tired and drawn ... But in a day or so I was just as dirty and felt more at home. My horse got shot on the first day and that was the worst that happened to me.

At the Battle of Romani, forces had been deployed to the south and west, to prevent the Turks from turning the flank of the defenders, but this was never attempted. The forces were the 5th Mounted Yeomanry Brigade, the NZ Mounted Rifle Brigade, the 3rd Australian Light Horse Brigade and the 42nd East Lancashire (Territorial) Infantry Division and all were now released to join in the pursuit to Katia. They were in reasonable fettle, and except for the New Zealanders and the regiment of Yeomanry that had captured Mount Royston (and then retired south-west again because there was no water to spare for them), had not yet been in action.

The 3rd Light Horse Brigade was new to this front and not only strange to the country but also underequipped, enduring the cold nights in only shirtsleeves. They had so far spent the summer guarding a section of the Canal well to the south and had seen little or nothing of the enemy since Gallipoli. But the men were in hard condition and eager to acquit themselves well.

Their first mission was to capture Hamisah, a hod four miles west of Katia, which they did boldly and swiftly. From the extreme right, they were positioned to make a strong flanking movement on Katia, which might well have tipped the balance against the Turk. The three regiments were still fresh and keen to push on, but they came under light shell fire from the distant Turks and the commander, the rapidly promoted Brigadier General Antill, pulled them back four miles to Bir Nagid, where they spent a peaceful night.

Jack Antill, a regular soldier, bordered on a martinet and was, in the end, a dud. He had a bold reputation in the Boer War and was lauded by correspondent Banjo Paterson, yet in the Boers' attack on Prieska in Cape Colony he hurried his squadron away from the enemy. We are all affected by the inner counsels of experience, and it may be that his failure to advance at Katia was related to The Nek bloodbath. At any rate, it was said that he lacked the cavalryman's instinct for exploiting fast-moving situations and he left Sinai to command an infantry brigade in France, handing over the 3rd Light Horse Brigade to Royston on 9 August.

All other mounted brigades advanced. They made a long north–south formation, in order from the south (or right) front: the NZ Mounted Rifles Brigade, the 1st and 2nd Light Horse Brigades and the Yeomanry nearest the coast. Ion Idriess of the 5th Light Horse Regiment, temporarily attached to the NZ Brigade, gives us a trooper's-eye view:

> Dawn came with a crimson sky. From a ridge we gazed behind at a grand sight all lit up in pink and grey and khaki stretching right back past the redoubts of Duedir, a winding column of New Zealand and Australian mounted troops. The sun blazed at Bir el Nuss where we watered the horses and waited a hard and expectant two hours, while up rolled more Australians, more New Zealanders and finally the helmeted Yeomanry. And then came the Somerset and Leicestershire Batteries of the Royal Horse Artillery, all chirpy and spoiling for a fight, the spare battery horses prancing and fat. Regiment after regiment, brigade after brigade … the oasis was surrounded by a dark brown cloth of horses and men. But the faces of the [1st and 2nd Brigade] men who had been fighting day and night were haggard, their eyes stary, their horses very tired.
>
> We moved off again whistling and singing, laughing and joking, the horses of us fresh brigades pulling at their bits, careless of the fierce desert heat.

As they rode, they heard the stories of the fighting of the last three days and 'Through it all, we can sense a battle very, very narrowly won'.

Approaching Katia, the rattle of machine-gun and rifle fire became continuous, with intermittent artillery bursts. They halted before a ridge while the 'heads' went up on it to confer with the Auckland Mounted Rifles and to reconnoitre. Then the two regiments were ordered forward again and 'straight down in front of us was a mile-long slope of hard sand leading right to the first oasis of the great El Katia system'. White shrapnel was bursting all over it.

Except for an absence of cover, it looked like good going for a mounted infantryman, but this proved to be a fatal illusion. The Turks had chosen their ground well: it was in part a salt flat and a morass, in which despairing and exhausted troops were to flounder, beset with Turkish fire.

Colonel L.C. Wilson of the 5th pointed ahead. 'A battery of heavy Austrian guns has been located in that oasis. We have to charge and take the guns. Regiment: Fix — bayonets!'

A mounted charge! Every trooper's hope — and the very first of the Australian Light Horse. They were awed, exalted … delighted. The 5th's 500 bayonets flashed, click-click-clicked onto rifles, and were borne aloft. They were unaware that all the mounted brigades were to charge across the salt pan at the same time, and Idriess seemed even unaware of the Aucklands, to the 5th's immediate left.

Unlike modern automatic and semi-automatic weapons, the .303 Short Magazine Lee-Enfield rifle with bayonet fixed was an unwieldy weapon and would have required concentration to the exclusion of all else to manage one-handed on a galloping horse. It was obviously not the most effective way to use the weapon, but the 'cold steel' effect against a defensive enemy was worth a try. It was the first time in the campaign that bayonets had been drawn by mounted men.

The 5th went forward at a brisk trot, with the Aucklands on their left. As Idriess tells it:

> The colonel with the adjutant rode in the lead, the squadron majors leading their squadrons, the old doctor and the padre riding knee to knee, laughing as if at a great joke. We held the horses in so as to have their strength in the last great clash. But they were getting excited … we rode knee to knee … and our bodies felt the massed heat of the horses that tugged and strained as the squadrons broke into a swift canter. Then a horse reared high and screamed and we were into a mad gallop, the horses' mouths open and their great eyes staring as the squadrons thundered on.
>
> Then to our right, I glimpsed a sandbagged trench. *The right flank is gone*, I thought, and stared straight ahead with gritted teeth — but not a solitary machine-gun rose above the parapet as we thundered by.

Hesitant men lined the oasis edge — even in those last mad moments I sensed they were too terrified either to run, or fire. We crashed right through the oasis out onto a plain surrounded by palms. And there was the colonel out in front, with his horse pulled back on its haunches, his hand held high.

'HALT!'

The guns were not there. The charge had ended in nothing, except a trap. Hundreds of sweating, rearing browns, bays, chestnuts and blacks surged and plunged around the colonel in a heaving welter. Then came the thud of bullets into horse flesh and the colonel's horse fell dead. Panting horses with crimson chests were sobbing up against their fellows. Their riders backed them into the palms, sorted themselves into troops, dismounted, and handed them over to the horse holders. Now they must get out of this.

Machine-gun bullets chipped laths off the trees, rifle bullets kicked up the sand, Turkish shells crashed among the palms. Together with the Aucklands, the men of the 5th started working round on foot towards the right.

On their left, all other ANZACs had charged together, with bayonets glinting in the sun, shouting with exhilaration. But here, the hard ground of the salt pan gave way to swamp and the horses floundered to a standstill, bogged to their knees. Successive waves of riders concertinaed, presenting a massed target.

Quickly, orders were passed to dismount and continue the advance on foot. The horses were galloped back to cover and the riflemen squelched into the morass. The Yeomanry, on the extreme left, had also been checked.

The suffering 1st and 2nd Brigades picked their way forward until they were within 600 to 1000 yards of the enemy. They had been three days without sleep and struggling in the bog, their progress was slow and feeble, their return of fire insufficient to shift the well-placed Turks. Chauvel that morning had told them he was sure they would 'continue to show in the pursuit the magnificent spirit of yesterday'. The spirit was still there, but the task was impossible. On dusk, the whole line was at a standstill and Chauvel ordered a general withdrawal.

The NZ Brigade spent the night near Mount Meredith, while the 1st and 2nd Brigades marched back to Etmaler, which they reached at midnight. Some men had been constantly in the saddle or the firing line for 59 hours — a squadron of the 6th Regiment for 60 — and as many horses had been without a drink for the same period. Approaching Katia, where they had often been watered on reconnaissance, the poor brutes revived enough to deliver one more full gallop for the charge, only to be denied again, and still dry, carried their riders right back to Romani. The capacity of these big (New South) Walers, bred for many years for army service with the British and Indian Armies, to continue working, especially since they would refuse food in intense heat, was unsuspected even by their owners. They treasured them accordingly.

As the ANZACs dragged their way back to Romani, the nearly prostrate Turks abandoned Katia and struggled on to Oghratina, seven miles further east. Only the desert won.

In all this, if the worst thing that happened to my father was having his horse shot, his account of Katia must surely be understated. I have wondered if he came to regret his impulsive gesture: as the years of fighting went on, he did develop a more barrack-room philosophy, if still a soldier's.

IT REMAINS TO RECORD WHAT HAPPENED TO THE 42ND INFANTRY DIVISION. WHILE the 52nd may have been nursed, these pitiable Lancashiremen were marched all that terrible day over the sand towards Katia. That their advance guard did almost get there as the ANZACs pulled out is to their great credit: by noon, the battalions of the 42nd were acutely distressed; by evening, thousands of exhausted stragglers had fallen out, 800 from one brigade, 300 from one battalion. Many lost their senses and dug madly with their hands in the burning sand for water, or tore their clothes off and rushed about laughing. Many more fell unconscious and not a few died.

Keeping constant pressure on the Turks resulted in one engagement tending to merge into the next, as was the case with Katia and Bir el Abd. This was an oasis 22 miles east of Romani, on the track to El Arish.

El Arish was on the south-east corner of the Mediterranean and came to be considered by the ANZACs as some far-off holy grail. If the enemy could be dislodged from Bir el Abd, he must retreat the 50 miles further on to El Arish because there was almost no water between the two places. El Arish was close to the Palestine border, where the Sinai desert ended. Hopes and dreams began to form and tantalise. They could get off the sand! Mirages, milk-and-honey visions of plains and trees, cities, grass feed, roads, water, flowers beckoned.

First things first: attack the enemy rearguard, capture his guns, destroy the remainder of his force. Reconnaissance early on 8 August showed that the Turks had abandoned Oghratina. Patrols probed forward and found him at Bir el Abd.

Chauvel shifted his HQ forward to Oghratina, with the New Zealand and Yeomanry brigades. Royston, temporarily in command of both the 1st and 2nd Light Horse Brigades, was to march from Katia overnight and at daylight on the 9th take up a position just north-east of Abd. The New Zealanders and the 3rd Light Horse Brigade were to start the advance, the first directly on the Turks' centre, the second to swing round behind them from the south, blocking their retreat. The Yeomanry were in reserve.

The whole ANZAC Mounted Division would be engaged, though it was reduced by sickness and exhaustion of both horses and men to 3000 dismounted rifles. Two regiments of Royston's were down to 180 rifles and the 7th Regiment mustered 214. But the Turks were said to be weak and the operation looked to be relatively easy. Because of the distances, no infantry were to be used and the job fell to the mounted troops again.

The Turks proved to be decidedly strong: 6000 men deployed on commanding sandhills, well supported by artillery.

The overnight ride by the 1st and 2nd Brigades was marked by precipitous sand cliffs, up or down which no horse would have gone, had it seen them. With daylight, the troopers were awed to see what they had come through.

At 4 am, the New Zealanders attacked the Turkish centre and the 3rd Light Horse Brigade started its encircling movement from the south. They encountered strong resistance. Royston's brigades, coming in from the north, were also checked. The dispositions left large gaps between the ANZAC units: 800 yards between Chaytor's New Zealanders and the 2nd Brigade on the left, a mile between Chaytor and the 3rd Brigade on the right.

Suddenly, things started to look grim. There were fire fights all along the line. The scattered ANZACs, after galloping in until the machine-gun and artillery fire became too heavy to risk the horses, dismounted and sent them back. For some hours, it was a near stalemate of no advance and no retreat, though marked by particular strokes of brilliance such as a bayonet charge by the Wellingtons, before which the Turks refused the steel and bolted, and the 'admirable tenacity and reckless courage' of the out-gunned batteries of Royal Horse Artillery, which from close behind the dismounted men waged an unequal contest with the Turkish guns.

About midday, the Turks counterattacked from one end of the line to the other and threw Chauvel's troops on the defensive. There were seesawing attacks and counterattacks for two hours, and while the ANZAC front was unbroken, they suffered a net loss of ground. Sniffing victory, the Turks' fire reached a pitch of concentration never experienced before, even at Gallipoli.

By 4.30 Royston's left had been almost completely turned and the Turks threw between 2000 and 3000 men against his centre. The ensuing crescendo of fire was most destructive to both sides. The New Zealanders gave no ground in their forward position, even as a retirement of the 3rd Brigade on their right and another by Royston's brigades on their left exposed them to enfilade fire on both sides. Still they hung on.

At 5.30, Chauvel ordered a general withdrawal. It was then a matter of getting away unscathed in a fighting retreat, another searching test of steadiness under fire, with troop deliberately laying back on troop and squadron laying back on squadron, while keeping the enemy at bay with their own shooting.

That accomplished, the ANZACs were once more exhausted. They had ridden all night and fought from daylight to sunset on a quart of water in the heat of a ship's stokehold. Their elbows were blistered from constant contact with the scalding sand as they fired their weapons. Chauvel's choice was between bivouacking that night nearby and resuming the assault next day, or retiring to Oghratina. After consulting his brigade commanders, he opted for the latter, posting the 3rd Brigade out on the flank.

Two hundred and ten wounded were carried out of Abd and greatly hampered the withdrawal, but with the exception of a few New Zealanders their countrymen could not possibly reach, all were borne back safely. The standard 'ambulance' was a camel cacolet, or litter — a narrow, swaying pannier atop the beast that so tormented wounded men they came to be feared by the ANZACs, and led to the Australian innovation of sand carts. However, these could not be deployed to the front line and the men were taken out on horses; and their preference then was to ride them home. Two men of the 5th Regiment with broken thighs rode home from Abd and one survived.

Lieutenant General Sir Harry Chauvel of the Desert Mounted Corps.

This 'law' about saving wounded men was dangerous and frowned on by anonymous high command mandarins, but the men went into action knowing that if it was humanly possible to be carried out, they would not be allowed to fall into the Turks' hands, or left to the murderous Bedouins who prowled around the edges of battlefields. As vindication, after two and a half years of constant fighting, only 73 Light Horsemen had been taken prisoner, most of them wounded, and not a single officer was captured. But they themselves captured between 40,000 and 50,000 Turks.

Casualties for Bir el Abd were 73 dead and 243 wounded. British casualties over all for the Romani phase of operations were killed, 202; wounded, 883; missing, 45. The vast majority of these losses were suffered by those who did the fighting: Australians and New Zealanders.

The morning after the battle, the Turks stole away again. The way lay open to El Arish.

SIX

The road to El Arish: Mazar

The War Office in London seemed to be slower than the troopers to apprehend that their Middle East campaign, set up to protect and defend the Suez Canal, had done that comprehensively and was now, almost willy-nilly, not defensive but offensive. There did not seem to be a conscious recognition of this, just a slow conversion of attitude, which found its reflection in the correspondence between the Commander-in-Chief, General Sir Archibald ('Don't take my ANZACs away') Murray and London. Even as late as October, the British government (Imperial General Staff) reminded Murray that while the occupation of El Arish seemed a good idea, because of its effect on 'certain malcontents' in Syria and upon friendly Arab operations in the Hejaz, the policy for Egypt in the immediate future must be, strategically at least, defensive. Murray, in his reply, expressed the view that the defence of Egypt should now rest on El Arish and just slipped in the notion of Palestine in the context of 'endeavours to prevent the withdrawal of enemy troops while threatening the Turkish communications with the Hejaz'. This seems to have been a way of hinting that, if we can pin down the Turks to defending Palestine (by, well, invading it) they won't be able to use their army somewhere else.

But there was no hurry: there couldn't be. Murray rightly would not countenance an advance to El Arish before the railway and water pipe, then not far past Romani, had been completed right across Sinai. This was a particular project of his, but despite all endeavours and unlimited Egyptian labour, it took nearly a year to build the 110 miles from Kantara to El Arish: extremely slow, but wartime shortages of materials were to blame. The railway was essential for moving troops to and fro, particularly infantry, and of course for supplies. The advance of the railway and water pipe therefore governed the advance of the troops guarding them, and for the next few months they resumed their old long-range reconnaissance and patrolling role, as at Romani.

At least, the end of the summer of 1916 was approaching. Colonel Richardson in his history of the 7th Regiment says of the time between the first occupation of Romani and Bir el Abd: 'endurance was so severely tested as to eliminate from active service any men whose physical conditions were not near perfection. Officers and men who survived the hardships became so seasoned that the rough conditions experienced later in Palestine … seemed to have little effect upon them. Utter and constant discomfort was the rule. Even in camp and when resting, there was nothing to make life worth living.' The men were so blackened by the sun as to be indistinguishable from the Bedouin Arabs.

The worn-out pioneer 2nd Brigade was at last taken out of the line and spent until early September refitting and recuperating at Romani. Unfit horses, many with sand colic, were replaced with remounts. But Romani had little to offer the men, unless it was just an absence of the unremitting strains and privations they had endured for five months.

There was a Turkish garrison at Bir el Mazar, only twenty miles short of El Arish on the direct track, believed to be 2200 strong and made up of Romani survivors. It was decided to mount an attack on this on 17 September, but there was no water supply for horses between Mazar and Salmana and it was necessary to improvise one to avoid a dry round trip of 37 miles. The mid-September weather was still hot.

Seven hundred camels no less, each carrying a twenty-gallon fantass of water, were to rendezvous with Chauvel's troops ten miles east of Salmana on their return journey. This was only one oddity in this untypical and, in the end, controversial operation.

On 15 September, Chauvel's three Australian brigades marched to Salmana. They were sighted there on the 16th and machine-gunned by a German aircraft which no doubt informed the garrison at Mazar of its discovery. After dark, the 2nd Brigade, now once more under Brigadier General Ryrie, and the 3rd Brigade under Royston, marched on Mazar while the 1st Brigade followed about seven miles in rear.

At dawn, Ryrie's 5th and 7th Regiments dismounted and advanced to within 700 yards north and west of the Turkish trenches. There was stiff resistance from enemy mountain batteries and rifles. The 3rd Brigade swept right round the position and began attacking it from the south and east, so that the Turks were virtually defending on all sides. A battalion of the Imperial Camel Corps should have attacked with them, but was late due to a difficult passage through single-file gullies and soft sand.

That was the situation soon after daylight, according to Gullett's Official History. Despite the absence of the camels, all ranks were confident of carrying the position. They had carried harder ones. From this point, however, differences in reported events and perceptions appear in Gullett's account and Colonel Richardson's history of the 7th Regiment.

Richardson said the regiment was checked close to the Mazar ruins, where the enemy was strongly entrenched in commanding positions, but it seemed possible to assault the place and preparations were in progress. Then the 7th received a message that the 3rd Brigade had been held up and was withdrawing. 'Some of their troops crossed our frontage and being in close formation, received concentrated fire from the enemy and sustained a number of casualties. Our field guns had opened fire, but although the enemy were firing in plain view from our position, and messages were sent to that effect, no attempt was made to shell them.'

Gullett said that the ANZACs' field guns had not up to this time come into action, but Richardson said he saw them firing. According to Gullet, Royston had advised Chauvel of his 'unfavourable view of the project' and after the 3rd Brigade had been held up for 'nearly three hours', at 7 am Chauvel decided to break off the engagement. But Richardson sounds as if the 3rd Brigade's withdrawal was a surprise to him: he was not preparing to leave, but was preparing to assault the enemy. This begs the question of whether the 7th got the message to break off at the same time.

When the order did come, the 7th could not leave the front line until they got a man, badly wounded in the abdomen, away in a sand cart. In the rescue three more men were wounded and 'our casualties for this ineffective little action were 1 killed 5 wounded: and two men subsequently died of wounds'. Richardson was not happy. 'As no bivouac had been indicated, it was presumed that Ge' Eila would be the place, but we arrived there only to find it deserted. Much trouble was experienced watering the horses from buckets and at 8 pm, it was decided to return to Salmana.' He concludes: 'The Mazar stunt was most strenuous and tested the endurance of men whose vitality had been greatly decreased by the fighting, fatigue and heat of the last few months'. One suspects he wanted to add, 'for nothing'.

Gullett acknowledges the engagement was always afterwards referred to in terms of strong disapproval by regimental officers who participated. Not only officers. Idriess says, 'We retired at midday, furious about it all, certain that a determined gallop would have ridden down the redoubts ... We swore at the Heads, whoever they might be. With this little lot, we should have eaten Mazar.'

It seems that different beholders, Rashomon-like, interpreted the same things in different ways, and as a whole the abortive battle could be seen in two ways. Either as an unimportant sideshow, not worth the sacrifice of any more lives, or, however it was, the Light Horse should not have been committed if it was not intended to win. The withdrawal diminished their proud service.

Chauvel has absolute right to the last word. He had categorical orders from General Lawrence that if 'the garrison was not taken by surprise and overrun in the first rush, he was to consider the operation a reconnaissance in force and withdraw'. On no account was he to seriously involve his brigades. When 'Galloping Jack' Royston, the last man in the army to vacillate before unfavourable odds, took a poor view of his chances after being held up for three hours, Chauvel's duty was clear to him. He would doubtless also have been influenced by the wretched prospects for his wounded, so far from aid, should the engagement prove expensive. He acted, and a commander in battle does not argue his case.

But there could be no equivocation over the scheme for watering the horses. It was a shambles.

That the 700 camels were in place and on time says something for the project, but the watering of 3000 desperate horses calls for expert handling, experience and skill. The Light Horse had their own methods and equipment, in which long canvas troughs were instrumental, but the supply camels carried only buckets. At one or two horses per bucket, it seems an entangling, burdensome method, even with quiet and biddable animals. Idriess described it:

By Jove, I was thirsty. The heat of the sand rose up to a man's face.

After another nine miles, we were surprised to see a long convoy of camels coming towards us between the hills. I don't know whether the horses sighted the fantasses or smelt the water in them, but a faint ripple of neighing, seldom heard now, broke out down the column. Horses threw up their heads, open-mouthed, sniffing eagerly …

We met the convoy — the horses went mad — they rushed it — at sight of the water we could not hold them — they swarmed like mad things, pawing, panting, jostling, straining. Two of us held back the section's horses while the other two vied around the fantasses for water, but immediately we got our buckets full, all horses rushed us. A dozen gasping mouths into one bucket, struggling animals, shouting men, rattling of stirrup irons, pressure of horses' bodies, spilled water — open-mouthed men trying to catch the splashes — plunging circle after circle around each fantass, horse holders with straining arms finally dragged over the sand … the horses struggled to lick wet sand, frantic-eyed, swollen-tongued.

There was not sufficient water — not even a squadron in our regiments got a drink! And the regiments coming behind — there had been other regiments in front.

The regiment pushed on rapidly and … passed all the Camel Corps making for water, water, water! How my bones ached! I thanked Christ when the sun went down. Eventually, we saw lights among the black palms of Salmana. The horses were frantic — they couldn't go faster than they did. Within the oasis, spelling troops had filled the water troughs — the horses rushed these troughs, their heads in rows went down, stayed down. We could not drag them away. They felt like the weight of elephants. The water was brackish, too.

Two days later, the Turks abandoned Mazar. Some strange imperative caused them to throw away the fruits of victory: this was the third time.

The long-range patrolling and reconnaissance resumed. Richardson says: 'Reveille at midnight was followed by a tedious march to the [supposed enemy line], reached just at dawn; then came the pleasant operation known as drawing fire and defining the enemy's line in which squadrons pushed slowly forward, then rode back very rapidly, followed by a hail of bullets. Next came the forming of the day outposts to watch the enemy movements and prevent his advance. Darkness brought relief, but … camp often was not reached until 10 o'clock. A hasty meal and the sleep of exhaustion followed.'

My father wrote to his sister Hope on 2 December 1916:

We are still in the desert keeping a good watch for Mr. Turk and at the same time advancing nearer his base, everything points to a dinkum argument before long, a big and tough affair. Advancing … is a slow proposition, everything must be made safe and secure as we go, bases made and garrisoned and a railway built and guarded along the whole length so that supplies and dismounted troops can be transported to the front. Since we first came out here last April, we have come 60 or 70 miles in this way and everything is fortified behind us. To reach the Canal now, the Turks will have to put up a great fight and break through these fortifications … no doubt they have been doing the same on their side and now that we are drawing near, will be quite ready to receive us warmly. A big clash when it comes. One thing for which we are truly thankful is the cool weather, we do not feel the lack of water and have much more energy — the same can be said of the horses, who have all earned VCs. The nights are very cold, too much so for sleeping out on the sand dunes and the dew is heavy, so by morning our blankets are pretty wet — of course tents are out of the question as we move about so much and must travel light. If we stop for a while, we build palm branch gunyahs and live like Bedouins.

Well old girl, buck up and carry on with that cheery spirit which is your special gift, that you well know how to use for the benefit of others …

Hope's husband was with the 13th Battalion in France.

In October, the British General Lawrence had proceeded to Aldershot and Lieutenant General Sir Charles Macpherson Dobell took command of Eastern Force, the name given to the army advancing east of the Canal; and another British leader, Major General Sir Philip Chetwode, took command of the Desert Column, Dobell's advanced troops, consisting of the ANZAC

Mounted Division, 52nd (Lowland Scottish) and 42nd (East Lancashire) Infantry Divisions. With the Commander-in-Chief in Cairo, it was an ever-spreading and sprawling command and still had the seeds of division and confusion in it, as at Romani, but no practical alternative seemed to offer.

However, the ANZACs found in Chetwode an experienced cavalry leader and far-seeing tactician as well as a man of strong and attractive personality, and with one damaging exception he guided their destiny well. Like most British senior officers, at first he was offended by the troops' apparent lack of discipline and casual ways, their failure to salute him and their scarcely disguised hilarity at the rigid bearing and precise, stiff horsemanship of his aides, but he had the expansiveness of spirit to trade that for their discipline where it counted, in the firing line, and their prowess in the field.

SEVEN

'Take that damned thing away': Magdhaba

There was a last night ride in Sinai on which nobody complained, or grew tired, or spared a thought for the desperate, gruelling return journey. It was on a cold and luminous desert night when the stars were brilliant points in a bluish dust, seeming to hang low and beckon the riders on. They gazed at them, and let themselves be drawn to the promised land.

At dawn on 20 December 1916, the 1st Brigade of the ANZAC Mounted Division (less the 2nd Brigade) reached the Mediterranean coast on the far side of El Arish and suddenly the horses stepped off the sand onto the wide, firm flat that flanks the great Wady (streambed) El Arish. They started prancing and Brigadier General 'Fighting Charlie' Cox called a halt just to watch them. 'That night,' Cox said, 'will always seem to me the most wonderful of the whole campaign. The hard going for the horses seemed almost miraculous after the months of sand; and, as their shoes struck fire on the stones in the bed of the wady, the men laughed with delight.'

Sinai was behind them. It was a perfect dawn arrival: the 1st Brigade to the east with its flank on the silver sea, the Camel Brigade to the south, the New Zealanders to the south-west and the 3rd Brigade at Masaid, a Turkish post five miles west. Each brigade was on time, none more than 200 yards out of position and they didn't have to fire a shot. The substantial Turkish army of occupation that had held the place for over two years had gone.

The dramatic appearance at dawn of this ring of tough-looking foreign horsemen right round the town sparked wild excitement and apparent demonstrations of delight from the Arab villagers, whatever their true loyalties or feelings. Bearded elders in many-coloured, flowing dresses crowded round the grinning ANZACs, grasping their stirrups and kissing their boots, while women and children swarmed around them, shouting. The chief sheikh formally surrendered the town and handed over one hapless Turk and some alleged Turkish spies.

The troopers wandered down the evil-smelling alleyways between the squalid mud huts. After the great region of nothing, the village was at least a place of human habitation and there were some mosques and minarets. Besides the familiar date palm oases, they came upon planted crops and fields of melons, vegetables, an orange grove. Fig trees! This was more like it.

The ANZACs camped in the wady bed and set up a series of strong outposts. They were on Turkish territory now, invaders not defenders, and could be attacked — and so, to keep the enemy off balance, should strike first. And how much more effective they would be, on firm ground, with good water and better feed for horse and man.

But where was the Turkish Army? If it was not at El Arish, it must be at Rafa, 26 miles further north-east along the coast, 'around the corner' of the Mediterranean, or at Magdhaba, 23 miles inland to the south, along the dry Wady el Arish ... or at both places. It was Sir Philip Chetwode's intention to advance on both simultaneously. On 22 December he arrived in El Arish from Port Said by naval ship and announced to Chauvel while the men were eating their last rations that he had already arranged for supplies to reach them that night, from railhead and by sea. Also, the 52nd Infantry Division was even then marching into the town and would secure it in the absence of the mounted troops. The attacks could begin.

However, during the day intelligence, notably from ten Australian airmen who had bombed Magdhaba heavily, revealed the place was well defended by a strong garrison and Chetwode then decided to send all his mounted strength against Magdhaba first. Accordingly, the ANZAC brigades and the Camel Corps Brigade, plus its Hong Kong and Singapore Mountain Battery, set off along the Wady el Arish that night. Fresh and eager, they marched fast, though the horses, while revelling in the firm and level going, were not used to it and frequently over-reached and stumbled.

No smoking, no talking. The clink of stirrup irons meeting, an occasional neigh or snort. Ride for forty minutes, lead for ten, halt for ten. Each soldier depended on the wellbeing of each horse for his life; each horse carried about 440 pounds weight and such variation eased their burden. The riders, aching from the bitter cold, welcomed every chance to walk and exercise.

Chauvel halted just before dawn, and while the men fed the animals and breakfasted he took his brigade commanders forward to make a reconnaissance. However, much of what they wanted to see was obscured by the smoke of Turkish cooking fires. He waited until 6.30, when the first British air attack arrived on schedule. The pilots flew low, bombing, and the Turks replied with machine-guns and rifles, disclosing the position of their redoubts to the party by muzzle flashes.

At 8.30, all brigades moved into position for the assault. The few buildings of the settlement were on the east side of the wady and here the Turks had concentrated their redoubts, each able to cover the next. However, there were redoubts on the west (Sinai) side, too: the Turks appreciated that the enemy would probably approach on the 'good' east side, but then must cross the wady, under fire, to take these western fortifications. The ground favoured the Turks. And both combatants knew it would be another gamble for water: the ANZACs must secure Magdhaba by nightfall, or march back dry to El Arish. Already, the men had made inroads on their bottles and the horses had had no water that morning.

Chauvel planned to keep to the east side of the wady, relying on the force and speed of his advance to drive the Turks across it, and away from their water.

The Camel Brigade started the attack, cantering straight at the Turks southwards, up the flat. The New Zealanders, with the 3rd Light Horse Brigade following, were on the Camels' left, both under the NZ Major General Chaytor. Cox's 1st Light Horse Brigade was in reserve.

The Imperial Camel Brigade, raised and trained by the British Brigadier General C.L. Smith, VC, consisted of Australians, British and New Zealanders from all arms of service, and was now making valuable contributions to operations. Camels could carry about as much water, equipment and rations as could be piled on them. The men were true infantry, because once dismounted for action they stayed dismounted: camels could not be raced up close to enemy positions, nor kept nearby for a galloping escape if need be. But they gave Chauvel a solid pivot to manoeuvre on in action and he now had what he had lacked at Katia and Bir el Abd: a considerable body of infantry to attack a sector firmly, in depth. The slender Light Horse line did not have that stability, weight and depth, but the horsemen could be moved about as required, ideally using the Camels as a pivot.

As soon as the advance started, British airmen reported some mounted Turks were escaping up the wady to the south and Chaytor ordered Brigadier General Royston's 3rd Light Horse Brigade to intercept. Galloping Jack Royston, of South African origin, was nearly 60 and as colourful a character as any of that exceptional company who made up the Light Horse leaders. At the Battle of Romani, he commanded the 2nd Brigade temporarily and wore out thirteen horses in one day, racing up and down his firing line, exhorting his troops on to victory. 'Stick to it, boys,' He would shout. 'You've got them on the run!' A trooper said, 'I looked up, and the buggers were coming at us in hundreds'. Getting first aid for a bullet wound in the leg, Royston suddenly saw something requiring his attention and galloped off, bloodstained bandage streaming out behind. Royston was the boldest of cavalrymen and was held in great affection and respect.

In response to Chaytor's order, he despatched his 10th Light Horse Regiment southward, on a wide, galloping detour round the Turks, of course accompanying them himself, in an attempt to cut off their retreat. The 10th reached the wady bank, took many prisoners and then became engaged with an enemy force from almost due east. The move of this regiment was serendipitous in relation to a pivotal development and opportunities to come.

A pilot landed his aircraft on the flat and reported the Turkish retreat to the south appeared to be gathering momentum again. Chaytor's and Royston's 10th Regiment might not be able to cut them off in time. Chauvel committed Cox's 1st Brigade from reserve to advance directly on Magdhaba along the wady, to the right of the Camels. The brigade trotted, encountered fire from mountain guns, deployed into the spread-out artillery formation, increased to a gallop and for a wild, brief burst, charged, the horses fighting for their heads. They ran straight into heavy machine-gun and rifle cross-fire, from ahead and to their left: Cox realised the evacuation report must be wrong, the ground was still heavily defended and nothing but destruction lay ahead. Still at the gallop, he swung his regiments instantly down into a deep fissure of the wady and dismounted.

By 11 am the Hong Kong and Singapore Mountain Batteries had been shooting effectively for some time, but there had been little territorial gain. The New Zealanders' advance was enfiladed by fire from redoubts on both banks of the wady, the Camels were held up on the flat in the centre where the ground was almost devoid of cover, though they did serve the purpose of drawing fire away from the mounted brigades. But they were still well away from their objective, the same No. 2 Redoubt that had stopped Cox's gallop.

Then a number of hard, separate fights developed, all with the aim of taking the No. 2 Redoubt. From the wady bed, Cox sent his 3rd Light Horse Regiment, dismounted, to the assistance of the Camels and at the same time the Hong Kong and Singapore Battery's Indians opened effective fire on the redoubt. The 3rd Regiment had to cross a wide, exposed bay of

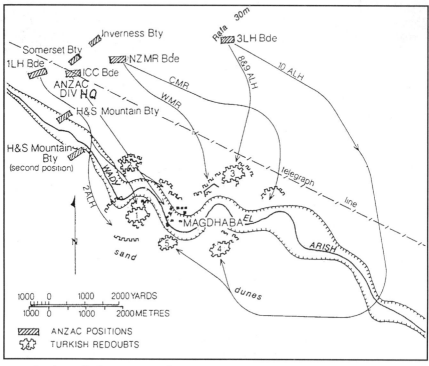

Battle of Magdhaba, 23 December 1916.

The Hong Kong and Singapore Mountain Battery was manned by Sikhs. All guns and equipment were carried on big Indian camels. They gave good artillery support to the ANZACs, but in Trans-Jordan operations struggled on the mountain tracks and were less effective.

COURTESY 2ND/14TH L. H.REGT [QMI] MUSEUM ENOGERRA

the wady as they advanced, but they did so steadily to within 100 yards of the Turks' trenches. All three battalions of the Camels were now also closing on the redoubt in section rushes, as were the New Zealanders from the east, with great dash, in the open. The resolve of them all carried the day. The 3rd Regiment paused briefly to adjust and stiffen their line, then with two companies of Camels leaped from the ground shouting and charged with their bayonets. The Turks poured intense fire at them, but the men flung themselves on to the trenches at their full momentum and the Turks stood up in a body and surrendered.

This was the turning point, but even as the redoubt was falling, Chauvel had decided to withdraw: Cox's 1st Brigade was out of sight and he had not yet learned of the 3rd Regiment's and the Camels' great success.

His engineers had not found water and the short winter day was fading. He telegraphed Chetwode of his intention and issued the order to retire to brigades. This order reached Cox just as his 3rd Regiment had gathered themselves for the bayonet charge and he said, 'Take that damned thing away and let me see it for the first time in half an hour'.

By then, the 3rd Regiment had run on to the next Turkish redoubt and the 2nd Camel Battalion had made touch with the New Zealanders, who with the 8th and 9th Light Horse Regiments were also going forward. Now abreast of all developments, Chauvel telephoned Chetwode to rescind his message and called off the withdrawal.

Meanwhile, Royston's 10th Regiment, having cut off the column of 300 Turks retreating up the wady and accepted their surrender, galloped north again and enveloped entirely the enemy's right flank. After that, they tackled more Turkish redoubts in a succession of mounted rushes, galloping from the cover of one bush to another, dismounting, firing off a magazine rapid, remounting and repeating the tactic. Two troops, numbering no more than 40 men, galloped straight on to a position occupied by over 300 Turks and, despite casualties, maintained momentum right over the earthworks and on to the cover of a ridge. Galloping Jack rode up to a Turkish trench and was instantly covered by five enemy rifles. He brandished his cane and shouted at the riflemen in Zulu to surrender, whereupon they held up their hands.

A squadron of the 2nd Light Horse made a mounted dash at the redoubt previously ridden over by the 10th's troops, jumping and swerving over their dead and wounded men and horses. The 2nd was severely mauled, too, but reined in on the redoubt and started firing from the saddle. The Turks immediately broke and ran.

With the New Zealanders and the 8th and 9th Light Horse closing swiftly from the east and the 1st Brigade and Camels still pushing north, more by accident than design the Turks were now inside an irregular but closing ring. The opposing forces were everywhere clashing at close quarters, but inevitably now, the remaining redoubts began to fall until all were accounted for. Some isolated pockets resisted longer, but by 4.30 pm, as the light was dying, the last shot was fired.

Then thousands of the victors met in the circle, celebrating, trying to find their led horses, camels and water, securing prisoners, succouring wounded and separating regiments and units all tangled together. Great animation and confusion continued for hours in the darkened, confined space and it was not until 11 pm that Chauvel could lead the column off to El Arish. They arrived just before dawn on a cold, fine Christmas Eve, with that same star glittering in the east.

There would have been ten or a dozen chaplains riding with the Light Horse and Camels, and while sharing the satisfaction of victory they surely would have sought out that star and reflected on it, perhaps a little wryly. No doubt they would have offered up a prayer for our dead and wounded and charitably, we may imagine, one for the infidels.

Turkish casualties were 97 dead and 300 wounded, with 1300 taken prisoner. Chauvel's were 22 killed and 124 wounded, all safely got away.

Magdhaba set a pattern that was to be repeated successfully for the whole campaign: of a slender but mobile and, above all, resourceful ANZAC column prevailing through enterprise and dash over the dogged, entrenched Turk.

A Night March

The following account, by 'Aram', appeared in *Australia in Palestine* — 'a Soldiers' Book'— edited by H.S. Gullett and Charles Barrett and published in 1919:

At twilight, when the air is cool, we prepare for our second consecutive night march. Overcoats and mufflers are put on, saddles are inspected to see that all is secure. Later it will be too dark, and we too tired to attend to such matters.

After a short wait we move off. Two or three hours of steady plodding through the darkness, with the effects of fatigue scarcely noticeable. Then, suddenly, an utter weariness assails us, numbing limbs, distorting vision, and rendering minds a prey to tantalising and disturbing thoughts — thoughts that mock and taunt; thoughts of feather beds and roaring fires; thoughts that accentuate our weariness and awake us to the realisation of the cold.

We ride with drooping eyelids, a swaying body, and a precarious seat, surrendered to the inevitable.

The column halts, and simultaneously we fall forward on our horses' necks, hoping to ease our aching limbs. Hoping against hope to hear the order dismount. A jerk, our horses move forward again, and disappointedly we resign ourselves to the further delusions of minds tortured from want of sleep.

Visions become distorted, we visualise the objects of our thoughts. A thought of water, and the road becomes a flowing stream. Thoughts of houses and trees, and in the darkness arises a village — a village that remains ever in the distance and endures only so long as our thoughts are of villages. The horse ahead moves strangely; it appears to be dancing, and has taken unto itself the shape of a beast of prehistoric ages. By an effort of will we shake off this state of semi-somnolence, and, for a time, see things in their normal shapes again.

At last, the order to dismount. Tumbling off we throw ourselves down at our horses' feet, indifferent to our position and its possibilities. With heads pillowed on arms, water-bottles or haversacks, we endeavour to win a few minutes respite. Follows sleep and blissful unconsciousness, until friendly hands awake us, and wearily we rise to a repetition of the last hour. On moving off some walk and lead their horses, stepping out briskly in an endeavour to dispel the ever-increasing drowsiness. It succeeds whilst walking, but a reaction sets in on regaining the saddle, leaving the walker in worse plight than ever.

With nerves on edge, we curse the numerous and apparently purposeless halts, become uncomplimentary about our leaders, revile horses for jogging and stumbling, warn companions of the damage they are likely to do if they persist in being careless with their rifles. Cheerful and good-tempered soldiers are few at 03.00.

And so on until we hail with relief the approach of dawn, which dispels the hallucinations of darkness.

EIGHT

Palestine: Rafa

Changes of season in Palestine are most regular. The fine, crisp days and nurturing rains of autumn start the year's crops, but by the second half of December the weather can be relied on to turn ugly. It did so with particular ferocity in 1916: bitter winds and rainstorms beat in from the sea and did their best to spoil the ANZACs' Christmas. They lacked tents, living in bivouacs in the most primitive conditions, enduring always the rigours of nature with those of the battlefield. In the New Year, there was a khamsin, a bombing raid by enemy aircraft and more rain and gales.

Worst of all, the evacuation of wounded from Magdhaba was dilatory again and they had to share these conditions. ANZAC medical officers had settled them in sand carts for the journey to the railhead, still some distance from El Arish, then were advised that the evacuation would be by sea. However, for five days the weather was too rough for embarkation and they were told to go overland by sand cart again. The wounded reached hospital after seven to nine days' delay, at least some of which could have been saved, to the fury of those who had rescued them under fire.

On 27 December, the Commander-in-Chief, General Sir Archibald Murray, visited the front. Few of the men had seen him and were at best indifferent, at worst, it must be said, resentful. After heaping full praise in his cables and dispatches to the War Office on the ANZAC Mounted Division and Chauvel for winning the Battle of Romani on their own, General Murray's account of it for publication played up the British part and minimised the ANZACs' out of all recognition. Chauvel visited the Western Front and England after the battle and read Murray's account of it in the *Daily Mail*. He reacted in a letter to his wife: 'I am afraid my men will be very angry when they see it. I cannot understand why the old man cannot do justice to those whom he owed so much and the whole thing is absolutely inconsistent with what he had already cabled.' (Chauvel's biographer A.J. Hill.)

His men were very angry. The long list of honours and awards for Romani bore out the C-in-C's fecklessness: the Imperial list was a good deal longer than the Dominions', and Chauvel was not even mentioned. It seems that he did decline a Distinguished Service Order, a fairly routine reward for good work to senior officers, as a slight to the ANZAC Mounted Division and this perhaps explains why his knighthood in January 1917 was for his services 'at El Arish, Magdhaba and Rafa' but not Romani. Praise is the only reward a servicemen gets and those of every rank share vicariously in their commander's recognition.

On the evening of 8 January 1917, the same two brigades of Light Horse and three battalions of Camels, with the important addition of General Chetwode and the 5th Mounted (Yeomanry) Brigade, set out for Rafa. Clear of the cultivation round El Arish, they were in sandhills again.

Atmospherics, pathos and drama have no place in military reports, which is why histories such as this can short-change readers seeking the heart of reportage, to 'know what it was like'. We are not able to embellish 'the regiment took the trenches with the bayonet' because it has been our good fortune not to have experienced such a thing. But rarely, an eye-witness does set down some contemporary — as opposed to recollected — observations and they are preserved.

One such piece was by Lieutenant Colonel Guy Powles, a New Zealander on Chauvel's staff. This is his description of the Desert Column on the march to Rafa:

Let us stop and watch them go by in the moonlight. The great wonder of the desert is its all-embracing silence — all sound is swallowed up — and so in silence they go by, each troop riding in line with its troop leader in front. Over the swelling sand hills they come, line upon line — noiseless they go — no song, no laughter, no talking, not a light to be seen; no sound but the snort of a horse as he blows the dust from his nostrils; or the click of two stirrup irons touching as two riders close in together; or the jingle of the links of the pack horses; or perhaps a neck chain rattling on the pommel. No other sound is heard unless one be very close, then there is a slow swish as the sand spurts out in front of a horse's foot, slithering on from step to step. All are intent on the work in hand, all with faces turned to the Promised Land.

Here come the Light Horse, with their emu plumes waving, here the quiet grim New Zealanders — here the yeomanry in helmets from many counties — and on the road itself go by the guns with their Scotch and English crews — and away out on the flank stretching out mile after mile into the black darkness come the Camels, riding in sections four abreast.

There are Australians among them and our own New Zealanders, and following them a band of tall, silent swarthy Sikhs on huge Indian camels. These are the Hong Kong and Singapore Mountain Battery, who so ably serve the Camel Brigade. And lastly, far behind, softly and slowly, come long streams of laden camels led by Egyptians bare footed in the sand.

They cleared the village of Sheikh Zowaiid at 1 am on the 9th and ten miles further on, approaching Rafa at first light, the leading men began standing in their stirrups, waving their hats and pointing ahead. Surely not at the Turks? They were grinning. Then the horses started snatching at green grass and daylight revealed a wide expanse of it, with patches of poppies, irises, anemones and wild flowers, interspersed with young barley. The jaded riders were intoxicated and it was all they could do to keep their mounts going forward with their heads up.

Soon they came to a clear view of the prospective battlefield. From the south, it was a diamond-shaped knob, with strong earthworks at the southern, eastern and western points and a hill, called Hill 255, at the northern point. There was a smaller knob to the south-east marked by another large, single tree. The two trees were the only vegetation, let alone cover, except for young barley and grass less than a foot high. In essentials, the objectives were similar to those at Magdhaba — a group of defended earthworks — and it was clear that encircling them from open ground, then drawing the ring tight, was the best tactic to employ.

At 10 am the New Zealanders rode at the eastern earthworks, from the east. At the same time, the 1st Light Horse Brigade closed on some earthworks from the south-east and the Camel Brigade advanced on foot towards the southern defences. The 3rd Light Horse Brigade and the 5th Yeomanry, under Chetwode's direct control, were in reserve.

The New Zealanders were successful at once, the Canterbury Regiment galloping down parties of Turks trying to escape from the eastern redoubt. They captured six German officers, two Turkish and 163 other ranks. The Auckland and Wellington regiments drove into sandhills between the earthworks and the sea, clearing them of enemy. Then slowly the whole NZ Brigade began to close on the eastern garrison against sustained fire.

By 11 am all forces were thrown in, including the reserve 1st Brigade and the Yeomanry. A general dismounted attack against the south and east enemy positions developed, but with the riflemen still a thousand yards from enemy trenches, the circle was too wide. Each brigade's flanks were exposed and the clever placement of the Turks left them open to enfilade fire. When they did gain ground to half a mile away, the Turks laid down a fire curtain of unremitting intensity and they were halted. The horse artillery and Hong Kong and Singapore Batteries shot well, but the effect of their small calibre shells on the earthworks was insignificant.

Nevertheless, at 2 pm the encirclement was complete and remarkably regular. North, at 12 o'clock, were three regiments of NZ Mounted Rifles, then round to 5 o'clock, five regiments of Light Horse, then three battalions of Camels until 7 o'clock, with the three regiments of Yeomanry closing the circle to 11 o'clock, where they linked up with the Canterbury Mounted Rifles. A pleasing symmetry indeed, but at no stage were they able to establish and maintain superiority with it. The Turks fought too well.

Stationary, the regiments could keep enemy heads down with rifle and machine-gun fire, but once that stopped to enable the squadrons to advance, the Turks shot standing up on their parapets and forced them prone again. The ammunition reserves had been left at Sheikh Zowaiid ten miles away and were slow to arrive: the New Zealanders had four machine-guns out of action and at 3 pm the Inverness Battery fired its last shell. Galloping Jack Royston galloped right round the whole circle seeking an opportunity to break the developing stalemate, perhaps by something similar to his coup with the 10th Light Horse Regiment at Magdhaba. If anyone could do it, he could, but nothing presented itself.

The battle had become a duel of small arms between attackers and defenders. Constant fire was required to keep the Turks off their parapets, from where they could sight and aim at the advancing men.

Three companies of the Camels worked round to their left, to face a section of earthworks that looked a little less impregnable than the rest and there they prepared to charge it. Luck then played a hand as, independently but simultaneously, the New Zealanders were collecting themselves for a charge from the opposite side of the ring.

The time was just before 4 pm. Reports from British aircraft and a scouting detachment of Light Horse confirmed that 2500 Turkish reinforcements were advancing on the ANZACs' rear, while another 500 were approaching from the north-east. Chetwode's Yeomanry were at a standstill, all reserves were committed, the light was fading, and if the ANZAC troops were to contend with this new threat they would need to redeploy. That meant breaking up the circle. Chetwode consulted Chauvel by telephone and at 4.25 decided to break off the action and withdraw. It seemed beyond the capacity of mounted troops to prevail. He pulled the Yeomanry Brigade out at once and, accepting failure, mounted his horse and started riding back to El Arish.

The order was received by 'some brigades', but whether this vague expression was meant to mask disobedience is irrelevant, because both the Camels and the New Zealanders were now out in the open, charging with fixed bayonets and beyond recall. The New Zealanders had received the report of approaching Turkish reinforcements, and in the brief time left General Chaytor had determined to bring the issue to a head and a decision. His objective, Hill 255, was a mile away on the crest of an absolutely bare grass slope: the men knew they were charging against time as well as Turks and went at it at a blistering pace. It was a headlong rush, rather than a controlled, steady advance. Inevitably, this became ragged and they paused 800 yards from the target to adjust the line and catch their breath. The Turkish resistance matched their courage: they could be seen standing up to take aim under a barrage of machine-gun and rifle fire supporting the New Zealanders from the circle. But as always under pressure, the Turks' aim was poor.

The re-formed regiments renewed their charge up the remaining slope in two strenuous dashes and leapt at the trenches, yelling. The Turks resisted the wildly scything blades only feebly and surrendered. Their trenches were strewn with dead and wounded, two and three deep in

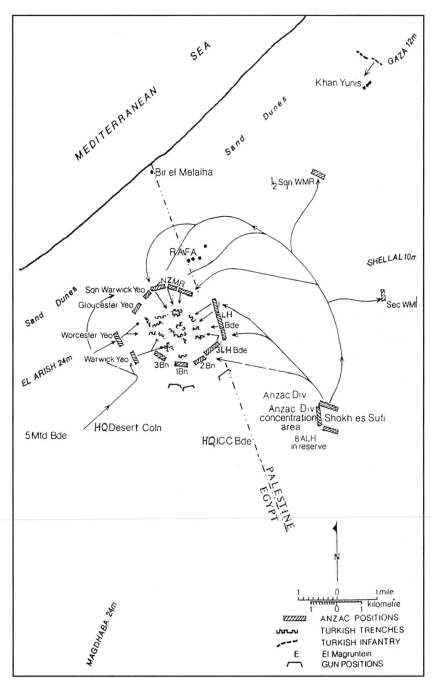

MEDITERRANEAN SEA

GAZA 12m

Khan Yunis

Sand Dunes

Bir el Melalha

½ Sqn WMR

RAFA

SHELLAL 10m

Sand Dunes

NZMR

Sqn Warwick Yeo

Gloucester Yeo

Sec WMl

Worcester Yeo

LH Bde

El ARISH 24m

Warwick Yeo

3LH Bde

3Bn 1Bn 2Bn

Anzac Div

Anzac Div
concentration
area

Shokh es Sufi

5Mtd Bde

HQ Desert Coln

HQ ICC Bde

8 ALH
in reserve

PALESTINE
EGYPT

N

MAGDHABA 24m

1   0   1 mile

kilometre

0   1

ANZAC POSITIONS

TURKISH TRENCHES

TURKISH INFANTRY

E   El Magruntein

GUN POSITIONS

Battle of Rafa, 9 January 1917.

places. But fortune did favour the brave: the New Zealanders suffered only seventeen men killed and 93 wounded in the whole day.

And from the south, perfectly timed, came the charge of 600 Cameleers. Two of their three companies were Australian, one British. They too had to ascend a bare slope to the southern earthworks that had resisted so stubbornly all day. The Camels' line gathered speed against heavy but inaccurate fire. At the 200 yard mark, the men actually saw the Turks fixing their bayonets and this apparent challenge was accepted with 'a great roar'. They rushed the stronghold, and as they reached it the Turks, ever shy of the savage steel, raised a number of white flags they must have had ready and surrendered. 'A moment later,' says Gullett, 'the panting assailants were shaking hands with the enemy all along the line.' He says there were many such examples of the ANZACs being unable to sustain their battle fury for a moment after the fight was won, and even when the enemy continued shooting from the security of his trench until the last possible moment he was spared as soon as he dropped his rifle.

With the two earthworks lost, all Turkish resistance collapsed. The New Zealanders even pushed on, securing other entrenchments, and Cox's 1st Brigade regiments got to their feet and dashed forward as soon as they saw the New Zealand charge. The rest of the Camels now joined in the renewed general assault and the 5th Yeomanry Brigade, advised of the dramatic transformation, returned to the battlefield to participate in the closing stages. With the surrender, Chauvel ordered a prompt withdrawal, for his flank guards were already exchanging shots at long range with the Turkish reinforcements.

Total British casualties at Rafa were 91 killed and 415 wounded. The Turks lost 200 killed, 168 wounded and 1434 captured. When the weary victors rode back to El Arish that night they were delighted to find that the Scottish Infantry had turned out to fill the water troughs for their horses.

There were some curiosities. British, and aircraft of the 1st Squadron, Australian Flying Corps, overflew the battle throughout and, for the first time, directed artillery fire by wireless from the air. One of the pilots was Lieutenant Ross Smith, late of the 3rd Light Horse Regiment and veteran of Romani, now at the start of his new and illustrious career.

It would seem that surrendering Turks transforming themselves on the spot from foe to friend in order to gain sanctuary was a current issue in the Light Horse, and my father takes a different line from Gullett's. He writes:

The Turks are not fighting as gamely or as cleanly as they did on the Peninsular. When our fellows charge their positions, they fire on them till they are on top of them, then throw up their hands and surrender, knowing they are safe ... It is hard for our fellows to refrain from ignoring the surrender and using his bayonet on a wretch who has shot his mates right up to the last second, then put his hands up to save his cowardly skin. At Romani, they also abused the white flag. One dirty dog threw up his hands to our colonel, then picked up his rifle and took deliberate aim at the colonel, but one of the boys handy was a bit too quick and the wily Turk went down before he got his shot in.

It can't have been a new problem in warfare and if there was official guidance or orders about it, these could only have said that an enemy clearly laying down his arms and surrendering must in all circumstances be treated as a prisoner of war.

In the same letter of 16 January, my father says:

I expect you have already read about the latest fighting out this way. Brigadier General Royston has been doing some more great work and proving himself a fine soldier, as he did with us at Romani. They attacked a very strong position and had a bad time of it and were ordered to retire, which other brigades did, but General Royston as is his wont, would not accept the defeat and got his brigade together — or rather what was left of it — went to the attack again, capturing the position and 1,700 prisoners. His casualties were heavy of course, but he did the job.

My father's 2nd Brigade was still in Sinai, far away from the Magdhaba and Rafa actions, but on the dates there were no other engagements he could have been referring to. Nothing like this concerning Royston occurred, but the story does accord with Brigadier General Cox's Nelson-like conduct at Magdhaba. No explanation is possible, other than that my father was relaying inaccurate but harmless hearsay. Indeed, good could have come of it to both distinguished brigadiers general, had they known. To a commander, the sweetest praise comes from his own men and I fancy both gentlemen would have shared and savoured that of Corporal Baly, as he was then.

The letters home of a young major of the 7th Regiment were always succinct and restrained. Most soldiers avoided direct reference to the horrors and dangers they experienced in their letters, especially to women, but Nathaniel Dunbar (Nat) Barton, a squadron commander at 23, is at his most cryptic when we look for enlightenment. He actually enjoyed the Sinai campaign for its open mounted work and never mentioned its heat and hardships. With rare discursiveness, he wrote: 'We really are having an enjoyable time here, as there is a prospect of a scrap ... the life is active, riding about patrolling and outpost duty, quite different from the confinement and deadly monotony of Gaba Tepe [Gallipoli]. I was in command of a patrol last night. We started out at noon yesterday and did not return until 2 am this morning and were riding hard practically all the time.'

Mostly, he was enigmatic.

On Katia: 'The Yeomanry on our left, the first we have seen of them when they were cut up in April when they fled for their lives, let us down again. They are the limit.' In other accounts, there is merely an absence of the mention of Yeomanry and we don't know the story.

On Bir el Abd: 'We had a very stiff little go on the 9th [of August], for which I see the London Times gives us great credit, but after that, we have done *no scrapping*' (Barton's emphasis).

On Mazar: 'We are all fearfully disgusted with the Mazar stunt ... Since then, we have not done anything much.'

The 2nd Brigade remained in Sinai policing the conquered territory and guarding the advancing railway and water pipe, while the rest of the ANZAC Mounted Division marched into Palestine and fought the Battles of Magdhaba and Rafa. 'We are still loafing here instead of where the fighting was,' Barton wrote. 'We call ourselves now "Ryrie's Sporting Brigade" or "The Australian Yeomanry". I think we shall always regret having missed these last shows.'

The collected letters of Nat Barton on World War I were published in 1999 and have been incorporated into the Australian War Memorial's records. Despite the gaps, the writings of this outstanding young leader broaden our perspectives, and on occasion dovetail with my father's accounts.

NINE

Gaza miscarriage

The two minor miracles of Magdhaba and Rafa had a strategic influence far beyond the tactical: now British thinking swung entirely behind a plan for the conquest of Palestine.

All the portents were propitious. General Murray's railway line was almost at El Arish and regular supplies were coming in by sea as well. The weather was cool and would remain so for four months, and the troops were seasoned, fit and at the height of their morale. The better going was ideal for mounted work and, at last, suitable for infantry. The huge camel trains, a burden in themselves, could be reduced, if not entirely replaced, with motor and horse-drawn transport. As a preliminary to full-scale Palestine operations, Sinai was entirely cleared of Turkish remnants.

After Rafa, the Turks left a garrison of 4000 troops ten miles to the north-east, but by March had withdrawn another ten miles to the Gaza–Beersheba line.

Gaza, then a city of 40,000 inhabitants, is two miles from the coast. It had always been a bar to access to the Philistine Plain and all country to the north. From the earliest civilisations its conquest had been necessary for either an invasion of Egypt from the north or an advance from Egypt into Palestine. It has been called 'The outpost of Africa and the door of Asia'. One of its strong defensive features was a maze of tall cactus hedges all round it.

Beersheba was a village trading centre 30 miles to the south-east. It linked the hinterland with the port of Gaza by rail and road but it offered little of material consequence to an army, except an abundance of good water fed by many springs.

To close the gateway to Palestine to the Desert Column, the Turks spread a force 15,000 strong between the two places.

Early in 1917, the Scottish 52nd Infantry Division was joined by the 53rd (Welsh Territorials) and 54th (East Anglian) Divisions, while the ANZAC Mounted Division was augmented by two new Australian Light Horse Brigades and two British Yeomanry brigades, named the Imperial

A camel train in the Wady Ghuzze. AWM H11642

Mounted Division. Not without controversy: the Australians wanted their name to be associated with the new division, and while they had no objection to a British commander, pressed for a proportional number of experienced Australian officers on his staff. They were rebuffed on both counts and this caused more resentment. The British officers who were appointed had little or no front-line service and it seemed that they were not only insensitive to Australian desiderations but also reluctant to trust its service officers, despite their record of two years' fighting in this theatre. After constant pressure, later in the year the Imperial Mounted Division did become the Australian Mounted Division, made up of two Light Horse and one Yeomanry Brigade.

On 18 March, Chetwode conferred with Chauvel and the British commanders Major General H.W. Hodgson of the Imperial Mounted Division and Major General A.G. Dallas of the 53rd Infantry Division to make final plans for an attack on Gaza. It was decided to concentrate all forces for the attack at Deir el Belah, a small native village ten miles south-west of Gaza. There were palm trees for concealment, clean sand at Belah for a good winter camp, and firm flat ground for movement towards the objective.

However, to reach that, the great Wady Ghuzze had to be crossed. At that season it was fordable at many places, but its floor was 30 to 40 feet deep between precipitous and shifting banks, and where the crossings needed to be made it was more than 100 yards wide. Still, it was less an obstacle to be surmounted than a feature to be negotiated, and in the event of a Turkish counterattack its weird gulches and prominences would offer good defensive positions. This wady was said to be Gustave Doré's inspiration for his illustrations of Dante's *Inferno*.

Chauvel's 2nd Brigade had now rejoined him from Sinai, to their mutual satisfaction. Colonel Richardson claims that after the long spell of cool weather and comparatively light work in Sinai, 'the health and spirits of the 7th Regiment were perhaps now better than they had ever been before, and the keenness and smartness displayed in patrols and reconnaissances had never been equalled'. He added that this was just as well, for there were severe tests of their mettle to come.

My father remarked on how this front had grown 'since we first crossed the Canal 12 months ago. We were just three regiments [2nd Brigade], had nothing but our rifles and a few machine-guns. Now, we see thousands upon thousands of Infantry, Light Horse, Cavalry, Camel Corps, plenty of artillery and other things I may not mention [amongst which, no doubt, were the first experimental tanks]. This brigade are the pioneers of this front and very proud of that ... but I don't think we will ever have such a hard time as we did that summer.'

The build-up of the Palestine front was to double and treble again. And there were just as hard times coming. Unfortunately, our correspondent's account of the First Battle of Gaza, in which his regiment played a key role with flair and exhilaration, was written too soon after the event and contains too many misapprehensions to quote.

On 25 March, a reconnaissance of Gaza was made by the 3rd Light Horse Brigade. After crossing the Wady Ghuzze, their screen dashed up close to the town and drew the Turks' attention, while staff officers rode about in the rear, making a survey of the ground over which the main force was to advance the next morning. The Turks opened fire from a distance, but gave no indication that they suspected a large British force was anywhere near.

As darkness fell, the Desert Column moved in quietly to their camping area at Belah. Final preparations occupied all hands for most of the night and few men slept. The infantry in particular, having marched over the last three nights, were tired, but also fit and keen. The two infantry divisions, two mounted divisions and the Camel Brigade could provide a total of 22,000 effective rifles, while the defenders' force of 15,000 was spread over ten to seventeen miles. In Gaza itself, the garrison was believed to number 4000 troops.

At 2.30 am on 26 March, Chauvel led the ANZACs out. The 7th Light Horse Regiment formed the screen and led the division to the Wady Ghuzze in pitch-black darkness. Then as the leading files were about to cross, a thick fog enveloped the whole force. The Imperial Mounted and 53rd Infantry Divisions and the Camels followed the ANZACs across without mishap, although there were instances of horses absolutely refusing to go forward and it was found they were standing on the edge of banks with a 50 foot drop. From the wady, it was intended that the mounted divisions take different directions, for the plan was for them to repeat the encircling tactics that had brought victory at Magdhaba and Rafa. The 54th Infantry was held in reserve, to support the 53rd and/or Imperial Mounted, if required.

Clear of the wady, the guides, an officer of the 7th and one of the 6th, checked their bearings and led on, confidently but slowly. The fog became so dense that one horseman was almost invisible to the next and contact between the advance guard and main body had to be maintained by means of gallopers dashing between them to show the way.

This generation of Australian countrymen had of necessity a good capability for finding their way over country, and the experience of trackless Sinai had developed this to an almost uncanny degree. Chauvel's brigades had surrounded El Arish before first light after a 20-mile night march and not one brigade was late on their start line or out of position by more than 200 yards. Brigadier General Ryrie of the 2nd Brigade set the inconvenience of such a fog at nothing, compared with the advantage it gave him of moving unobserved. The British infantry, however, took the view that to proceed in it courted confusion and calamities, such as losing the way.

Soon after 6 am, the fog started to lift and the 7th Regiment, 'noted for its dashing screen work', was fired on by an enemy patrol when still six miles south of the city. The regiment charged the Turks at the gallop and almost ran into two German aircraft on the ground, frantically preparing to take off. These taxied just clear of the galloping horsemen, took off and turned towards the main body, machine-guns firing. One squadron from each regiment dismounted and fired at the planes. This startled two of General Ryrie's favourite chargers, which broke away and galloped right into Gaza — the only mishap of the air raid. Even then, only hours later some Turks were captured with the two horses in their possession.

The pace quickened. The 7th, trotting and cantering on a wide front through open country and olive groves, were making contact with small bodies of Turks and galloping down any show of resistance. They crossed the Gaza–Beersheba road and cut the telephone wires. The 5th Regiment, following, galloped down a convoy of ten wagons carrying supplies for German aircraft; others captured 30 German pioneers.

The sun rose on an excited cavalcade of horsemen enjoying such an adventure as rarely came their way. The whole ANZAC division was now deep in enemy territory, but as yet ignorant of the fortunes and movements of the other mounted division and the infantry. That the enemy were taken utterly unawares was shown by one of their small mounted patrols escorting a Turkish general, en route to Gaza to take command of its garrison, blundering into the 7th's path. There was a wild yell, thundering hooves and suddenly the general was looking from his carriage at four grinning, unshaven foreign soldiers, leaning down from huge horses that steamed gently in the morning air. The flabbergasted general produced his gold cigarette case and offered it round: a trooper fished from his breeches pocket a half-smoked fag, and with a courtly flourish offered it to the general. Eventually passed to the rear, the Turk kept protesting at the indignity of his capture by common soldiers and demanded an escort of equal rank. General Chauvel's regrets that he was too busy were conveyed to him.

The 7th Regiment, now abreast of the north-east of the city and close enough to observe its individual buildings, stopped briefly to block a number of roads leading from Gaza northwards and led on. Uninterrupted, they soon reached the sand dunes, then the sea. A long, slender line of horsemen stretched behind them: the 5th Regiment, the New Zealand Brigade, then snaking round to the city's southern extremities, the 22nd Mounted Brigade. If the 22nd was in touch on its left with the 53rd Infantry Division, and if any of that division had reached the sea, Gaza would be encircled, as planned. A battalion of the 53rd and two squadrons of Yeomanry under Lieutenant Colonel N.E. Money had in fact reached the sea: their primary role was a feint, to draw the Turks' attention away from the main body.

The ANZACs deployed on a three-mile line that followed the contours of a hill through olive groves to the coast, and from there they looked straight down over the city. It appeared the Imperial Division and the Camels had taken up their appointed posts on an outer defensive perimeter, again approximately circular. But, where were the infantry?

The tasks of Major General Dallas' 53rd Division were to throw a strong bridgehead over the Wady Ghuzze by 5 am, seize two high features called Mansura and El Sheluf, then attack Ali Muntar as soon as possible. This was a strongly fortified 300-foot knoll half a mile from the city, overlooking its south and eastern quarters. The feature was flanked by small fields and cactus hedges on both sides. The British assessed that if Ali Muntar could be taken early in the day, the rest would be easy and the fall of Gaza would be assured.

It was anticipated that the 53rd would have commenced its assault by 8 am at least. But having crossed the wady, Dallas had to wheel his division from the right over unknown country and he feared that his brigades would come under heavy fire from Turkish artillery before his own had been able to deliver a softening-up bombardment, or even register, in the conditions. There had already been some confusion in the brigades and he decided to wait. His division stayed put near the wady for two hours, until the fog lifted.

Yet his attack started well, with the capture of the two ridges, El Sheluf and Mansura. From that point, however, the enterprise was wrecked by extraordinary and unexplained delays, wasted opportunities and a total breakdown of communications.

There were two generals running this battle, Chetwode, the Desert Column commander, and Dobell, the overall commander of Eastern Force — that is, all British forces east of the Suez Canal. They had adjacent headquarters and seemed able to keep out of each other's way, but the pitfalls inherent in such an arrangement might have played some part in their control. When the situation with Dallas could not be resolved from headquarters, there was nothing to prevent one of them riding forward to see him, but neither did so. Could such an obvious move possibly have fallen between two stools?

They conferred and noted anxiously that no attempt had been made to bring the 53rd's artillery into action and that its advance had stalled. At 9.30 am Chetwode signalled that he should push his attack vigorously. But for some reason, Dallas had gone up with all his staff to one of his brigade's headquarters and for over two hours, he was out of touch.

1005 — Chetwode's Chief-of-Staff to Dallas: 'The General Officer Commanding wishes me to press on you the extreme importance of the capture of Gaza before reinforcements can reach it ...'

1130 — Chief-of-Staff to Dallas: 'I am directed to inform you that (1) you have been out of touch with Desert Column and your own headquarters for over two hours; (2) no gun registration appears to have been carried out; (3) that time is passing and you are still far from your objective; (4) that the Army and Column Commanders are exercised at the loss of time, which is vital; (5) you must keep a general staff officer at your headquarters who can communicate with you immediately; (6) you must launch your attack forthwith.'

1200 — Chetwode to Dallas: 'No message from you for over two hours. When are you going to begin your attack? Time is of vital importance. No general staff officer at your headquarters for two hours.'

Half the daylight had gone and Dallas was already five hours late. When he did return to his headquarters, he signalled: 'Where are infantry brigade and field artillery brigade which are to come to my support if required? I should like them at Mansura now, as I am not sure what the enemy strength is.'

By then it was clear that, even if the 53rd Division advanced at once and met the formidable opposition undoubtedly waiting for it, Dallas would be unable to reach Gaza by nightfall.

Cavalry to the rescue. At 12 o'clock, Chetwode had put both mounted divisions on stand-by. They were 'to reconnoitre immediately with a view to closing in on enemy at Gaza, to assist infantry if required'. An hour later he and Dobell took the decision to use them. Chauvel was placed in command of both mounted divisions, Hodgson's Yeomanry were to take over Chauvel's line and the Camels were to move to Hodgson's former position.

But at that time, Dallas at last committed his two forward brigades to their advance. They had to cover 4000 yards of uphill, naked plain against a bristling enemy that had waited to pounce on them all morning. They let the Welsh battalions come to some cactus hedges 1000 yards away, then poured concentrated rifle and machine-gun fire on them. The battalions changed their tactics to short rushes and with the greatest gallantry, struggled on. They suffered dreadful casualties. The 18-pounder batteries supporting them were inaccurate and did not correct their aim despite spotting reports by aircraft.

Ion Idriess was watching from the Light Horse line on the hillside. 'It was a terrible sight of massed human courage,' he wrote. 'I wonder what other madness the human race will go through before the end of the world … We know now that Ali Muntar was taken and lost three times with the bayonet and then taken again.'

After 1 pm, Dallas committed his reserve brigade to the assault. They endeavoured to roll up the Turks' left flank, but by yet another failure of staff work, an artillery brigade of the 54th Division was three hours late with its fire support. The infantry was now in amongst the maze of cactus hedges, which afforded some cover but impeded progress. Just before 4 pm, Dallas had committed all his troops, he had sustained heavy casualties, his men were exhausted and the afternoon light was fading into dusk.

Chauvel had meanwhile been managing the reorganisation of his front for the dismounted assault from the opposite side of Gaza. At 1 pm, he was ordered urgently to the attack. But although movements were carried out at the gallop, such a redeployment of a whole division of Yeomanry and a brigade of Camels, as well as repositioning his own ANZAC brigades for the attack, re-siting headquarters and final briefings of staff, took time and it was 4 pm before they could start.

The 2nd Brigade and New Zealanders, well-rested spectators of the incredible squandering of their good work in the early morning, set off at a willing canter. They were seething to set things right and if it meant hand-to-hand fighting with the bayonet in those hedges, so be it. But they were spread very thin, only five regiments over three miles (the Australian 6th Regiment was at Deir Sineid, five miles north, guarding the northern approach to Gaza).

First into action was a squadron of the 5th Light Horse, galloping with fixed bayonets down the Jaffa–Gaza road. When they struck heavy fire from the cactus hedges they dismounted and swung right, towards the enemy fire. Their advance was covered by the 2nd Brigade's machine-gun squadron repeatedly packing their guns onto horses, trotting forward, unloading and setting up the guns again so as to enfilade the opposing Turks. Then all the squadrons were among the cactus hedges, cutting gaps through the plants with their bayonets to reach the Turks just feet away on the other side. According to Idriess:

> The colonel threw up his hand — we reined up our horses with their noses rearing from the [prickly] pear — we jumped off — all along the hedge from tiny holes were squirting rifle-puffs, in other places the pear was spitting at us as the Turks standing behind simply fired through the juicy leaves. The horse holders grabbed the horses while each man slashed with his bayonet to cut a hole through those cactus walls. The colonel was firing with his revolver at the juice spots bursting through the leaves — the New Zealand Brigade had galloped by to the left of us, the 7th Light Horse were fighting on our right. Then came the fiercest individual excitement — man after man tore through the cactus to be met by the bayonets of the Turks, six to one. It was just berserk slaughter. A man sprang at the closest Turk, thrust, sprang aside and thrust again and again — some men howled as they rushed, the shivery feel of steel on steel — the grunting breaths ... the sobbing scream as the bayonet ripped home. The

Turkish battalion simply melted away ... men lay horribly bloody and dead; others writhed on the stained grass while all through the cactus lanes our men were chasing demented Turks ... I saw the finest soldiers of Turkey go down that day.

'The Turks,' said an officer of the 5th, 'ran in and out like rabbits and we shot them as they ran.'

For its part, the 7th went for the town with all their heart and soul. Night fell with the moon only in its first quarter, but the troops and squadrons kept in touch by means of whistles and lamps as they pressed to the city's threshold. When the fight went out of the Turks, even the men with led horses pushed through the mutilated hedges after the riflemen. A party of horse holders shot a number of Turks and accepted the surrender of twenty. Some of the gaps cut with bayonets would admit passage in single file only: junior officer troop leader first with his revolver, then a call to his men to scramble through — and these gory apparitions with bloodied bayonets were enough now to induce surrender on sight.

The New Zealanders had galloped in from the east and attacked towards Ali Muntar. They came under hot fire from cactus hedges between them and Gaza, and enfilade fire from Ali Muntar itself. The ground was more open than on the Australians' front and their regiments went forward in good formation. Heavy fighting fell to the Wellingtons, who overran an ambulance station, then cut briskly through an olive grove to cactus enclosures at the town's edge. Again, they had to hack their way through with the bayonet, but they were checked by fire from some of the more determined Turks. Two troops rushed the position, some Turks surrendered but most resisted until 32 were killed with the bayonet.

On the right, two heavy-calibre Krupp guns were located and a squadron of the Wellingtons swooped on them. Fifty-six Turks were bayoneted and twenty captured. Then the enemy opened fire from a house 75 yards away and a considerable enemy force started a counterattack from another direction. They were first seen by an officer of the 7th, who ran into the open with a Hotchkiss gun, rested it on the shoulder of one of his troop and shot down many of them at close range. The New Zealanders dispersed the rest by rifle fire.

Then, joined by some of the troop from the 7th, they laid one of the big Krupp guns through its open breech onto the house, from which the enemy was still firing. Sighting along the barrel, they loaded and fired two shells. These burst in the building. A great many Turks were killed and twenty dazed survivors surrendered. Teams were improvised and brought up and the guns hauled away to brigade headquarters. In all these encounters, the Wellingtons had only one man killed and nineteen wounded.

Two squadrons of the Canterburys closed on the town with the Wellingtons, while the third squadron went further south and made touch with Dallas' infantry, still engaged. Simultaneously, the two forces reached the sheikh's tomb on the height of Ali Muntar. This fortification was now a reeking, smoking hulk lit only by its own fires and blackened by their smoke. It had already changed hands several times, and at the last, fell with all honour to the 53rd's Welshmen.

The time was then 6.40 pm. The Australian 2nd Brigade and the New Zealand Brigade were entering Gaza from the north and east, the infantry had carried that 'key to Gaza's defences', Ali Muntar, and its labyrinth of cactus hedges and trenches at the base. The Turk had been dislodged from his southern front line by the sustained fighting of the 53rd and the ANZACs had secured most of his territory to the north. But now, coming through to the front-line units was a signal from Chetwode, drafted after full consultation with Dobell and Chauvel, but opposed, and strongly resisted, by the Australian leader: 'Retire. Retire. Retire.'

It was utterly bewildering. Every rifleman knew that they had won. The Turks were demoralised, disinclined to fight, the ANZACs had suffered minuscule casualties and every indication pointed to a Turkish rout and general surrender at any moment. General Chaytor demanded to have the order in writing. General Ryrie ordered none of the 2nd Brigade to move until every man had been collected. As Chetwode's order went from brigades, to regiments, to squadrons and to troops, it was everywhere received with disbelief, then disgust. Distraught officers ordered signallers to confirm it and when the crushing, bitter truth was forced on them, they felt as men could only feel who had won a battle and been ordered to accept defeat.

No less shattered were General Dallas and the infantry. He had failed to advance through the fog and was therefore the first cause of all subsequent failures, but when the 53rd did finally attack, its men showed complete disregard for their lives in prevailing against their formidable objective. Ali Muntar remains a celebrated feat of British arms.

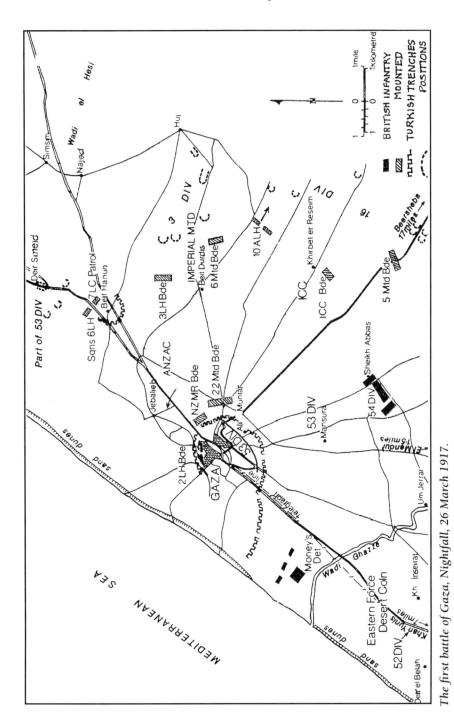

The first battle of Gaza, Nightfall, 26 March 1917.

What prompted Chetwode's order was the reported approach from various quarters of Turkish reinforcements, numbering 10,000. He, and Chauvel, had been fully aware of the risk they took in withdrawing the mounted troops from dispositions where they could guard against such developments. When they threw them against the town, they took away most of the outer perimeter of defence. In his report on the operation, Dallas said: 'Towards sunset … General Chauvel pointed out that my right was in the air and that he could give me no protection during the night'. Chetwode had then ordered Dallas to close this gap by joining his right to the left flank of the 54th Division. 'I explained,' continued Dallas, 'that it was quite impossible to do this without abandoning the positions the division had gained. I asked for time to consider. Finally I received definite instructions that I must bring my right back and get in touch with the 54th Division.'

So Dallas's brigades gave up the stronghold they had struggled for and won at so great a price. They had held it for less than an hour.

The ANZACs' withdrawal was a miserable business. Richardson, leading B and C Squadrons of the 7th Regiment through the prickly pear, said with his clipped understatement: 'The buildings and streets of Gaza were within a few hundred yards of us, but an anxious silence had fallen [as the advance and the Turkish resistance had both stopped]. The prisoners taken had been sent back and an officer was sent to Lieut. Colonel Onslow for orders … apparently there was no-one on our right or left, no-one behind and it was not known what was in front. It was now nearly 9 o'clock and nothing could be seen of the horses, though where they were to have been was close by.'

At last, an officer from Brigade Headquarters brought the 'astonishing news that a withdrawal of the whole force was in progress'. The 'anxious silence' was explained. The messenger 'urged the necessity of haste, but without horses, little could be done'.

The account is typical of the scattered 2nd Brigade's efforts to extricate itself from the cactus maze in the dark, re-form, and of course locate its horses, which in many cases had been led forward when their holders joined the fight. Brigadier General Ryrie's order to account for every man was practical, as well as owing much to rebelliousness, and in the end there was uncertainty about only one individual, who later turned up.

It took four hours for the ANZAC Mounted Division to reassemble and start the wretched ride back to Deir el Belah, with Ryrie's regiments as rearguard. As well as smashed morale, the men were suffering their third night without sleep and most horses had not been watered. The familiar hallucinations from exhaustion plagued the column, but no Turks harried them — an indication of how soundly they were beaten — and the brigadiers were so confident they were in no danger from reinforcements that they allowed lights to be shown, smoking and talking. The bodies of the single Australian and two New Zealanders killed at Gaza accompanied them on gun limbers.

The aftermath was long and bitter and affected profoundly the attitudes and destinies of every man in the theatre, as well as the future conduct of the campaign. If they believed two divisions of Turks were about to reinforce Gaza, Chetwode and Dobell needed to take some action, but the ANZAC and other senior officers were adamant that they overreacted. It emerged that these reinforcements were organised by the energetic German General von Kressenstein and he complained of 'typical Turkish delays' which meant the new columns constituted no real threat that day. The 6th and 10th Light Horse Regiments in their advance posts north of Gaza were, among others, in contact with some of the columns and said that there was no enemy pressure on their front when they were withdrawn.

Every brigadier in the line believed that the occupation of the town could have been completed and the enemy held off without any trouble. There were, after all, two divisions of mounted troops and two of infantry to call on, half of whom were still fresh, against two divisions of Turks.

Gullett suggests that the distortion of the two generals' view could have come about, at least in part, because of their remoteness from the field commanders. Had they moved among them, they might have absorbed some different perspectives. The British military historian Cyril Falls' summation is simply that the Turks were slow and the British muddle-headed. Dobell, of course, gave the actual order and Chetwode concurred. Dobell told Chauvel by telephone of the intention and he protested, 'But we have Gaza!' Dobell replied, 'Yes, but the reinforcements are all over you.'

Prisoners taken later confirmed that the Turks intended to surrender at dawn and white flags had been distributed. A captured Syrian doctor asked Brigadier General Ryrie why he had pulled out. 'You can damn well search me!' he answered. The Syrian observed that when the Turkish garrison commander learned of it, 'he laughed for a long time'.

Regrettably, only Chetwode's account on the public record is clear and frank. Much was made of the necessity to water the horses, but this was not a pressing issue to those who owned them, and some were watered in rain pools. The C-in-C General Murray's report to the War Office concludes: 'it was a most successful operation, the fog and waterless nature of the country just saving the enemy from complete disaster, and proved conclusively that the enemy has no chance against our troops in the open'.

For this soaring flight of fancy and others, including the rigging of casualty figures in British favour, the Commander-in-Chief received a congratulatory telegram from George V.

Nat Barton was at his most heartsick and trenchant after this battle and wrote only: 'I found this last stunt very unsettling and it has only been during the last few days that I have felt inclined either to read or write'.

TEN

Second Gaza engagement

The Turks had a talent for earthworks and wielded pick and shovel as if this was the highest of callings. After First Gaza, their morale rose just as their enemy's sank and they set about fortifying the southern approaches to the town zestfully, with the aim of denying it permanently to the British.

Just south of the Gaza–Beersheba road ran an irregular series of low ridges: rough ground, on which they built a new system of trenches and redoubts. The approach to the ridges from the south was over long, open slopes with no cover and the Turks' fields of fire could command every skerrick of it. Gaza itself was still protected by the cactus hedges known as the Maze, the Labyrinth and Green Hill. And despite its pounding by artillery, Ali Muntar was not nearly as badly damaged as it looked and it was quickly refurbished. There was a gap of 800 yards between Ali Muntar and the fortified ridges — the bare plain on which the 53rd Division had suffered so terribly. The plain was still completely overlooked by Ali Muntar's defences and just as vulnerable. As for fighting men, the Turks had positioned between 20,000 and 25,000 between Beersheba and the sea by early April 1917.

Both Generals Murray and Dobell had made quite indefensible claims to the British government about the 'success' of the engagement of 26 March, and so should not have been much surprised when the War

Cabinet urged them to proceed with the capture of Gaza, the defeat of all Turks south of Jerusalem and the conquest of Jerusalem itself, 45 miles further north. The new British Prime Minister, David Lloyd George, favoured an offensive in Palestine, indeed anywhere but on the Western Front, where the news kept going from bad to worse. Dobell appeared to be genuine, and not self-serving, in his view that such an offensive would succeed and certainly, with the addition of the 74th Division brought forward from El Arish, he had numbers of two to one. However, Murray, while supporting Dobell's plan, continued to stress to the War Office that fighting in this theatre would be fierce and casualties heavy, and to draw attention to 'my never varying estimate of the troops required'. He was directed to further his operations with all energy, but told that no additional troops would be sent as his present force was considered adequate to deal with the Turks in their somewhat beleaguered state.

Dobell's plan was nothing less than a frontal assault on Gaza with all his strength. His troops were still at Deir el Belah and could no longer have the advantage of surprise. The infantry divisions were to crush the enemy round Gaza, while the mounted divisions were to force his flank back on Beersheba, preventing the reinforcement of the Gaza garrison, and then be in readiness for the pursuit. The 52nd Division was to assault Ali Muntar, while the 54th, on the 52nd's right, was to fight its way through some new redoubts two miles south of the city at Khurbet el Bir, then swing round the town to its north and take Anzac Ridge — so named for the ANZACs' occupation after their epic ride around the city in the first stage of the first battle. At the same time, the 53rd Division was to attack from south-west of Gaza, over the sand dunes nearest the sea.

Neither Chetwode nor Chauvel favoured the scheme. One British commander, briefing his brigadiers, concluded with: 'That, gentlemen, is the plan and I might say frankly that I do not think much of it'. Such doubts of leaders in battle are always sensed by the men and there was no soldier present who did not believe that failures at the most senior staff level were responsible for the defeat snatched from victory of First Gaza. But no plan with any better chance of success seems to have been canvassed, and indeed, without surprise, it is difficult to conceive of one.

The preliminary bombardment started at 5.30 am on 17 April. Heavy artillery was well directed, as was fire from the French cruiser *Requin* and two Royal Navy monitors offshore, but it all made little inroads on the earthworks of Gaza.

By 7 am, the 52nd and 54th Divisions had advanced on a five-mile front across Mansura Ridge, with only six casualties, and had started to dig in. But most of them were in full view of the enemy, who opened fire, pinned them down for the whole day and inflicted 150 casualties.

The Desert Column, on the right, had started to deploy at 2 am, typically, in a long, thin, mobile screen, running approximately north–south. Reconnaissance by the mounted divisions soon located the enemy's line, lying roughly parallel to the Gaza–Beersheba road. There was little patrol skirmishing, but serious damage was done by an enemy aircraft bombing the 2nd Light Horse Brigade's limbers and spare horses at Shelal. Six men were killed and thirteen wounded, together with seventeen horses killed and thirteen wounded.

That night, the ANZAC and Imperial Mounted Divisions left a line of strong outposts extending from the 54th Division's right back to the Wady Ghuzze and withdrew across the wady. The infantry consolidated their line closest to Gaza, which, if the Turks had been in any doubt, confirmed to them the objective. The 53rd Division had not yet crossed the wady, but had reconnoitred in strength towards their sector by the coast.

On the next day, Chetwode's two mounted divisions repeated and extended their reconnaissance. He came to the view that if his brigades were to make a dismounted attack, they would be ineffective against such a strong enemy flank and asked Dobell to earmark part of the new 74th Division (in reserve) for an attack on the formidable Turkish trenches at Atawineh. But Dobell preferred to keep the 74th intact to await developments and refused. However, when the time came he did lend the horse soldiers a brigade of the 54th (East Anglia) Division.

That day also passed quietly, except for shelling of advanced infantry trenches. In the evening, Dobell decided to make his all-out attack along the whole line next morning and his final orders went out.

At 5.30 am on a fine, very cold morning, British artillery and the French and British warships opened again on Ali Muntar and the other targets. Two hours later, the 53rd, 52nd and 54th Divisions, together with the Camel Brigade, 4th and 3rd Light Horse Brigades and 5th Mounted Brigade, all went forward. On the extreme right, the ANZAC Mounted

Enemy machine gunners at the Second Battle of Gaza. The officer-in-charge at right is Austrian and the Turk next to him is the range-taker. The man at the rear is one of two spare numbers to replace casualties. AWM A00577

Division conformed. The whole British line was similar to a semi-circle, curving away to the east and south for twenty miles.

The infantry divisions made some ground against heavy fire, but the Turks never lost control and, with only one exception, all attempts by infantry and mounted men to reach enemy trenches were shattered. It was trench warfare at its most expensive, hideous and brave. There was no cover when the troops left their trenches and they walked into teeming artillery and machine-gun fire. The 52nd Division, striking for Ali Muntar, was restricted by topography to a very narrow front and made the plummest of targets. It did gain ground, capturing two small rises, but could go no further.

On the right, the 54th Division had better going and heedless of the cost reached the Gaza–Beersheba road at 9 am, where it cut the telegraph wires. The leading elements swung to their right towards a complex known as the Beer Trenches, and what was to be named the Tank Redoubt, both heavily fortified. Further right again, the Camel Brigade was also approaching Tank Redoubt, while on their immediate right the 4th and 3rd Australian Light Horse Brigades of the Imperial Mounted Division had closed to less than half a mile of the Turkish front line. But they had run up against the Atawineh redoubt and were pinned down.

The Turks mounted a counterattack at 9.30 am. It was repulsed by the 54th Division, but others followed and the readiness of the Turk to seize the offensive was rare evidence of his confidence and ascendency.

There was no opportunity for the infantry to manoeuvre or change tactics, and if they could not cross this bare ground in the teeth of enemy fire from concealed positions the battle must be lost. For nearly twelve hours, the two British divisions tried, but time after time their leading waves were shot down by machine-guns. They strove so finely, but in the end squandered their lives for nothing.

At the same time, the Camel Brigade and the 4th and 3rd Light Horse Brigades were trying to advance towards Tank Redoubt and Atawineh. Their ground had a slight upward slope but was floor-like in its smoothness, with scattered crops of barley coming into ear the only cover.

Six tanks were used experimentally at Second Gaza. At intervals along the front, they moved in advance of the infantry, but as individual, conspicuous and novel targets they attracted such concentrated fire that the infantrymen following were nearly wiped out by bursting shells. Had they moved as a phalanx, results should have been better, but as it was they were ineffective.

The disposition of the mounted troops early in the day was, from the Gaza or northern end, the Camel Brigade with the British 161st Brigade temporarily attached attacking Tank Redoubt, the 4th Light Horse Brigade attacking between Tank Redoubt and Atawineh, the 3rd Light Horse Brigade attacking Atawineh, the 5th Mounted Brigade attacking between Atawineh and Sausage Ridge, with the 6th Mounted Brigade in reserve. The ANZAC Mounted Division was demonstrating against Sausage Ridge to prevent the enemy from enfilading the attack of the 5th Mounted. As usual, the mounted troops suffered from the lightness of their artillery in this company, but Generals Hodgson (Imperial Mounted Division) and Smith (Camels) were promised the support of Dobell's main artillery.

The 1st and 3rd Battalions of the Camels (Australian) with the 161st Infantry Brigade (British, East Anglian) attacked Tank Redoubt, leaving the 2nd Camel Battalion (British) in reserve.

The infantry had a 200 yard start on the Camels, who had to travel fast to catch them, laden down with pick and shovel and 300 rounds of ammunition. Both Camel Battalions came under shrapnel fire at once, but casualties were light. They moved quickly, but the inspired British brigade, one of the 54th's best, had consecrated itself to vindication and victory after having defeat imposed on them before. They frequently broke into the double and the Camels found it hard to catch up.

Tank Redoubt loomed up slightly to the Camels' left, through a haze of smoke and dust. When the leading men were 1200 yards away, a tank called by its crew 'The Nutty' took up the lead of the infantry and the Australians and quickened their pace. But automatically, every enemy gun within range seized on it. Though it was bombarded, shattered and torched, it still went on. However, the troops in its wake were decimated.

The British brigade, still in the lead, received the heaviest punishment, and as they lost momentum the Australians pulled abreast of them. The two leading companies of Camels lost touch with other, but the No. 2 Company pressed forward to a slight ridge 350 yards short of their objective and halted. The men threw themselves down and fired their first shots of the engagement. Following waves quickly joined them and the company commander sent back for No. 3 Company, which was in support, to join him.

The plan of attack allowed for the British to take the position and the Camels to pass to their left, but the company commander Captain A.E.G. Campbell, a strapping, well-set Queenslander, observed that if the infantry did so — which he now thought unlikely because of exhaustion and the casualties they had suffered behind the tank — he would be exposed to cross-fire at point-blank range. He therefore decided to take the Tank Redoubt with his own and No. 3 Company, as soon as it came up.

Meanwhile, the tank was still going. It had been obstructed by rough ground, but once it had manoeuvred clear of it the crew lost direction and it careered sharply right, immediately traversing the Camels' front. Discovering its error, its commander reversed it over his tracks: the Australians, crouching with bayonets fixed within a few yards of it, were smothered in a barrage of shell fire and lost many more men.

The two companies of Camels had numbered 200 men, but by the time No. 3 Company joined Campbell about half of these had been killed or wounded. However, the tank was once again on course for the redoubt and the Camels followed it, their Lewis gunners shooting at Turkish heads showing above the parapets 'like cabbages on a wall'. Eight enemy guns were now shooting point-blank at the tank, but miraculously it rolled on, with the Camels and, to Campbell's enormous pleasure and relief, the British infantry again, charging with fixed bayonets in its wake.

The tank belched smoke and flame and was apparently red-hot in places, but it lumbered on through wire entanglements, over an outer circle of trenches and reached the very centre of the enemy redoubt, the highest piece of ground over several square miles. Here, riddled with shot, broken down, on fire and burning itself out, The Nutty finally succumbed. Gullett concludes the saga of the tank:

> The gallant crew had nobly fulfilled their task. If the tank had drawn terrific fire on the Australians and British infantry, it had served them as a lead and an inspiration. Of the hundred survivors of the Camel companies who attempted to follow it over the last terrible 350 yards, about seventy fell before the hail of Turkish fire. But the surviving remnant, undaunted, charged shouting with their bayonets at the Turkish trenches. At the same time that the thirty Australians … began to use their steel on the Turks, twenty gallant men of the British infantry also reached the redoubt.

There were 600 Turks in the redoubt and some German and Austrian officers. How could the 50 have prevailed? Only by roaring and jumping and hacking with their bayonets, each man trying literally to emulate the activity and strength of ten. With that frantic power lent to us in moments of physical and mortal danger, and probably too with some rational recall of the Turk's fear and loathing of the bayonet, they pulled it off. It would have been acting as much as fighting.

To an Anatolian peasant, the extraordinary spectacle of that huge, fiery tank (what was it?) lumbering at him could have seemed supernatural and was nerve-shattering enough; and now these horrifying whirling, lunging demons were trying to skewer him with long steel blades. Many Turks were killed and wounded, 40 were captured and the rest, numbering about 500, threw down their rifles, scrambled out of the trenches and ran to their main line 600 yards in rear.

Campbell, shot through his equipment and uniform but unharmed, placed his six Lewis gunners so that they could fire on the retreating Turks. Then he took the prisoners to the British side of the redoubt and told them to run for it. Already the enemy had opened shell fire on the position and swept it with machine-guns and rifles. Campbell was confronted by a German officer with his revolver yards away, but before he could snatch his own weapon a shell burst and the German was obliterated.

The remnant of English and Australians hung on to the knoll for two hours. They manned the trenches facing the Turks, but without support they knew the odds were insuperable. Five of the six Lewis gunners were killed and the sixth wounded. Campbell sent back a total of six runners with messages, but four were killed, two were wounded and no message got through.

At 2 pm, 'I issued orders,' Campbell said afterwards, 'to the few remaining men to return to a small wady on our right as best they could. I also communicated my order to the Englishmen. At the same time I got a message from a Hants officer on the other side of the redoubt to say that he considered the position hopeless and was going to surrender.'

Soon, Campbell and Lieutenant E.J. Aylwin, with whom he had enlisted at Toowoomba, were the only two Australians left. Campbell had told Aylwin to go first, 'which he did only after an argument'. He was hit as he ran, but survived. Campbell's luck held and he was one of only five men of his company of 102 who was not either killed or wounded. Five or six Australians, most wounded, were taken prisoner.

Along with Campbell's feat of arms, the other Australian Camel Battalion (3rd) was advancing well on the 1st's right. It was not in touch with the 1st, but ranged abreast of it, and when Campbell rushed the redoubt the 3rd overran a trench on some higher ground to its right. Its leading company then crossed the Beersheba road, where they were joined by a squadron of the 11th Light Horse Regiment, coming in from their right. This was the furthest penetration of the Turkish line — a claim General Headquarters was inclined to question until, months later, the bones of three 3rd Battalion men were recovered at the place and supplied grisly proof.

From two little mounds called Jack and Jill, the Camels and Light Horsemen were able to delay Turks massing for a counterattack on Tank Redoubt by effective fire and also shot the horses of an enemy battery limbering up, although the guns escaped. But, deep into enemy territory, they appreciated their success had to remain local without strong and immediate support. They had suffered severe casualties and soon the Light Horse squadron was ordered to withdraw by the brigade commander back to their regiment, and the 4th Light Horse Brigade's line.

The Camels asked the Light Horse squadron to stand its ground, but their orders were precise and they retired. The Camel Company hung on under heavy shelling and an infantry counterattack, but it too was soon ordered to withdraw some hundreds of yards back, to straighten the line.

These were the only penetrations of the Turkish defences at the Second Battle of Gaza.

As the British/Turkish front extended south, the opposing lines diverged, until the ANZAC Mounted Division guarding the southern flank were five miles away from Turkish entrenchments and spread over six miles of good, open ground — a rare conjunction of things to gladden a cavalryman's heart.

However, Hodgson's Imperial Mounted Division was well north (left) of the ANZACs and its two Australian brigades (4th and 3rd), fighting dismounted, encountered the same impenetrable resistance and heavy casualties as the infantry. The 3rd Brigade (late of the ANZAC Mounted) got off to a bad start because Galloping Jack Royston led it forward before dawn, when he should have advanced at 7.30 am with all other troops. His regiments were out on their own, being enfiladed from Sausage Ridge, in the incorrect sector (the 5th Mounted's) and had opened up a gap between themselves and the 4th Brigade, all nearly an hour before the battle started. Hodgson ordered Royston to halt while the battle line re-formed.

The 4th Brigade was only two regiments strong and could put just 500 men in the firing line. They made a dismounted attack on the Atawineh redoubt, advancing through a barley crop and red poppies akin to Flanders fields'. A dismounted Light Horse line was ever precariously slender and this one was utterly inadequate to assault heavy, bristling earthworks such as Atawineh's. No officer in the brigade, or the division, believed they had the slightest chance of taking it.

They walked forward on a front of 1000 yards until the fire became too intense, then crawled on their bellies in the barley, returning fire when they could. Within the hour, the enemy fire rose from steady to intense and they were raked by shrapnel, machine-gun and rifle fire. 'All seemed to be going well,' said the brigade major, 'when suddenly the whole show melted away — due to sheer dissolution by casualties.' The British artillery fire in this sector was poor and the enemy enjoyed shooting undisturbed at the exposed Australian line, 800 yards away.

The 4th could not possibly improve their situation and could only stick it out until 7.30 pm, when their line was withdrawn. Yet it was one of their squadrons on the extreme left that joined up with the Camels, as we have seen. On the day, they sustained over 30 percent casualties, but carried out all their wounded and dead, except one.

The 3rd Light Horse Brigade had the 4th on its left and the 5th Mounted Brigade on its right (south). Owing to Royston's characteristic but mistaken dash forward, they discovered they were well out on their own at daylight and had to wait while the disorganised line could be re-formed. They suffered badly for it. They lay down in the barley and kept firing, but the Turks' accurate artillery and machine-guns had them pinned down.

Another deadlock of attrition had developed. Then with calculated audacity, the 5th Mounted Brigade galloped right into the Turkish shell fire. They lost several horses, but otherwise their casualties were far fewer than if they had advanced on foot, as their commander had estimated. But when they did send back their horses, enemy fire was still too deadly for them to get up in line with the 3rd's regiments on their left.

Nevertheless, the move allowed these 9th and 10th Regiments to advance again until they were within 500 yards of Atawineh. They rushed some enemy trenches and took 70 prisoners, but were unable to consolidate by joining up with the 12th Regiment on their left and had to withdraw their own right to close the gap to the now-stalled Yeomanry.

Still at this stage, Dobell was prepared to commit more troops as the prospects grew grimmer. The only mobility in the fighting was that it gradually spread southward. The Wellingtons of the New Zealand Brigade made an advance along Sausage Ridge to support the Yeomanry but were at once stalled, and if they couldn't break out no-one could.

At midday, the 5th Mounted did advance slightly and the 9th Light Horse of the 3rd Brigade made another attempt on Atawineh. The 9th fell like the barley they stood in before the storm. To save it from complete destruction, the whole 3rd Brigade was withdrawn. But as the Turks made no attempt to pursue them and the 4th was still holding its ground, Hodgson ordered the 3rd forward again. Under terrible fire, they made it to their former position, but no further. Then a Turkish counterattack forced the 54th Division and the Camels to give ground, exposing the whole Imperial Mounted Division to fire from the west and cross-fire from Sausage Ridge.

The 3rd Brigade stood firm in the full blast of this and were greatly heartened when the 6th Mounted Brigade, brought forward from reserve, galloped in almost to the firing line. The 6th's regiments went to the support of the 3rd and 4th. At the same time Dobell ordered an artillery brigade of the reserve 74th Division into action. These moves dispersed the Turkish counterattack but, as was soon apparent, offered no hope of other gains.

It was 5 pm and in the gathering dark Dobell started to commit his reserves. Through intercepted radio messages he was aware that the Turks had not committed theirs. He said later: 'it was evident that the action could not be brought to a conclusion within the day ... and it would be necessary to consolidate the positions gained and postpone any further advance until the following day'. What positions gained he was thinking of is baffling — particularly since his next move was to evacuate the entire Imperial Mounted Division because their ground was too weakly held to be safe overnight.

This retirement was delayed for three hours because of difficulty evacuating the wounded, but it was carried out successfully and the division took up a new outpost line two miles in rear. But the move left Dobell open to a much-feared counterattack around his flank and on their fourth night without sleep the men turned to with picks and shovels and dug themselves in urgently all night and well into the next day.

While they did so, Dobell consulted with his division commanders and decided to postpone a resumption of his assault for 24 hours, apparently in the hope that if there was no British attack there would be no Turkish counterattack. It seems a sweeping and singular tactic, but was successful. Under careful observation, the Turks just made improvements to their earthworks while the Imperial Mounted worked hard building theirs, and when time was up late on the 20th, Hodgson was confident he could withstand whatever the Turks might launch at him.

Meanwhile, by the morning of the battle, the ANZAC Mounted Division, less the New Zealand Mounted Rifles in reserve, but now including the 22nd Mounted (Yeomanry) Brigade in place of Royston's 3rd Brigade, was spread widely south of the main engagement, with orders not to make a dismounted attack, but to demonstrate against the Turkish Hareira redoubt and generally protect the right flank of the British forces. Nothing could have suited Chauvel better. The southernmost 22nd Mounted advanced across the Wady Ghuzze at Tel el Fara and the 2nd and 1st Light Horse Brigades marched for Hareira and its surrounds. There were seven miles of elbow room between the 22nd and 2nd Brigades, from south to north.

The 1st Regiment of Cox's 1st Brigade drew light shell fire off Hareira. At 2.30 pm Cox relieved the 1st with his other two regiments and extended his line south, to join up with the 7th Regiment, which had advanced three troops under Major Richardson towards Abu Shawish. However, the 22nd Mounted, also advancing to link up with the 7th, mistook the galloping retirement of the 7th's led horses for a general withdrawal and evacuated its position, returning across the Ghuzze. This left Richardson's right flank in the air.

The ANZACs observed a regiment of Turkish infantry massing on the Gaza–Beersheba road 3000 yards away, and suddenly the 3rd Regiment came in contact with about 1000 Turkish cavalry.

The Light Horseman had long anticipated such a meeting, but contact with enemy cavalry had so far been fleeting: they had always kept their distance, avoiding a mounted conflict. And now, though armed with lances, the Turks left their horses and advanced on foot with rifles. They had a field piece and a battery of mountain guns with them. The 3rd Regiment spread out dismounted, with Maxims and the brigade's machine-guns, to await them.

Between 500 and 900 yards range, the machine-guns opened fire, and with good rifle shooting from the men the enemy advance was stopped. Then they retired, mounted their horses and made towards the 7th Regiment to their right. At the same time, they were joined by another much larger cavalry force and the combined body advanced quickly on the 7th. Now about a whole division strong, they came behind an extraordinary 'screen' of rag-tag Arab camels, donkeys and mares with foals at foot. Possibly these were intended as some kind of stalking horse. Whatever they were for, the Light Horsemen rubbed their eyes in amazement.

Yet the Turks themselves scarcely made a better showing, mounted on nondescript ponies in wretched condition and, it became evident, with no stomach for an attack, overwhelming numbers or not. Their artillery support was good, though, maintaining a constant and accurate fire at the Light Horse line.

Here, this consisted only of Richardson's three troops of the 7th. They retired slowly, firing four machine-guns with such precision as to keep the Turks at a standstill just out of range.

Richardson made for a line of outposts dug by the 5th Regiment. The Turks broke away as they approached this and the night of 19 April passed peacefully, right along the front. 'As far as the Regiment was concerned,' Richardson wrote, 'the day was full of interest and the work was ideal for mounted troops. Few will forget the excitement of hanging on to positions as long as possible in order to hold up the enemy's cavalry division. The Regiment's casualties were not heavy, for moving troops in shell formation present poor targets for either field or machine-guns, except at close range.'

But the Second Battle of Gaza had been lost. The beaten army still manned its trenches next morning in case of the dreaded Turkish counterattack, but the Turks had no need of it. As the British historian Cyril Falls says, they just sat in their redoubts and shot the British to pieces. They took all honours for their decisive victory.

There was music to face. The British government was shocked by the casualties, worse than those they had become accustomed to in France:

54th Division	2971
52nd Division	1365
53rd Division	584
ANZAC Mounted Division	105
Imperial Mounted Division	547
	5572

It was being said that Gaza was another Gallipoli.

Murray sacked Dobell, but his own reckoning was not long delayed. On 27 June 1917, General Sir Edmund Allenby arrived in Cairo to relieve him.

Contemporary views of General Sir Archibald Murray indicate a man of outstanding ability and versatility who was, in the end, swamped by his responsibilities. One of his faults was that he was a worrier over details properly the concern of subordinates and he could not afford this. His bailiwick was vast: as well as the army of the Near East, it included carriage of military affairs in the French/British imbroglio over Salonika, implementing British policy towards the Arabs of the Hejaz, subduing the 'troublesome' Senussi tribes in the Upper Nile, and the internal security of Egypt itself, with its burgeoning seditious movements working for revolt. It is no wonder that he seldom left Cairo. But the time had come for the army, having secured Egypt from the Turk, to have a commander who would put his stamp on it and concentrate on the new problems of the Palestine campaign; and that Allenby could do this without distraction says much for Murray's work on the other matters.

General Dobell had a reputation built on his success in colonial wars against rebellious natives, but the experience had little application to fighting the comparatively modern and sophisticated Turks — and their German advisers. It was said that he had such boundless self-confidence that he was unable to see this. His spirit was dauntless but his judgments in the Gaza battles were faulty.

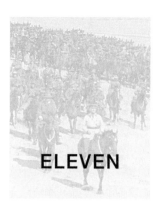

ELEVEN

Allenby transcendent: before Beersheba

For the first time since crossing the Suez Canal, Eastern Force became defensive. The troops took to their picks and shovels like the Turks, and on the very night of their defeat started digging. For weeks, they dug and laid barbed wire without pause, creating a British line running first from the sea for two miles and only 400 yards from the Turks. Then it curved back in a series of strong posts to the Wady Ghuzze, following this watercourse for the next nine miles to Gamli. There it turned right (directly south), because lack of water prevented further extension to match the Turks' defences around Beersheba. The line was 24 miles long. It may be evoked as a set of teeth, with a few lower right molars missing: the infantry's works were the teeth, and the mounted troops sortied through these gaps to patrol and reconnoitre the hundreds of square miles of no-man's land to Beersheba and beyond. In short, the British held the territory as far north as the Ghuzze, while the Turks held it as far south as the Wady Imleih, conforming still to their original Gaza–Beersheba line.

Dry, hot summer weather approached and the good water at Beersheba was increasingly coveted. The Turks saw to it that its defences were as impregnable as they could make them.

The British government, far from losing interest and shelving work on the Palestine front after the Gaza reverses, decided not only to continue the offensive but to invest it with fresh spirit, new leadership, more troops and at least some new materiel, including new Bristol fighters which could at last match the German Rumpler, Taube and Albatros aircraft.

Chetwode was appointed to command Eastern Force *vice* Dobell, who was not replaced. With the arrival of a new, entire division of Yeomanry, the mounted strength was now three divisions of three brigades each: the ANZAC Mounted (with Camel Brigade), the Australian Mounted — its name having been changed from Imperial — and the new one under Major General Sir G. de S. Barrow, later to be reconstituted as the 4th Cavalry Division.

The Desert Column then became the Desert Mounted Corps and Chauvel, having just handed over the ANZAC Mounted Division to the New Zealander Major General Chaytor, so as to succeed Chetwode in command of the Desert Column, found himself commanding a whole British Army Corps. He was the first officer from any Dominion to do so and the first Australian to attain the rank of lieutenant general.

The Desert Mounted Corps of 1917 numbered 20,000 troops, just short of Napoleon's two cavalry corps in the Grand Army of 1809. In 1918, a fourth division was added to Desert Mounted, and it then surpassed one of Napoleon's (Bessière's Reserve Cavalry) in strength. However, Desert Mounted never deployed more than three divisions in battle.

Chauvel rejoiced, but had his hands full, with the new division of British Yeomanry under his wing and the sometimes rival demands of the three nationalities (four, including the 'Bing Boys' — the Indians of the Hong Kong and Singapore Mountain Battery) for distinguishing service and positions of influence. British policy, with which he agreed — and was therefore not one of those who had pushed for the Australianisation of the former Imperial Mounted Division — was that the troops could all learn from each other, under their respective flags.

The new C-in-C was not having anyone run his army but himself and, before he arrived, abolished the Eastern Force command. Chetwode was instead appointed to command one of two newly created infantry corps, the 20th, and Major General E.S. Bulfin, arriving with a division of Londoners (60th), took command of the 21st.

Field Marshal Viscount Allenby, Commander-in-Chief Middle East.

Chetwode, always in spirit a cavalryman, regretted his separation from the ANZACs and wrote in reply to Chauvel's letter of congratulation:

> Very many thanks for your kind letter. You and I have worked together in the greatest harmony. We have together helped write a small page of history, which if a small affair in so great a convulsion, is at any rate creditable in the highest degree to the splendid troops who took part in it. I shall always be very proud of having had such a fine body of men under my command as your Anzac mounted troops and grateful to you for the able way in which you have led them.
>
> I cannot say how much I envy you the command of the largest body of mounted troops ever under one hand — it is my own trade — but fate has willed it otherwise.

These airs of change blew through at a time when the army needed them to lift its spirits, inevitably lowered after two successive major defeats (at least, on the record), with the heaviest of casualties. Suddenly the airs became a hurricane. General Sir Edmund (The Bull) Allenby had arrived.

The force of Allenby's personality was rare, even among generals. Tall, heavily built, with a broad oval face, wide grey eyes, a straight, strong nose and a small, rather pursed mouth — the opposite of generous — it is easy to conclude his photograph is witness to what he was: a fiery, impulsive, hard-driving man with a temper. He had one indeed, and it was explosive, though not routinely unleashed at full pitch. The ANZACs inflamed it on one occasion.

He was a cavalryman in a cavalryman's war. He did not get on with some of his peers, notably Field Marshal Haig, and enjoyed being on his own. First he removed his headquarters from the Savoy Hotel in Cairo to Kelab, a few miles north of Rafa, no doubt to the dismay of some of his staff living in fashionable Cairo hotels. Then he got to know his army. Gullett records that: 'He would dash up in his car to a Light Horse regiment, shake hands with a few officers, inspect hurriedly, but with a sure eye to good and bad points, the horses of, perhaps, a single squadron, and be gone in a few minutes, leaving a great trail of dust behind him. His tall and massive, but restlessly active figure, his keen eyes and prominent, hooked nose, his terse and forcible speech, and his imperious bearing, radiated an impression of tremendous resolution, quick decision and steely discipline.'

A system rapidly established itself. When the C-in-C left camp, a signals officer at General Headquarters would send out the warning message, 'BL'. It stood for 'Bull loose'. A Light Horse brigade major said, 'I could not count the times I have shaken hands with Allenby. Between the Canal and Gaza, I never set eyes on Murray.'

Allenby had most impact where it most mattered, in the ranks. Where there had been a vacuum, there was now very much in the flesh a leader with one of the most dramatic personalities and reputations of the war. The men had a lively curiosity in him, that soon turned to approval and confidence. A somewhat desultory, if not dejected, spirit had been abroad, but a new wave of energy and optimism began to replace it. This bloke knew what he was doing.

And he did have a gracious side. The 2nd Brigade of ANZACs held a race and sports meeting in September 1917, to which Allenby was invited. Major N.D. Barton of the 7th Regiment — who boasted that his own 'Cossack', bred on the family property, was the fastest horse in the regiment over 300 yards — recorded that a wet canteen was operating for the occasion 'which, as always, had rather disastrous results'. His regiment was not sometimes called 'the Drunken 7th' for nothing. There were no fences or crowd controls and the Chief appeared to be jostled by men somewhat the worse for wear, on foot, or mounted on horses, donkeys and mules, all trying to get to the trackside. Dust enveloped Allenby and he seemed in danger of abuse, if not rough treatment.

Afterwards, Brigadier General Ryrie wrote to him apologising for his treatment and 'received a very nice letter [saying he] had quite enjoyed himself, he considered the events were very good and he had been treated everywhere with respect by the men. Without barricades and ropes it was very difficult to keep them from crowding and he was sure anything he asked this brigade to do would be carried out well.' Nat Barton concludes: 'He is a gentleman, isn't he?'

Allenby's task, given by Lloyd George when he left London, was to take Jerusalem 'as a Christmas present for the British nation'.

Lawrence of Arabia remarked that Allenby's mind was like the prow of the *Mauretania*: there was so much weight behind it that it didn't need to be razor-sharp. He turned the prow towards Jerusalem, and a plan the energetic Chetwode had made for the first step of breaking through the Gaza–Beersheba line. It had to depend on deception. The still superior

Turkish defences and ground ruled out a frontal assault, even supposing the previous failure had not. Any overt attack would fail.

There was a gap of eight miles between the Hareira redoubt and the Beersheba defences, well observed and covered by artillery. Further east, beyond Beersheba, the Turkish redoubts were also less developed. This waterless, open country and its lack of roads seemed to preclude any threat of a British attack in that quarter.

The essence of the deception was to persuade the enemy that the British would attack Gaza again, while in fact they would have concentrated secretly and in overwhelming numbers against Beersheba. Bulfin's 21 Infantry Corps would demonstrate and bombard Gaza from the old infantry ground, to keep the enemy's attention on that end of his line; then when the trap was sprung, Chetwode's infantry corps would attack north-west towards the Hareira redoubt and north-east towards Beersheba, to cover the eight-mile gap, while Chauvel's mounted corps would swoop on the town from the barren and lightly defended east and seize the wells. With Beersheba secured, Allenby would roll up the Turkish left flank from it towards Gaza, while Bulfin would keep up his bluff of the major infantry assault. In boxing terms, Allenby would first feint with his left, and while the Turk's guard was up drive a right to his ribs, then combine left feints and rights to the head and body, keeping him groggy on his feet, his attention divided and his ability to counterpunch curtailed.

Allenby insisted that Beersheba be captured on the first day. Any longer and the Turks could destroy the wells which were Chauvel's only prospect of water on his long march. Also, the enemy might be allowed time to readjust, meet the attacks on a more even footing and maintain his line. Bulfin's 21 Corps and Chetwode's 20 would not move on Gaza and Beersheba to the north-west until Chauvel had progressed his attack from the east. If Chauvel ever quailed at the carriage of responsibility, this must have been such a time. But he thrived on it.

In strong terms, Chetwode set some conditions. One was, 'Divisions must be divisions and mounted divisions mounted divisions'. The plan provided for seven infantry divisions and three mounted divisions, but it was useless moving these about on paper when the deficiencies in some units of both arms ranged from 30 to 50 percent. All of them not only had to be at full strength, but also have reserves of 20 percent, never less than 10, on the ground. 'Divisions ... such as the 52nd, 53rd and 54th with no drafts to keep them up, will disappear in three week's fighting.' And there needed to be an eye to the immediate and strenuous pursuit of the enemy, particularly by the mounted troops, after breaking through.

This plan, Chetwode was saying, can only succeed if the War Office provides the men. He would not accept any more raw territorial divisions liable at any moment to be withdrawn to France. If the government wanted Palestine, they must put this campaign on a par with the Western Front.

Allenby was just the man for such an issue, but he found the government compliant and got exactly what he wanted.

There was work of staggering proportions to do in two months. Allenby's weather 'window' was September, after the summer heat and before the heavy autumn rains turned the dust to mud. Even so, he had to accept a risky postponement until the end of October, because elements of the army itself were not quite up to operational pitch. Most of the work on the Beersheba front had to be done in secret, at night. It included the laying of railway tracks, new road construction, installation of new watering points with associated pumps and piping, stock-piling of munitions and supplies. Apart from troops, 50,000 Egyptian labourers, 20,000 camels and thousands of horses and mules were engaged.

Deception was a small industry in itself and it proved to be entirely successful. As examples, the British helped convince the enemy that the blow would fall on Gaza, with some fake props of a seaborne assault landing north of the town. There were naval bombardments, naval craft took soundings and surveyed the 'landing area', a flotilla of small craft appeared off Belah. A British officer appeared to be wounded in a skirmish with Turkish cavalry, and as he galloped away he dropped a bloodstained haversack containing, among personal things, fake papers designed to confirm Gaza as the objective. The haversack was observed to be recovered by the enemy.

Chauvel's reconnaissances on the Beersheba flank were often in divisional strength, to persuade the Turks that large bodies of horse near the town were just routine.

A DRY HOT SUMMER TO RIVAL SINAI'S PASSED — IN FACT IT WAS THE SAME AS SINAI'S, including khamsins, but with dust instead of sand. There was hardly nostalgia for Sinai, but at least the sand had been clean and it blew about only in the strongest winds, whereas the continuous traffic of 30,000 men with their horses and wheels over light clay soil raised a permanent, suffocating pall of dust. Men could not see the stars, or their compasses at night.

The mounted divisions were rostered on a month's patrolling, reconnaissance and the occasional stunt, a month's rest and a month's training. The rest was at beach camps at Belah and swimming was popular, but a poor diet and minor ailments such as septic sores kept them below the peak of fitness. The horses suffered on operations: after a 36-hour patrol they had to be marched another twelve miles to water and they returned to Belah from operations jaded and having lost condition.

There were some sparkling little operations. When two troops of enemy cavalry appeared to a squadron of the 7th Regiment, the squadron commander Major Bird withdrew his centre troop, but sent the two flanking troops forward on either side. The Turks thought they faced only one troop and rode forward with a great show of lances and swords, whereupon they were set on by the whole squadron. They fled and there was a two-mile gallop in pursuit, with the speed and endurance of the Waler wearing down the Arab until, finally, those Turks the Light Horsemen could not club off their saddles with rifles were yanked off by their collars and all were taken prisoner.

C Squadron of the 7th under Major Nat Barton was entrusted to escort a detachment of engineers with a large bomb to place under the Gaza–Beersheba railway line, fourteen miles inside enemy territory. This called for the darkest of nights and utmost clandestinity. Barton writes of being out all night on a brigade enterprise the night before, 'which was especially trying as we had a fair amount of walking and then did not accomplish our objective … I do not think I have ever seen the men give way to tiredness more than on the next day.' He is circumspect in what he says, but apparently this was a first attempt at placing the bomb, which was aborted as they could not cover the ground in time to complete the task in darkness.

The next morning, the operation was repeated. Turning to at 0200, Barton 'summoned up enough energy' to open a newly arrived parcel and put some good things in his haversack.

They spent most of that day waiting for darkness in the abandoned orchard of a sheikh, 'so had a good time, all except the horses, who were a bit short of water'. Then with darkness they set off again, marching by the stars, 'to do the same job as before and this squadron had to go a mile further than the remainder of the force'. The remainder consisted of B

Squadron. 'We did not waste ... time, but I thought we were never going to reach the end of that journey. At last ... we got into position and had been there twenty minutes when along came a Jacko patrol of seven.'

The ground was unexpectedly hard and all of that time was spent digging the bomb's hole. Just as that was completed, the Turkish patrol stumbled on the expedition and opened fire. The Australians' orders were to respond only with the bayonet in case of trouble: Corporal R.G. Moore charged the Turks with his, killed one and fell dead himself, riddled with bullets. The Australians then opened fire and wounded and captured the rest of the Turks. Nat continues his letter home:

> Although the object of the affair was not finished, I ordered the squadron back at once and we got back ... in pretty quick time. I was very anxious to know what those in authority thought of the show and was rather worried ... so was very relieved when the Colonel told me that Division was satisfied.
>
> Next day we slept all morning, but there was a funeral in the afternoon [presumably Moore's, whose body was carried back, together with the bomb] and after that the men had to be paid so I was glad when night came.

On 18 August the 2nd Brigade moved back to the beach at Marakeb for a rest period. It must have been badly needed. Nat Barton, that most restless energetic and exacting of squadron commanders, wrote that he would be happy 'so long as they let me lie on my back and loaf'.

My father mentioned that the Turks demonstrated against his part of the line and 'we had to get out in a hurry to hunt them back. There were thousands of us operating in open, flat country, all our movements could be seen and we were under constant shell fire. The Turks fired over 1,000 shells at us, yet we had only two casualties. That's wonderful, what I call providential care. Of course, we had other casualties from other causes, bombs from planes, etc.' He announced his promotion to temporary sergeant to replace one sent to hospital, but in the next letter said the sergeant had returned and 'I fell back to corporal with a sickening thud'.

By dawn on 31 October, Chauvel was to have the ANZAC Mounted, and the Australian Mounted Divisions to the east and south-east of Beersheba, ready to strike simultaneously at the town and at the old

Hebron road leading out of it, cutting off the potential escape route for the Turks. Barrow's new Yeomanry Division was in reserve.

He must reach his starting position undetected, and with his horses watered and fresh enough for at least one day's hard work without a drink. After that, the two divisions had to fend for themselves: and what might befall them if they failed to find water that night — that is, capture the Beersheba wells — was not something to let the imagination dwell on. This was the major gamble of the whole offensive.

After reconnaissance and investigation, a way was found to at least start the great day watered. At Asluj, sixteen miles due south of Beersheba and at Khalasa, fourteen miles south-west of it, Desert Mounted Corps engineers found old and damaged wells, blown up by German engineers but capable of rehabilitation. If there was sufficient time and manpower to dig them out, the horses of both mounted divisions could be watered there before they marched on their objectives.

On 20 October, Chauvel's and Chetwode's forces began the movement east from Belah to their start lines on the right flank. They marched at night and in daytime hid in the wadys, keeping quiet and still. As soon as they could get to them, the ANZAC field engineers and the Camel Brigade started work in the Khalasa wells and Brigadier General Ryrie's 2nd Brigade started digging out the Asluj wells further east. Huge quantities of masonry and earth blocked them and had to come out. Ryrie's men had only six days to do it in and worked against the clock, up to their waists in mud, but with a great will, knowing what was at stake. And, as they had done since clattering across that pontoon bridge over the Suez Canal eighteen months ago to be first in the field at Sinai, they would do anything for 'the Old Brig', their most printable term for this most colourful of all the Light Horse leaders.

Granville de Laune Ryrie was 52 and the heaviest man in the Light Horse: sixteen stone of bull-necked, hulking, ungainly bulk. The field service cap, which he seemed to prefer to the slouch hat in photographs, sits on his bullet head like a schoolboy's cap. He looked anything but a cavalryman, yet he rode lighter and better than most of his troops — Gullett called him 'the most perfect horseman in Palestine' — and he shot better, skills that he learned as a boy in the Australian bush. He could throw and treat a sick horse as well as any veterinary officer, and wield a boomerang with the best Aborigines. In his youth, he had fought in the finals of two amateur Australian heavyweight boxing championships.

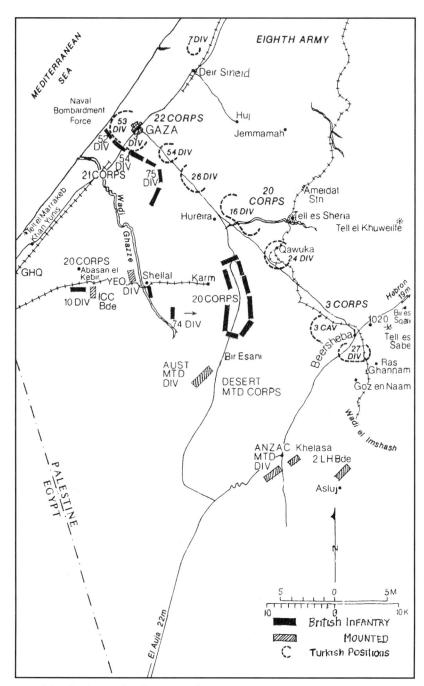

Eve of the third Gaza battle, 29 October 1917.

He was no deep student of war, but relied on instinct, common sense and courage to carry him, and from first to last made no serious mistake — a rare record in a dashing, mobile force that saw so much action. He and the men appeared to have a symbiotic understanding: we'll do what you want if you get us out of trouble. Both parties kept the bargain.

Some considered Ryrie a careless disciplinarian: he did like to share the troopers' rations and vicissitudes, and was more indulgent than other commanders, but his directness, humour and humanitarian good offices made him a force for improvement and no-one could count on more loyalty and affection. He was a member of the Federal parliament, entitled officially to be called 'The Honourable', though on leave from parliamentary duties for the duration.

As for Chauvel, he chose his two old ANZAC brigades, the 2nd and 1st who won Romani for him, to lead this enterprise. Who else?

The wells were cleared with a day to spare and all was ready.

Brigadier General G. de L. Ryrie, commander 2nd Brigade ANZAC Mounted Division, on Plain Bill.

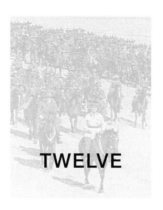

TWELVE

The pageant of the plain: Beersheba

Before a battle, the soldier becomes short of speech, brisk of movement, somewhat brittle of temper and withdrawn. He is alone with his thoughts. He keeps active. He feels his horse's legs for heat, checks for loose or worn shoes and picks the sole of each hoof clean. These must work as pumps with the paces, forcing blood from the four extremities back to the heart again, far above. He brushes and curry-combs the quiet horse, trying to produce that satiny coat that is the sign of wellbeing. Grooming is a form of communication. The 'bivvy sheet', with blanket and greatcoat rolled inside, is rolled tighter. Water bottle, haversack with three days' rations, quart pot and mug, grain bag, canvas bucket and case with spare horseshoes and nails are checked and secured on his Universal saddle; the spare bandolier to buckle round the horse's neck is topped up.

He pulls his rifle through, takes the little oil bottle out of the base plate, lubricates the bolt and works it back and forth repeatedly. The magazine is smacked on, taken off, hit home again. Eyes shut, he selects a cartridge clip from his bandolier, positions it and jams the five rounds down into the magazine, then working the bolt, ejects them. He repeats that, still unsighted: in the dark, sure and nimble fingers can save his life. He checks that the foresight is clean, the backsight slides easily, the safety catch clicks on and off. The spring-loaded bayonet catch is oiled, the bayonet point tested for sharpness.

Before Beersheba, the prescient Major General Hodgson of the Australian Mounted Division, orders all bayonets sharpened. The soldier scrawls a letter home, eats something and rests …

'MOUNT UP!' IT IS 6 PM ON 30 OCTOBER 1917 AND QUITE DARK. THE soldier is glad to go. So is his horse: his kind sense they will be thundering into action again and they snort, reef for their heads and pull at the bits. This horse and rider are in the dark moving mass of the ANZAC Mounted Division and the Australian Mounted Division, 13,000 strong, moving off from Asluj. The Australian Mounted started from their wells at Khalasa and have already ridden eight miles.

The 7th Regiment of the 2nd Brigade of ANZACs, in what has become its place of honour, is leading at a brisk walk over unknown, barren and stony hills. It is difficult country with troublesome tracks. At 2.30 am on 31st, the track forks and the column separates: the 2nd Brigade of ANZACs is going on to the Hebron road, to secure it against either retreating Turks from Beersheba, or Turk reinforcements to Beersheba advancing from the Judean hills.

The main body, now led by the Wellington Mounted Rifles, takes the left fork towards a destination just south of the Wady Saba, five miles east of Beersheba town. Silently and smoothly, the formations separate: our soldier is in the 2nd Brigade's 5th Regiment and in the bright moonlight he is one who raises a hand in farewell to the Australian Mounted as it curves away. A few raise a hand in reply. The 2nd Brigade, with the 7th Regiment still leading, quickens its pace, as if its long tail has slowed it down.

But they go faster because they are now on a metalled road: the horses' hooves clatter and the gun wheels of their faithful Scottish and English Royal Horse Artillery batteries rumble.

So does the British artillery at Gaza over 30 miles away, now pounding at the Turks and throwing up angry glimmers of light into the night sky.

The 2nd Brigade halts at 7 am by the Hamam well and Brigadier General Ryrie dispatches patrols forward towards Tel el Sakati, their objective adjacent to the Hebron road. But with the daylight, all eyes are turned west, looking down on Beersheba six miles away. It seems not unlike a small country town in Australia, except for its white mosque shining in the early sun.

Chetwode, too, has started his 20 Corps bombardment of the enemy's Hareira and Atawineh redoubts. Two hundred and forty field pieces and howitzers are shaking the earth and the air; and that is so still that the smoke of the shell bursts just hangs like a curtain, obscuring the targets. The soldier breakfasts on his vantage point to the sights and sounds of battle: the roar of heavy guns and their smoke and flame all along the line.

Then the 2nd Brigade is ordered to 'advance with all speed on Sakati'. The 7th Regiment leads off north-west at the trot, but over such good and open ground that Colonel Onslow soon increases to an extended canter. The soldier has to hold in his horse, but his eyes are still on the panoramic battlefield on his left and the attack unfolding there. He sees a four-mile wide plain, which he has ridden over often enough, but which now holds unfamiliar fascination. Running away to the right ahead of him is the white Hebron–Beersheba road, ascending between forbidding hills of rock.

On the plain, the clouds of red dust swirl as infantry and cavalry are moved about. Then simultaneously, obviously on signal, he sees hordes more infantry pour into the open, brigade after brigade, dust cloud after dust cloud, all advancing on the Turks' bristling mounds and trenches, to the accompaniment of a curious, dull undertone that permeates for miles: the drumming hooves of 18,000 horses of the Australian Mounted, ANZAC Mounted and Yeomanry Divisions and the wheels of 100 guns.

But the soldier has to look to his own situation. Inevitably, the exploding white puffs of shrapnel appear amongst them. The brigade disperses into shell formation, Colonel Onslow gives his horse its head and instantly the pace goes up the last notch to a full gallop. Experience tells them now they will move too quickly for the Austrian gunners: good as they are, they will not shorten their range fast enough to catch the horsemen. And sure enough, the shell bursts creep to the rear.

Suddenly the 7th runs straight into a Bedouin settlement of mud huts and the charging horses scatter donkeys, camels and goats, and send some of their owners flying. When the soldier passes through, the dark-cowled owners are scrambling after the animals and some of the shrapnel meant for him bursts among the fowls.

After Beersheba. DAVIES FAMILY ARCHIVE

The first machine-gun bullets are whining overhead, finding the range. The 7th gallop down a Turkish road convoy and press straight on. Some led packhorses of the 5th leap and buck so much with excitement that their too-loose packs slip round under their bellies.

A Turkish cavalry regiment with four mountain guns appears before the 7th. They stare open-mouthed at the (also open-mouthed) stampeding horde rushing to engulf them, wheel and gallop out of the way. But they thrash their teams up a hill behind the Sakati redoubt, deploy smartly and open fire. Their targets are nearly point blank and they drop their shells right amongst the Light Horsemen, but so effective is the artillery formation and so well has it been kept, that not a man is hit.

But it is clear now that the Sakati redoubt is too steep and too strongly defended to gallop down; and with that split-second appreciation, Colonel Onslow swings the 7th hard and sharply right, crosses the Hebron road and plunges down into the bed of the Wady Auja. The soldier beholds the amazing sight of a whole regiment of horse disappearing into the ground at full gallop, but has no time to wonder, for his own goggle-eyed regiment is upon the same crack in the earth and must plunge down after them. Down they flounder in billowing dust, he pulls up, dismounts, runs up to the wady bank with his rifle and joins the line already forming.

'God, what a stunt that was!' he pants to the man beside him, a reinforcement he knows only by sight.

'Best ride I've ever had! That colonel of the 7th's a goer. See the Jacko cavalry take off!'

Throwing back their heads, they laugh with delight and relief.

The 2nd Brigade is pinned down in their wady by machine-gun and rifle fire from the height of Sakati, but are precisely placed to secure the Hebron road and have no need to move. Their attention is again fastened on the intensifying pageant of the plain.

FROM DESERT MOUNTED CORPS HEADQUARTERS JUST EAST OF BEERSHEBA, Chauvel watches through field glasses the 2nd Brigade's brilliant dash to its objective with scarcely less satisfaction. The first obstacle to the grand design has been overcome, and in the early afternoon Chetwode claims that his 20 Corps infantry has cleared the enemy out of his entrenchments to the south and south-west of the town.

The next barrier to getting at that Beersheba water this day or dangerously failing, suffering consequences of unendurable loss and tragedy, is Beersheba's Ali Muntar. Named Tel el Saba, it is another massive mound rising out of the plain for hundreds of feet on the eastern approaches to the town. Flat topped, with a cliff face abutting the dry watercourse of Wady Saba, it lends itself in every aspect to defence and the Turks have made imaginative and formidable use of it for the purpose.

Chauvel intends to keep Hodgson's Australian Mounted Division in reserve for the final assault on Beersheba and that leaves Major General Chaytor's ANZAC Mounted Division, less its 2nd Brigade, to tackle Tel el Saba. Once again, a thin, fragile line of mounted infantry must attack over open ground an enemy many times stronger, in well-built fortifications. Chaytor sends the New Zealanders and Cox's 1st Light Horse Brigade against the bulwark: the Auckland Mounted Rifles close on it north of the Wady Saba and the 3rd Light Horse Regiment closes on it from the south. Neither is ever halted, but the closer they come the more intense the

Turkish fire grows and there appears to be danger of the ANZACs' complete destruction.

Chaytor 'feeds the attack': the Wellingtons are thrown in on the Aucklands' right and the 2nd Light Horse Regiment comes in on the 3rds' left.

The evolution of galloping up, dismounting and galloping the horses back is done so smartly by the 2nd that the Turks believe they are in retreat still mounted, and direct their fire accordingly. This allows the 2nd to push on quickly for a space: two squadrons of the 3rd have already gained the wady bank and the two New Zealand regiments are now starting to hold their own with intense converging fire.

At 3 pm the New Zealanders rise from their line and rush forward with the bayonet. When the Aucklands reach the first trenches on the slopes of Tel el Saba, 132 Turks simply stand up with raised hands. All the rest flee to Beersheba with the 2nd and 3rd Light Horse in pursuit. They shoot them on the run and drive off a Turkish counterattack coming out from the town.

It is over and, once again, dash, skill and that almost trick bluster the Camels show at Tank Redoubt, of seeming to be stronger and fiercer than they really are, or feel, carries the day. Yet, time stymies them: they are behind a tight schedule.

It is 3.30 pm. The sun will set at 4.30 and it will be entirely dark by 5. Had Tel el Saba fallen earlier, a dismounted attack of the Australian Mounted Division on the town would have been launched. But now, the waning day calls for speedier solutions, a bolder stroke, a neck-or-nothing *coup de main*. Chetwode's infantry and the Desert Mounted must drink.

The going is good, sloping upward slightly. Aerial reconnaissance has shown there are no barbed-wire entanglements or entrapment pits for horses. The Australian Mounted and the Yeomanry brigades are fit and rested.

Major General Hodgson, Brigadiers General W. Grant of the 4th Light Horse Brigade and P.D. Fitzgerald of the 7th Mounted (Yeomanry) Brigade are all at Chauvel's headquarters. The Yeomanry have their swords and are closest to headquarters. Grant's men have only their rifles and bayonets but are closest to Beersheba. There is a brief, tense discussion, both officers pleading for the honour. A moment's thought and Chauvel says to Hodgson: 'Put Grant straight at it'.

Grant gallops off to his brigade. All the Australian Mounted are scattered in troops as a measure against air attack: it is not usual to assemble large bodies of men on a battlefield any more. It takes until 4.30

pm to assemble 'Grant's Mob', and then only the 4th (Victoria) and 12th (New South Wales) Regiments are available. Grant's third regiment, the 11th, is too far away to co-opt for the front line — it is spread on a line of outposts towards the 7th Mounted — but is ordered to follow.

The 4th and 12th cast long shadows as they form up, in line, with a squadron frontage, three lines deep, 300 to 500 yards apart. There are no stirring addresses, no flourishes or gestures: they are too spread out to see, or hear, such things. Grant just has a good, hard look at them, and what he sees pleases him.

They set out at the trot, but there are only five miles to go and no point in conserving horses for long, though there is every point in speed, preserving surprise and beating the dying light. They extend to a gallop and spread the distance between riders to five yards. It is a spare, thin formation, typically Light Horse, but there is plenty of support: two gallant batteries of Royal Horse Artillery are in the open blazing away, the 11th Regiment is to follow in reserve as soon as it can and the 5th and 7th Mounted Brigades are to advance on their left.

Some troopers with bayonet in hand take the time to make practice swipes, others conceive of the rifle with fixed bayonet as a lance and ride with the butt of this cumbrous ensemble against the thigh. There have been cavalry charges of equal moment since the great Kurd Saladin's mounted men fought Richard Coeur de Lion in the twelfth century, but these modern antipodeans are only masquerading as cavalry.

Grant sets the direction, then falls back with his brigade major to the last line, from where he can observe better and direct if necessary, leaving Lieutenant Colonels W.M. Bourchier (12th) and D.C. Cameron (4th) in the lead.

The Turks open fire with shrapnel at once, but with trifling effect. Then at two miles, hot machine-gun fire comes at the left front squadrons, but the Essex RHA Battery puts them out of action with their first shells. Then the front line comes within rifle range and the Turks produce their best: sustained, accurate fire hits the horses and many crash. But this only serves to increase the pace. All riders from the game ground scouts ahead to the rear line, making a bee-line for Beersheba's white mosque reflecting the last sidelong light aswirl with red dust, dig in their spurs and lie flat on their horses' necks; and with frothing mouths agape, eyes bulging and long manes and tails streaming out, the galloping Walers find another ounce of gristle and bone and spirit to go up another notch. But the Turks know they are mounted infantry and, expecting them to dismount, conserve their full fire yet: the horde of horses thunders on, to the Turks' consternation, who neglect to lower their sights. According to Ian Jones, (screenwriter and co-producer of the film *The Lighthorsemen*, and author of *The Australian Light Horse*), rifles picked up afterwards are all set at 1500 metres.

They are nearly up to the earthworks, looming in the gathering dark. Now there will be fighting at squadron, troop, section and individual level. They find the first trench an easy jump, unfinished, shallow and undermanned, taken in their stride. Nevertheless, a squadron of the 4th rides through a barrage of stick grenades that kills fourteen horses, and of that troop only seven men stay mounted. Racing on through a clutter of bell tents and dugouts, the squadron bears down on the second trench.

It is ten feet deep and four wide, thickly lined with Turks and abutting a big system of redoubts beyond. The leading squadrons of the 4th soar over it, coaxing the horses high over the Turkish bayonets lunging up at their bellies. Some men and horses are shot. The riders rein in: now it is dismounted work. As the leading troop's horses are galloped away to cover and the men jump into the trench they have just crossed, a troop of the 12th Regiment arrives: two officers are killed dismounting. All go to work with the bayonet, the Turks are demoralised and their shooting and counter-strokes are wild. Over 30 are bayoneted to death and others throw down their arms, begging for their lives.

The advance of the 12th Regiment is just as headlong. Major E.H. Hyman, commanding the leading squadron of the 12th, dismounts to engage the Turks hand-to-hand in their trenches, but is followed by only twelve of his men. Captain R.K. Robey, however, sees a patch of clear going on Hyman's right, passes him, then perceives a way forward through the Turkish defences and gallops for it, followed by about half the squadron. They plunge on past gaping Turks and, scarcely believing it themselves, race right around the town's north side, reining up at its western end.

On Hyman's left, B Squadron's commander Major C.L. Featherstonehaugh is pitched from his horse as it falls wounded 30 yards short of the Turks' main trench. He puts the horse out of its pain with his revolver, then charges on foot into the trench, where he empties his weapon at the nearest Turks, then falls at last, shot through both legs.

The 12th Regiment engage the Turks with bayonets, killing 60 in violent, elemental, individual encounters. Many Turks violate their surrender. An officer confronting a Turk sees him throw down his arms and raise his hands, turns his back to hand over his horse and the Turk fells him with a shot in the back. The enraged horse holder jumps at the Turk and kills him, lunging repeatedly with the bayonet, yelling, 'You bastard! You bastard!' Colonel Bourchier is in the thick of it, killing six enemy with his revolver. A man pinned beneath his dead horse swaps shots with a Turk. The corpse of the 12th's Regimental Sergeant Major Wilson, firmly mounted, gallops on. A riderless horse at the lip of the trench rears and strikes out with its fore-feet.

Through it all, the mounted stretcher-bearers, always at the forefront of battle, calmly do their work.

Featherstonehaugh's second-in-command is Captain Jack Davies. On the extreme left of the advance, Davies registers that the Turks' main trench peters out a little to his left, swerves, and rides round it 'wildly excited and

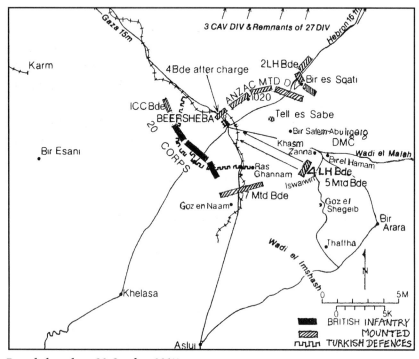

Beersheba taken, 31 October 1917.

galloping mad' according to a report, and 'while brandishing his sword, yells "Come on boys, Beersheba first stop!"' He is followed by thirteen men and the report — possibly in a newspaper of Davies' native Scone — adds that the men respond, 'You'll do us, Jack!' But it seems unlikely that anyone would hear them and the story may be one of the kind not to risk spoiling with facts. Davies had no sword.

At any rate, these thirteen follow Davies into the town and Turks, struck dumb and immobile with astonishment, see them career straight down the main street, to fetch up near Robey's party at the western outskirts. Beersheba falls as night falls, to these fewer than 100 men. Casualties for the two regiments are marvellously light: the 4th has lost eleven men with another seventeen wounded; the 12th, twenty killed and nineteen wounded. Seventy horses have been killed. Nearly all the human casualties are from the trench fighting.

The Turks have demolition charges laid at all important installations, including the wells, but succeed only in destroying two of the latter, some ammunition dumps that blow up with 'a terrific sustained roar' as the Australians ride in, and random buildings and railway points.

The way is now open for the 7th Mounted, approaching on the Khalasa road from the south, to take the remaining Turkish opposition along their whole line, in rear. But the Turkish defence is reduced to chaos by the wild charge of the 4th Brigade and individuals are left with only the instinct of survival. All ranks take off for the hills and personal safety.

In the lines and camps of the Desert Mounted Corps that night, the toast, of muddy tea made with Beersheba water in quart pots, is 'Grant's Mob'.

Thirteen days later, Featherstonehaugh writes to Davies:

I hear you arrived in Beersheba at the head of 13 men and captured many prisoners and booty. We heard you got the MC, I sincerely hope this is right. It was up to you and Hyman. I … hear there has been a good issue of decorations for the regiment. There's no doubt about it, those fellows of ours deserve the best that is going. So far, I have heard of 10 of our B [Squadron] killed: Flood, Beerfoard, Bradbury, Charters, Cork, Kilpatrick, Greenburgh, Hills, Smith, McLymont; and Smith, Moon, Melvaine in hospital here. Poor old Gerry is having a bad time. The bullet went in near his backside and ran up his back. They got it out, but it got a bit septic and they had to open it up today. I got a bullet through both thighs, it made a clean hole through the left but opened out and made a large gash through the back of the right, which will take a little while to fix up. I'll be back as soon as I can.

In Featherstonehaugh's absence, Davies is in command of B Squadron. The letter continues:

There must be many changes and promotions in B after all those casualties … I'm quite sure you've fixed things up all right; when you get this, I wish you would get the sergeants together and thank them from me for their work on 31st and ask them to let the other ranks know how I appreciated the splendid way they carried out their job. It was a treat to ride in front of a crowd like them. Remember me to Abbott, Lindsay and Easterbrook and tell them I'm glad they got through safely and hope to see you along (here?) some of these days yourself.

On 3 November, Jack Davies wrote to his wife Mildred, who was in Cairo with their three children:

My Darling Mill,

Am quite OK and the tummy feeling fine. I can't say this letter will get through but it may. The 4th Brigade were the first into Beersheba. It was the most exciting thing I've ever been in, just an absolute Bust Through. We wheeled on the north side of the town and collared all we headed … Feathers was not badly wounded I hear also Guy, otherwise the Regiment came off lucky as regards officers. Really very few casualties considering with fond love to all ever your Jack.

Three months after the battle, Davies writes to his brother Reg, whose colourful, singular story as a medical officer in the French Army also deserves telling. By war's end, he held the Croix de Guerre and the British OBE. 'It was rather peculiar you referring to the polo game in connection with it, I made the remark to Cameron that night, after the charge was over

114

and I had just finished counting my little lot of prisoners ... I said, "Well, I've played some good games, but that was the best run I've ever had".' Describing the charge, he wrote:

... then the fire started and we went at it hell for split, we struck trenches 1½ miles from town, some went over them, some went round one end, some through a gap a few yards in the middle and the remainder, including myself, round the left flank. Providence guided me that day and I rode into the town as if I knew all the roads leading into it. I've seen some surprised people, but those Turks were certainly not expecting us and it was just a camp rounding up, as many as we could handle. We had been told the ANZACs on our left and the 3rd Brigade were also going to ride into town and expected to find 7 or 8 regiments concentrating ... past the mosque, but to my surprise I found ... I had about 80 men ... Aubrey Abbott was close by with another troop and that was about all the Desert Mounted Corps I could see and I began to think it was time to go home, then sighted another troop ... so we just grafted as many as we could and made back to the wells, which was what we were really after. We did a 38 mile march the night before, so you can imagine Abdul hardly expected us where he found us ...

My squadron leader Featherstonehaugh had his horse shot and was later wounded himself. This left me the senior officer of the two squadrons, though I knew nothing of this until it was all over ...

Colonel Cameron got a DSO and Featherstonehaugh and Hyman a DSO each, Robey and myself MCs, three DCMs and five Military Medals. Bourchier of the 4th got a DSO, one of his majors a DSO, two captains MCs, two DCMs and four MMs. Not bad for an hour's job especially since Allenby personally gave [Brigadier General] Grant his bar [to the DSO] next day. I was jolly pleased Feathers got a DSO ... for the splendid, cool way he deployed the squadron in action ... he's a great old bird, son of the old man who drove a four-in-hand in the old days.

Davies goes on to describe Major Hyman's part in the action, then says: 'when General Hodgson was giving out the ribbons, he made a speech to us all and when he came along to me, said "Captain Davies has done excellent work. I hope soon to have the pleasure of pinning a DSO alongside that." I'll have a chance now for pukka promotion to major ... and shall be glad to have the rank, also glad I did not have to get anyone killed to get it.'

Perspectives

When from the wady bank near Tel el Sakati Major Richardson observed on the flat plain eight miles distant the deployment of the Australian Mounted Division before Beersheba, it made such an impression on him that he recorded it in the 7th Regiment's history: 'It was a fine sight to see the Australian Mounted Division moving forward to close on the town of Beersheba. Regiment after regiment, troop after troop, they moved forward until the whole plain to the east seemed to be covered with mounted men. This movement was to culminate in the gallant charge of the 4th Light Horse Brigade.'

Such a phlegmatic observer was seldom moved to mere description. The truth is, the Light Horsemen hardly ever saw themselves en masse and in their memorable moments really didn't know what they looked like. As Ion Idriess put it, 'Soon we would be too occupied to note anything beyond the regiment, then it would be the squadron, then the troop, then very likely the section'.

They were curious; and the cover photograph of the 2nd Brigade of ANZACs crossing the desert at Esdud was therefore sought-after. It is remarkable. Seldom have 1800 men in any activity been captured in such detail in one frame. With a magnifying glass, they may be counted. The square, unmistakeable figure of Brigadier General Ryrie rides ahead and the main body fans out in a massed, irregular arrowhead. The tail, echelon after diagonal echelon of troops, seems to stretch away to infinity, with a branch to the right across the picture, far distant but still clear. In that flat, bare setting, one can only speculate that the photographer Frank Hurley must have climbed a date palm to take the picture. The glass negative has a thumbprint and a fingerprint on the left, near the horizon: Hurley's?

The campaign was British, and the Dominions' contribution just that. Australia's official historian Sir Henry Gullett preserves scrupulously this relativity and the British historian Cyril Falls says his account is 'one of the best things of its kind I have ever read'.

The Gaza–Beersheba front was 30 miles long, with British at one end and the Dominions at the other. Cyril Falls covers Beersheba with: '[It] was duly captured, the final stroke being a charge by an Australian brigade, the men —

good riders but not cavalrymen — carrying bayonets for effect, a magnificent exploit'. The praise, if spare, is by no means faint and in the context of the intense activity and deciding breakthrough by British infantry, the summation is balanced.

The feat did attract intense professional interest, however, and was responsible for a brief restoration of the charge in the cavalry repertoire. The Australians had proved it could still be done against modern fire-power and the Yeomanry, who carried swords, emulated them with equal success in later fighting. After Beersheba, the Australian Mounted Division was armed with swords at its own request: however, the ANZACs preferred to stick to their rifles and bayonets.

THIRTEEN

Khuweilfe barrier and Kauwukah breakthrough

Twenty-five centuries earlier, the Chinese military sage Sun-tze had written in his immortal analects: 'The skilful tactician may be likened to the Shuai-jan. Now the Shuai-jan is a snake that is found in the Ch'ang Mountains. Strike at its head and you will be attacked by its tail; strike at its tail and you will be attacked by its head; strike at its middle and you will be attacked by its head and tail both.'

Chetwode appeared to have these principles in mind when he formulated his plan. If the Turks were a 30-mile snake, the fighting around Beersheba steadily drew reinforcements from the Gaza head; and for his part, General Allenby no doubt knew of the Prussian General Moltke, who consolidated the leadership of the German peoples in Prussian hands and remarked of plans, 'None survives contact with the enemy'.

Unknown to the British, the Turkish Army was in disarray owing to divided counsels, uncertainty in its aims and irresolution in its actions. Rations, clothing and munitions were not flowing and a chronic haemorrhaging of deserters wasted the front line. The German General von Falkenhayn, in Fall's estimation one of the greatest soldiers of the war, was at dangerous odds with Djemal Pasha, the tempestuous Turkish Commander-in-Chief who resented German interference. In his eyes, they were to provide technical assistance in aircraft, gunnery, transport and communications and no more, and he made an ostentatious point of ignoring German strategic advice. Djemal ran Palestine like a despotic potentate and sybarite of old, and a Turkish major general remarked to the German von Kressenstein, 'Now we shall go hungry because Djemal will have no interest in feeding us'.

In spite of all this, the Turkish Army after Beersheba summoned a creditable defence. There was less throwing down of arms and begging for mercy and more of the dogged rifleman who, having dug a trench to his liking, was not about to give it up.

The effect of this resistance on the British plan was that the envisaged 'rolling up' of the Turkish left flank from Beersheba towards Gaza by the mounted men did not take place. Instead, there was a series of chequerboard actions for the next week around Tel el Khuweilfe, a Turkish strongpoint with good water ten miles north of Beersheba. What influenced von Falkenhayn to fight here was the seizure of some high ground overlooking the Hebron road by Arab irregulars under a British officer. Falkenhayn was convinced they were Chauvel's advance guard and deployed six Turkish battalions against them. The Arabs fought well and their eventual surrender was dearly bought.

The British then had to tackle the enemy who still held Khuweilfe. This was rough, dry country and the summer lingered on with intense heat and a three-day khamsin. There was no water to be had beyond Beersheba and the infantrymen, Yeomanry and Light Horse had to march and fight on one water bottle in 36 hours, and the horses on nothing — they would not eat past the early stages of thirst — until they could be brought out of action and back to Beersheba, twelve to fifteen miles away.

Tel el Khuweilfe commanded the country to both west and east, and would therefore menace the British infantry and mounted troops when they struck at the Hareira and Nejile redoubts in the rolling-up process. On the other hand, its capture by the British would leave the Turkish left flank in the air.

The 8th Mounted Brigade of Sherwood Rangers and South Notts Hussars and the 8th Light Horse Regiment (which was under the mistaken impression it would be deployed for only one day and did not draw rations) advanced directly up the valley to three miles below the enemy stronghold.

Brigadier General J.T. Wigan considered a bold frontal attack offered the best chance of success and sent a squadron of the 8th Light Horse at it at the gallop. The squadron got to within 800 yards before it was forced into cover on its left by heavy fire. It was later joined by the rest of the 8th Regiment. After nightfall, Wigan endeavoured to link up the Yeomanry regiments with the Light Horse, but the Sherwoods could not go forward.

All night the 8th was under heavy machine-gun and rifle fire, but with good cover in the rocks, suffered little. At dawn, the enemy was discovered in strength much closer, within 200 to 300 yards of the Australians, who had now been 24 hours without food and had exhausted their water on the previous day.

The commitment expanded. The 53rd Infantry Division and Cox's 1st Light Horse Brigade advanced on the feature and Cox's 1st Regiment seized a ridge on its right, but there they were pinned down and isolated all day, suffering heavy casualties. Many officers were killed and one squadron was left with a sergeant in command. The Turks deliberately fired on ambulance carts sent in to collect the 1st's wounded in a gross breach of their previously honoured convention. A Turkish prisoner said this was at the instigation of Germans, who claimed the ambulance carts would be carrying ammunition.

Soon after the 1st Regiment's advance, Brigadier General 'Fighting Charlie' Cox took over the forward area, including the ridge called Ras el Nagb, from the Yeomanry and the 8th Light Horse came under his command. The Yeomanry were withdrawn but Cox ordered the 8th to hold on at all costs. The 8th endured and fought back until their ammunition was exhausted.

At 11 am the enemy launched a rare counterattack, but Cox dispersed it with the 2nd and 3rd Regiments. In two hours, fresh British regiments began to arrive and the 5th Mounted took over at Ras el Nagb. Elements of the 53rd Division marched up from the south-west and at 4 pm the British took over the whole line.

These rotations, a trial in themselves, where necessary for men and horses to be watered at Beersheba. The long-suffering 8th Light Horse arrived at Beersheba at 10 pm and their desperate horses heaved and struggled for the water troughs and their first drink in 39 hours. Many men drank too much, suffering the consequences of severe diarrhoea.

During the action at Khuweilfe, Ryrie's 2nd Brigade was vainly trying to break through from the east. The country was just as strewn with rocks and ridges over which men and horses could only pick their way and the Turks, on higher ground, had the advantage. Over two days, Ryrie tried three times to turn the Turks' flank, but the terrain, lack of water, shortage of supplies and ammunition, and constant enemy shell fire in which time after time the led horses were searched out and fired on, indicating Bedouin cooperation with enemy artillery, all conspired to frustrate the brigade. The truth was, it was being worked to exhaustion. Recognising this, Chauvel intervened to say the main object should be to guard the flank rather than advance and that Ryrie should just hold the line. The last of some rain puddles from an October thunderstorm dried out and Ryrie had to march back to Beersheba after a most strenuous and frustrating operation.

In the centre, on 6 November, Chetwode was to assault the Kauwukah Trench System, a typically labyrinthine Turkish gallery protecting the Hareira and Sheria redoubts, with three divisions of infantry. This plan also provided for the 53rd Division to capture Khuweilfe simultaneously.

The New Zealand Brigade had relieved the 1st Light Horse Brigade at Khuweilfe just as 2000 Turks attacked the Yeomanry on Ras el Nagb. The Yeomanry held them off until nightfall, when they were relieved by the Canterbury Regiment. The New Zealanders' orders were to hold their ground while the 53rd Division attacked Khuweilfe from the south-west again. The 53rd had suffered much for no gain, except to serve and to augment the flow of Turks from Gaza to the Beersheba operation.

A quiet night of the 5th ended with two hours of Turkish bombardment and an advance against the Canterburys at dawn. The Wellingtons went to their support, the enemy was stopped and there was no further action that day. But in the evening, the NZ Brigade had to return to Beersheba for water: they had been unable to complete watering before setting out, owing to congestion and insufficient flow at Abraham's Wells.

The Camel Brigade took over their line, less its 3rd Battalion (Australian), temporarily attached to the 53rd Division. Its task was to follow close in rear of the 53rd's advance and occupy Khuweilfe's commanding hill once it was captured.

The 158th Brigade of the 53rd Division set off before dawn on the 6th, unfortunately short of one battalion that had not arrived in time. The Hereford Battalion was ordered to close this gap in the line, but in attempting this movement they lost direction and turned a full circle to the left. The Camel Battalion, which had been following the Herefords, kept to the line of march and with daylight found themselves in utter isolation, with Tel el Khuweilfe looming ominously ahead. To Lieutenant Colonel N. de Lancey Forth's alarm, the Camels would obviously attract annihilating fire and he moved to cover behind a spur just as the Turks swept the open ground with machine-guns. At the same time, some 200 of the Herefords in the open were targeted: they lost all their officers and fell back in confusion on the left of the Camels, in the process abandoning to the enemy part of the ridge behind which the Australians sheltered. It was clear that unless the Herefords held that part of the ridge, the Camels would have to retreat from their part. Lieutenant E.W. Dixon with about 30 men rushed to meet the retreating infantry and, waving his hat, stemmed the confusion and turned them under heavy fire back onto the ridge, where they then held steadfastly. Later in the day, they repulsed a Turkish attempt to envelop them, at the same time saving the Camels from encirclement and likely disaster.

But from every approach, the Camels were still taking shrapnel, machine-gun and rifle fire and Forth asked for assistance. His official report says: 'At about 10 o'clock, representations were made by the 3rd Battalion to the General Officer Commanding the 158th Brigade for the infantry to come up and drive the Turks off the ridge ... to the left rear, and over which the infantry held commanding ground. This, for reasons unknown, they were not ordered to do; but the 2nd Light Horse Brigade's machine-gun squadron were ordered to gallop up a little valley commanded by the Turks ... They charged in a very gallant manner and at once came under murderous machine-gun and shrapnel fire, but ... led by Captain Cain, reached their objective ... They rushed their guns up the hill within forty yards of the Turks, and, although the teams were shot down almost to a man, their very gallant action caused the Turks to pause and gave the 3rd Battalion breathing time to size up their position.'

The machine-gun squadron maintained their precarious hold and their fire, along with the Camel Battalion's, all through the day, repelling repeated Turkish counterattacks that threatened to sweep them, and the 53rd Division's leading elements beside them, off their ground.

Shortly before dawn on the 7th, the machine-gunners were withdrawn, but the fire fights resumed with daylight, Turkish close-range sniping especially taking a severe toll. The action was deadlocked, with the Camels and 53rd units unable to move, and the Turks held at bay. At 3 pm, accurate artillery fire was brought to the support of the 53rd, enabling a general advance to be mounted towards evening. All troops had been marching and fighting for over 36 hours, but summoned their last reserves to attack determinedly. The Camels rushed the slopes of Khuweilfe with bayonets and hand grenades, and after brief resistance the Turks fled the grim mound. The 53rd went forward until darkness checked them. The night was tense but quiet, and in the morning it was found that the Turks, whose front had been comprehensively breached by Chetwode at Kauwukah, had abandoned all the Khuweilfe fortifications.

Khuweilfe was a piecemeal, reactive action. It seemed small scale, undeserving of proper plans and systematic reduction, yet the pinprick became a consuming canker that wore down and mauled three divisions for six days. Beersheba, from the time Brigadier General Grant got his orders to the fall of the town, took less than an hour.

The Khuweilfe operations dashed Allenby's hope of an early breakthrough and pursuit, yet in the sense that it did draw the enemy away from Gaza in strength, it contributed very much to victory. And despite the lack of an overall operational plan, no theorist has yet conjured any one that would have served well.

In the final action, the 53rd Division suffered the heaviest pro rata casualties. The 3rd Camel Battalion lost 22 men killed and 54 wounded, and Captain Cain's machine-gun squadron eight men killed and nineteen wounded.

THE FIRST PHASE OF THE THIRD BATTLE OF GAZA BEGAN TWO DAYS AFTER BEERSHEBA had fallen, when Allenby judged the confusion this thunderbolt had caused the Turks would be at its height. The preliminary two-day bombardment of Gaza was unprecedented in its ferocity, then on 7 November, General Bulfin, who had waited patiently through the summer until the Beersheba diversion was launched, was ordered forward with his 21 Corps.

Bulfin advanced over 1000 yards of no-man's land, spearheaded by the 7th Scottish Rifles. Then two brigades of the 54th Division carried no-man's land from end to end and overran the Turks' front-line trench. The enemy had been jolted from a line he believed invincible. His flank had not yet been decisively turned, but his protection against that had virtually disappeared.

Allenby was content. Within three days, a surprise attack had shattered the enemy at Beersheba, then a determined frontal attack over the sandhills between Gaza and the sea left him in confusion and apprehension as to where the next blow would fall.

He was still in that state on 6 November, when Chetwode flung his three divisions, with the Yeomanry Mounted Division guarding their flank, against the Kauwukah trenches in the centre of the line. His 20 Corps had an advantage in higher ground, but this was bare of cover and the resolution of the 74th Division particularly, in overcoming the most difficult sector, was applauded by Light Horsemen in the wings. The transformation in spirit between Allenby's army and Murray's was plain to see.

By 2.30 pm the 74th, the 10th and the 60th Divisions had all smashed though the Kauwukah defences. The 60th's Londoners were then to carry Tel el Sheria with the bayonet at night, but the Turks fired a large dump nearby and this shed too much light for the operation. The British then bivouacked in a wady bed.

At Gaza next morning, after another heavy bombardment, Bulfin attacked again on both sides and the Turks abandoned the city. At 9 am the Imperial Service Cavalry Brigade — an Indian independent states brigade with Indian officers but a de facto British commander — rode in to find it completely wrecked. The British shelling had been severe enough, but the Turks had demolished the buildings for every scrap of timber in them to revet their trenches in the sand dunes. The place was deserted and the Turks' notorious neglect of sanitation had rendered it nauseously foul and noisome. Later, when the Australians retraced their steps of the earlier battles, there was nothing left of the fine palm plantations and thriving olive groves they had ridden through; just plains of dust. The Turks had used the trees for their trenches and as fuel for their locomotives.

The divisions of 21 Corps were therefore the first troops to advance north of Gaza. They did so swiftly and, further east, Chetwode's 10th Division took the Hareira redoubt, followed by the 60th's occupation of the Sheria redoubt. The Turks re-formed on a slope a mile and a half north, pursued by the 60th, but as the enemy organised his new line the 60th themselves were thrown on the defensive. Their advance stopped and they lay prone.

When this new Turkish line was broken, the final obstacle to the Desert Mounted Corps debouching onto the Philistine Plain and starting the last and greatest chapter in the history of cavalry would be overcome.

Chauvel and his chief-of-staff climbed the Sheria mound to survey the prospect. He had at his disposal the Australian Mounted's 4th Light Horse and 5th Mounted (Yeomanry) Brigades about three miles back and the ANZACs' 1st and 2nd Light Horse Brigades (less two squadrons, one of them the machine-gun squadron still at Khuweilfe) a few miles west, after making a strenuous night march. Barrow's Yeomanry Division was to remain with the infantry and the New Zealanders were now supporting the Camels and the 53rd Division, also at Khuweilfe.

The great mass of the 7th Turkish Army was retreating up the plain and the immediate objective of the mounted troops was to seize the water ten miles north of Sheria at Jemmameh and Huj before the enemy got to it, either by driving through the Turks or skirting round their flank. The ANZACs could have been deployed on this at once, but Chauvel decided to first use the Australian Mounted to rescue the Londoners, still pinned down and prone in front of Sheria, and clear this direct way forward for their mounted pursuit.

Chauvel therefore ordered Hodgson's Australian Mounted Division to 'clear the enemy from the front of 60th Division'. This proved to be a messy and costly expedient and Chauvel has been criticised for not allowing the Australian Mounted to join up with the ANZAC Mounted as it started to advance, then take the Turks on the flank. Perhaps he was too anxious to get this irritating detail holding up the grand drive out of the way; he has said himself that he became 'infinitely more worried during the two days that followed Tel el Sheria than … at any time during the Battle of Beersheba'.

It was in fact an attempt to repeat the Beersheba triumph, dependant on a galloping advance to panic the Turks into submission. And again, the task fell to Grant's 4th Light Horse Brigade.

The 11th and 12th Light Horse Regiments rode into the Wady Sheria under heavy shell fire, but as their horses had been dry for 28 hours they paused to let them drink. This cost them momentum. They emerged from the steep banks as fast as they could, but not fast enough to miss the swathes of machine-gun and rifle fire ranged accurately against them. Cameron, who had commanded the 12th at Beersheba, appreciated that there was no chance of repeating such a coup in this case and dismounted two of his squadrons, sending back their horses.

On his left, the 11th emerged from the wady at a better pace and two squadrons galloped forward, careless of enemy fire and riding hard. They

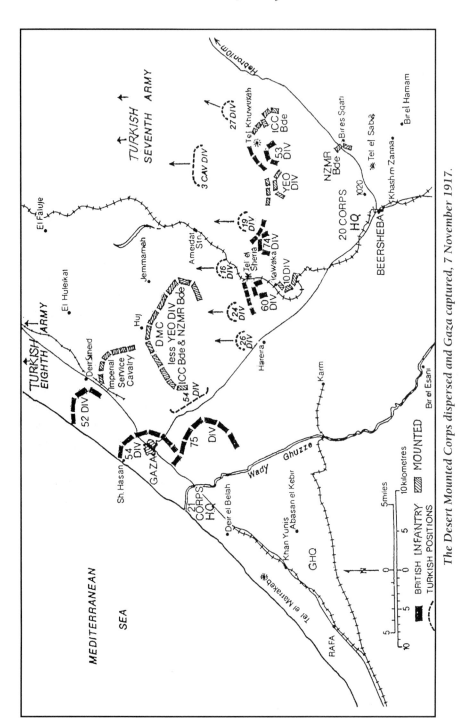

The Desert Mounted Corps dispersed and Gaza captured, 7 November 1917.

passed dead Londoners, then live Cockney soldiers who rose and cheered them. But the Turks were not to be demoralised this time and a few hundred yards further on, under still heavier fire, the order was given to dismount and the horses were galloped back.

But one troop of 21 men missed the signal and galloped on, right to the enemy trenches where some Turks held up their hands as the horses jumped them. The men tumbled from the saddles and rushed in with the bayonet, but the Turks who had surrendered now attacked again and others closed in around them. In seconds, every horse was down, eleven men were killed and all the rest, save one, wounded.

The remaining dismounted men of the 11th's squadrons were now some hundreds of yards forward of the infantry, under heavy fire, shooting at individual Turks creeping forward with the bayonet. They hung on all day, shooting in that deliberate, economical way that always distinguished the Light Horse. Colonel P.J. Bailey of the 11th dashed back to the Londoners and persuaded an officer to run forward with a machine-gun. The officer and two gunners were killed, but the remaining young British private carried on operating the gun himself. 'He was,' said Bailey, 'the coolest man I ever saw.'

Towards sunset, relief arrived in the form of the reserve brigade of the 60th Division, advancing in waves from the left. It was the Light Horsemen who then cheered the Londoners, as they had been cheered by them that morning. 'How far away are they?' asked a sergeant. 'Five hundred yards,' replied an Australian. 'Then in five minutes, we'll be into them.' Some of the Australians rose to join in the advance. With a crescendo of fire and a culminating bayonet charge, the Londoners broke through the Turks and the gateway to Palestine was open.

This marked the start of a close and enduring partnership between the Cockneys and the Light Horse in the campaigning to come. But the whole day's delay at the start of the pursuit resulted in a longer and harder campaign for both.

WHILE THE 60TH DIVISION WAS ATTACKING TEL EL SHERIA TO ALLOW THE Australian Mounted through, Major General Chaytor's ANZACs further west were ordered to drive through to the north-west, seize the enemy's ammunition dump at the railway station of Ameidat, and then (hopefully) being joined by the Australian Mounted, continue north-west at all speed across the enemy's communications.

The ANZACs were lacking the New Zealand Brigade and two squadrons, one machine-gun, from the 2nd Brigade. They were weary and worn after a night march from Beersheba in a khamsin and of course thirsty, with the time and place of the next drink anybody's guess. But as the first mounted troops to take up this pursuit role in the new territory they were abuzz with anticipation, and no doubt with some sense of history — larger than they probably would have recognised at the time. They were on the best of all cavalry missions and, if nothing else, were assured of a grand ride.

Cox's 1st Brigade led off at 6.30 am. Riding briskly, with the 2nd Brigade in support, the 1st was soon within three miles of Ameidat station on the railway line between Beersheba, Jerusalem and all points north. The going was good over open downs country, but the brigade was under constant, though not concentrated, shell fire. Passing the 60th Infantry Division, the 2nd increased the pace to a gallop, and with whoops and shouts swooped on Ameidat station. There was little resistance and the Light Horse captured 400 startled Turks, enormous quantities of ammunition, stores and a complete field hospital.

Cox pushed on towards Jemmameh, but in the afternoon was held up at the village of Dilakh. At 1230, Chauvel had told General Chaytor that Gaza had fallen and that he was to press on to Jemmameh and engage large bodies of retreating Turks making for it. However, the Turks at Dilakh, on commanding ground, with reinforcements arriving and an accurate battery keeping the Australians' heads down, were still resisting.

Chaytor ordered the 2nd Brigade to charge it. The 5th Regiment, from a mile and a half away, went at it with their usual resolution. They occupied part of the village, but discovered that the enemy guns were not there but three miles further on. Ion Idriess wrote:

> We formed artillery formation and galloped straight for the guns. How they plastered us with shells! By Jove, it was a grand gallop with the horses reefing for their heads ... then A squadron galloped on alone — into a burst of machine-gun fire, vicious rattle of rifles ... we galloped over a low hill down into a gully as the major shrieked 'Halt!' We peered over the sheltering bank at a flat, running for six hundred yards

in full view of the German machine-gunners — and just beyond … the guns waited — and relays of Turkish infantry lying … waiting too!

Our first troop faced the gully bank, then at a signal, dug in the spurs. The horses plunged up — we caught our breaths at the hail of shrapnel as their tails swept up over the bank! The gunners had point-blank range … Our turn came. The first three sections jammed knee to knee … we waited until two shells exploded crash-crash! — we spurred up, horses pawing the bank and were racing for our lives.

The 5th advanced mounted and dismounted until almost sunset, when they were called back for the night.

All through the afternoon of 7 November, Chaytor had looked out anxiously for Hodgson's division to arrive. He knew that opportunities for striking blows at the enemy were slipping away, but the ANZAC Division, less a brigade and with the other two undermanned, were too thin to be effective on their own. Indeed, should the Turks turn on them in numbers they could be ambushed or surrounded. At present, all Chaytor's troops were in the firing line, his horses had not been watered since Beersheba and many of them had missed that drink. He concluded that he must rest on his ground that night, watering as many horses as he could, and postpone the taking of Jemmameh until next morning.

The ANZACs' difficulties were not lost on Chauvel and on the same day he made an attempt to bring the Imperial Service Cavalry Brigade, near Gaza, across to Chaytor's support, but before the message reached the brigade the Turks were streaming past Huj and it was too late. The 7th Mounted Brigade did reinforce the ANZACs for the attack on Jemmameh next morning, however. The 60th Division was to strike for Huj at the same time, and the Australian Mounted, free of the Sheria imbroglio at last, was to advance in the wedge of land between them.

The 52nd Division was also to march up the coast north of Gaza; and in the best outcome, the cavalry and infantry might even yet join up across the front and cut off the retreat of still large enemy forces.

The 7th Mounted (Yeomanry) Brigade was positioned between the two Light Horse Brigades as they went forward. Now, as they topped each ridge, they saw column after column of the blue-grey army hurrying north over the miles of wide plain extending to the sea. But they were safe: just as the Light Horseman and British trooper might instinctively check the ground and collect his horse for the charge, the first shells and bullets fell around him. In the 24 hours lost, the enemy had been able to protect his flank.

The advance to Jemmameh was slow and hard, the Turks offering strong resistance. First the 5th Light Horse Regiment, then the 7th Mounted, were checked and counterattacked. The Yeomanry stood firm against waves of Turks for three hours. The 1st Light Horse Brigade at last took the village with a slow dismounted attack, passing through the 2nd Brigade, but it was then after 3 pm and, except for water, the village was no longer of such significance.

The ANZAC line was established to guard the water at both Jemmameh and Nejile and immediately the Turks counterattacked it. From 3000 to 5000 infantry with artillery support marched forward against the 5th and 7th Light Horse Regiments, with no more than 500 men in their line. But they were on good ground and 'never shot so calmly and surely in their lives', according to one of their leaders. The Turks reached to within 40 yards at times, but withdrew for some miles at dark, no doubt to prepare for the next move, another mounted advance against them in the morning.

The ANZAC horses were fully watered that night. With few exceptions, it was their first drink in 50 hours and they had long since refused forage. The men had either been in the saddle or fighting on foot for three days and nights without sleep, and on short rations. These last needs were met, but with watering horses, outpost duties and incidentals, there was again no sleep.

The Australian Mounted had meanwhile advanced with the 60th Infantry on Huj. The 5th Mounted Brigade and the 3rd Light Horse Brigade combined in, respectively, a successful dismounted attack and establishing contact with the ANZACs on their left. The 3rd Light Horse Brigade had lost Galloping Jack Royston, who had returned to his native South Africa, it was said at his own request, but it seems more likely due to the government's policy that Australians must be commanded by Australians. The former commander of the 5th Regiment, L.C. Wilson, a Brisbane solicitor, now commanded the brigade. It took a good man to fill Royston's shoes, and while he could not but be a quieter and more orthodox personality Wilson did so with distinction. He had led the dashing 5th through all the hot spots since Romani.

The Londoners of the 60th marched briskly on in the Huj advance, scattering a Turkish rearguard in their confident stride. Without exception the British infantry had fought well, but the Londoners had a particular bearing and spirit that seemed to make light of anything in their way and, despite having marched and fought for nine straight days, had the carriage and energy of perfectly fresh troops. General J.S.M. Shea, their commander, went ahead in a car, picking the way forward through wadys and rough ground.

Shea saw a strong Turkish column passing across his front a mile and a half away. Difficult, rough country lay between. The Turks halted and brought some of their field guns into action, apparently with the intention to engage his column. Shea saw troops of the 5th Mounted Brigade a mile to the right and drove over to them. He pointed out the Turkish force to Lieutenant Colonel Gray-Cheape, who commanded the Warwickshire Yeomanry Regiment, and asked for his help.

Gray-Cheape had only about 200 men of the Warwicks, but he at once decided to charge, leading his men straight for the guns at the gallop. The route led down a slope, then across a valley fully exposed to the enemy, for a mile and a half. The artillery shifted target from the infantry to the charging horsemen, firing rapidly, shortening the range until the shells were bursting right at the muzzles as the yelling Yeomanry, with swords aloft, galloped up to the batteries through a torrent of shrapnel. They sabred the gunners, re-formed and charged again at the machine-gun nest, killing the crews.

The Warwicks suffered heavy casualties, but had struck a great blow. They captured eleven field guns, three machine-guns and 30 prisoners, and their charge enabled the Londoners to advance again and Wilson's 3rd Light Horse Brigade to occupy the village of Huj. The charge mauled the enemy's rearguard and he was unable to offer stiff resistance again for another twelve miles.

The 5th Mounted Brigade, through the Warwicks, had covered themselves with glory. Their failure to resist the Turks' surprise attack in the Sinai desert, that triggered the whole Middle East campaign so long ago, had been hard to live down and their performance since had been patchy, but the Australians in particular, some of whom saw the charge, were lavish in their praise. Idriess wrote: 'The Australians are enthusiastic about a charge by the Yeomanry regiments (sic) who ... with drawn swords charged straight into the mouths of eleven guns. The Yeomanry will have their tails up now. By Jove, they've earned it. Eleven guns!'

FOURTEEN

The worn and ragged armies drive on

Now well into autumn, the weather at last turned cooler, but water levels in the wells of the Philistine Plain were at their lowest, some over 200 feet down. The water had to be hauled up by any improvised means that would work: buckets on the end of telephone wires, bridle reins buckled end-to-end, baling twine. A horse might have to walk the 200 feet drawing up his bucket, then having drunk that, pull up his next bucketful. By working all through the night of 8–9 November 1917, the 1st and 2nd Brigades of the ANZAC Mounted Division and the 7th Mounted Brigade managed to complete watering, but the Australian Mounted had to be sent back to the already overtaxed supply at Jemmameh and could not resume the pursuit until late on the 9th.

Therefore on that morning, only the 1st and 2nd ANZAC Brigades and the 7th Mounted were able to resume the pursuit. Barrow's Yeomanry Division — and the New Zealand Brigade — were yet to arrive from Khuweilfe and the melancholy fact that only one of Chauvel's three divisions could be in action, and it was under strength, was starkly illuminated.

With the exhausted 5th and 7th Regiments leading, Ryrie's brigade struck north and Cox's brigade north-west, with orders to establish a line between two villages ten miles away. It was the day of the enemy's greatest confusion and disorganisation, and again the opportunity to shorten the war slipped through Allenby's fingers through lack of water. Two brigades could scarcely defend themselves, let alone capture an army; and after the 9th, the Turk's retreat became more orderly and his defence better.

But, hungry and sleepless though the ANZACs were, the sense of occasion, the good, open going and the new country, with the forbidding hills of Judea to the right and glimpses of the blue Mediterranean to the left, buoyed them up. They were moving on again and driving the enemy before them, having been stalled behind the Gaza–Beersheba line for seven months. All could now see that 'Jerusalem by Christmas' was no longer just a catchphrase, but a possibility.

Richardson records in this stage of the pursuit the winning combination of the 5th and 7th Regiments: 'the two regiments moved North into more rugged country, near to Wadi Hesi. B Squadron, under Major T.J. Willsallen came into action across the wadi ... and although checked, held its position against strong enemy counter attacks. At 2 pm [on 9 November], C Squadron under Major Barton was sent to support the 5th, which was holding a long line on our left. They arrived just in time to help beat off a desperate enemy attack. The enemy, doubtless, wished to deny us the water supply of the Wadi Hesi. This squadron, in conjunction with a squadron of the 5th, checked all counterattacks and retained the position.'

In mid-February 1918, Nat Barton wrote: 'I received a letter from Harry Barton [a cousin] a couple of days ago, congratulating me on being mentioned in Allenby's dispatches on January 18th; it must be a pretty long list to have me in it!' He might have also thought that the Chief was well behind with his dispatches. The family papers describe Nat's exploit as 'taking his squadron across the face of the enemy at the gallop to take a hill [Tel Abu Dilakh] to assist the 5th Australian Light Horse Regiment'.

Ryrie's two regiments then advanced at a lively trot. The 7th suffered a dreadful blow right at the start when half a troop was destroyed by an enemy shell burst. The 7th's screen galloped down a convoy of 110 wagons and took 360 prisoners — and many loaves of brown bread fresh from the ovens, which the troopers declared the best they had ever eaten and an acceptable breakfast.

The 5th, and B and C Squadrons of the 7th, 'with great dash' galloped in pursuit of another north-bound convoy. For seven miles they urged on their weakened horses, eventually overtaking the convoy and capturing another 100 wagons and 300 more sick and exhausted prisoners. But they were now deep into the enemy's rearguard and at great risk from concentrated enemy artillery and machine-gun fire on either side, their own horses were spent and the Turkish prisoners were beyond marching. The Australians had more than their own number of prisoners and were surrounded on three sides by Turkish troops of uncertain temper. The two regiments were ordered to concentrate and remain in position.

Just after dark, a body of Turks with fixed bayonets advanced on two troops of B Squadron, on outpost. The Australians fired and their officer shouted in Turkish, 'You are surrounded!' A Turkish officer approached, and after a brief parley 230 more prisoners were added to the total. They had surrendered to 40 men.

'This day,' said Richardson, 'had been a great one for the Regiment as well as the Brigade. The Regiment alone captured six guns, 110 wagons and over 500 prisoners and had assisted the 5th Regiment in the capture of 100 more wagons and 300 men. Our casualties for the day amounted to only 21.'

Once captured, convoys were shelled by their own side. Idriess of the 5th provides a description. There were, he writes:

hundreds upon hundreds of Turkish wagons in jumbled masses of wreckage and confusion. Some were piled upon the other where bomb and shell had blown them. Streets, houses, cactus hedges were littered with fragments of wheels, wagons, limbs and entrails of bullocks. But hundreds of wagons were quite unharmed, their horses and bullocks and mules still yoked to the wagons, in a pitiable state. Those that had been killed outright ... were the happy ones. Many had dropped dead toiling under the knout until their hearts burst. Others were still alive, moaning with the piled up wagons on top of them; others were being slowly strangled by the yoke and weight of the loaded wagons ... slowly dying of wounds, exhaustion, hunger, thirst and strangulation.

Coming and going ... to the wagons were swarms of Arabs, men women and children staggering under loads of loot ... sweat pouring down their faces in their greed to get all away before the more distant rival villagers should rush the spoil ... the women hysterical, shrieking almost crying in their excitement as they clawed the contents of the wagons ... They didn't think to end the misery of the poor moaning beasts upon whose mangled bodies they climbed ... over hundreds of yards ... were countless rifles, stacks of cases of ammunition, wagons loaded to the brim with shiny brass bombs, farriers' gear, saddlery, armourers' gear, wagons loaded with doctors' gear, provisions, confusion indescribable; the baggage of an army in full retreat.

Among the huge litter lay dead Turks, their dusty faces trodden on ... huddled Turks used as a footstool by women and children whose bloodstained feet were covered with dust.

That night was a repeat of the night before, only worse. Water, water, water! For over two years now, it had dominated the Light Horsemen's waking thoughts and dictated what they did and they had come to detest the name of it. The regiments had strong outposts to find and its horses to water again. Nobody slept. The Light Horse supply wagons had caught up with forage and rations as they always did, to the envy of the British — but not with water.

All night, the men coaxed up the water from 250 feet down, a bucket at a time. The crooked alleyways in the mud-walled, straw roofed villages were jammed with 2000 gasping, fractious horses and gaunt and dusty unshaven men working ceaselessly to relieve them, keeping going on just the idea of finishing the work. And the war. An occasional ancient waterwheel wobbled round, but the canvas buckets and improvised ropes carried most of it. Crowding the troops were dirty, ragged, picturesque natives, clamouring for water themselves, denied them during the fighting.

Until late the following day, the work had to go on. Turkish prisoners sick with malaria and dysentery cried and moaned, 'Moya! Moya!' (Water! Water!) and the Light Horsemen could not but give it, sometimes from their own jealously harboured bottles. However, organised relief had to be attempted and Richardson records that at daylight, the 7th Regiment's captives were taken in parties of twenty to the wells; then as soon as they started to drink, orders came to send all prisoners to the rear and complete watering horses urgently.

Early on the 10th, Ryrie sent forward patrols towards their objective, the villages of Beit Durdis and Kustine. Like all the men, the patrollers were almost insensible for want of sleep and only half their horses had been watered. The ANZAC Division commander Chaytor had ordered a 'vigorous' resumption of the pursuit: Ryrie decided, not lightly, that he had to act. He signalled that this would mean the loss of most of his horses, but he would proceed if it was essential. No-one was better informed about horsemastership than Ryrie, Chaytor accepted his judgment, and the brigade spent the day at the wells.

Cox's 1st Brigade, with the 7th Mounted in support, had advanced to the left of the 2nd, diverging north-west to the village of Burier. They captured that with 164 prisoners, then further north, towards Beit Durdis, encountered strong rearguard resistance. Cox swung towards the coast and bivouacked overnight south of Esdud — the biblical Ashdod, one of the five cities of the Philistines. Both the 52nd and 75th Infantry Divisions were advancing almost parallel to the mounted troops at the same time. A little later, the 75th entered Deir Sineid, completing that phase of the

Rest camp at Hamame, Palestine. COURTESY 2ND/14TH L.H. REGIMENT [QMI] MUSEUM ENOGGERRA

infantry's task. They had done so in good time, admittedly against little opposition, but the 52nd's brisk march up the coast from Gaza was particularly fine. The next morning, Cox occupied Esdud.

For practical purposes, the junction of the mounted troops and infantry at this point represented cutting through the enemy's retreat from right to left flanks, though by no means cleanly: the Turkish front was not square, looping away to the south-east from the coast. Nevertheless, it could be said that those Turks below the line were vanquished, while those above it lived to fight again.

Chaytor recognised that the 2nd Light Horse Brigade was close to collapse and he must save not only the horses. At dusk on the 10th, the 75th Division took over Ryrie's line and the 2nd Brigade moved to the coast, at Hamame. There was good spring water, the weather was kind and for three days the horses drank, rolled in the sand and rested. The men had their first bath and their only sleep beyond broken snatches in over a fortnight. The sky was blue, the sea peaceful and the air balmy, with no speck of dust. They did summon the energy to bury some dead Turks on the sand dunes and the war could still be heard, faintly. But they could shut their ears to it.

TO RELIEVE THE CONGESTION AT THE WELLS, THE AUSTRALIAN MOUNTED DIVISION had been sent back to the Jemmameh and Nejile areas to water on the 9th. They were joined there by Major General Barrow's Yeomanry Division fresh from Beersheba–Khuweilfe. That evening, the two divisions resumed the advance: Hodgson's Australian Mounted moved north-east towards El Faluje, ten miles distant and approximately in the centre of the maritime plain, and Barrow's Yeomanry, designated corps reserve, marched on Hodgson's left rear.

The night was dark, the ground was rough, but the advance guard of Wilson's 3rd Light Horse Brigade moved surely by the stars and at 6 am entered a village on the Jerusalem–Beersheba railway three miles east of El Faluje. The brigade spent nearly all that day watering horses, again with the usual difficulties. Some wells were 300 feet deep and the enemy had destroyed the pumps. They also constantly shelled the position.

Hodgson determined to strike at Summeil, a few miles north of El Faluje. The 4th and 3rd Brigades were to attack with the 5th Mounted

Brigade between them, on a broad front. However, the attack did not develop. The 9th Light Horse Regiment advanced to within 1000 yards of the enemy, but could not make touch with the 4th Brigade, which had been committed to a long dismounted advance against heavy fire from higher ground. The attack was abandoned and Grant's 4th Brigade withdrew to a line of outposts for the night.

The Australian Mounted did occupy Summeil at dawn on the 11th, but the prospects of going on immediately were not good. The rough ground was nullifying the advantage of mounted work and Turkish opposition was still building.

Chauvel had hoped for a rapid advance similar to the ANZAC Division's, but recognising that the opposition was stiffer and the going much less favourable, thought he could better the situation and perhaps kill two birds with one stone by ordering Barrow's Yeomanry Division to move with all speed to the coast and take over the ANZAC Division's sector. Barrow's Yeomanry were impatient for action, having seen none of it in the preceding fortnight; and as corps reserve the Yeomanry should be more gainfully employed on that front than supporting the struggling, nearly stalled Australian Mounted in its sector. It mattered little which flank advanced, as long as one did.

Alas for the corps commander's good intentions. When the order came, it was dark and late for assembling the scattered brigades, for forming 7500 men into columns for the march together with their artillery, supply train and ammunition limbers, and for navigating the cavalcade from one flank to the other over rough, unfamiliar country. Such moves required preparation, patience and time. That there was not enough time was no-one's fault, but in the end the move was ineffective, its original prospects largely overtaken.

Then without the Yeomanry Division, Hodgson felt obliged to cancel orders for a strong fighting advance in the morning. Chauvel admitted his miscalculation and ordered Hodgson to watch the enemy's south-eastern flank, but not to advance unless the Turks withdrew. He should demonstrate with strong mounted patrols, but the rest of his division should prepare to repel any counterattack dismounted.

The water problem bedevilled the Australian Mounted most of all. So deep were the wells and so limited the supply that it took seventeen hours to water a single regiment. The horses fell away rapidly in strength and condition.

Operations developed north of Summeil, around the villages of Burkusie and Balin, recently seized by the 5th Mounted and the 3rd Light Horse Brigades, respectively. Six thousand Turks, a number indicative of a major offensive, were reported to be moving south towards the villages and enemy cavalry were seen west of Balin. An attack on the Yeomanry Brigade seemed imminent, but Hodgson could send only the 8th Light Horse Regiment to their assistance. The attack came, but at the same time the Turks attacked Burkusie, held by just a squadron of the 9th Light Horse. Two squadrons of the 8th therefore rushed to reinforce them, leaving only one squadron to assist the Yeomanry.

General Allenby decorating a Light Horseman. General Chauvel is second from left. 2ND/14TH L.H.REGT [QMI] MUSEUM ENOGGERA

Under attack, the line holding Burkusie fell back to better ground, then the three squadrons held it until 3.30 pm, when the 10th Regiment, having watered, arrived at the gallop. At Balin, a fierce fight developed and at 3 pm the Yeomanry had to withdraw, whereupon 4000 of the Turks marched south on either side of the railway line, and when abreast of Burkusie swung left in large numbers against its defenders — whose left flank was exposed by the withdrawal of the Yeomanry. The Australians fired effectively with Hotchkiss and machine-guns, but were overwhelmed by numbers and had to leave the ridge. At the same time, the enemy force thrust for the 4th Light Horse Brigade's position further west. They reached to within 200 yards of the 11th Regiment, who held them until reinforced by the brigade's machine-gun squadron, when the attack was broken.

The 5th Mounted had re-formed two miles south-west of Balin and, reinforced by elements of Wilson's 3rd Brigade and Royal Horse Artillery batteries, stopped the Turks finally. At 5 pm, the 75th Infantry Division became available to defend Hodgson's left, if necessary.

The enemy remained on the ground he had taken overnight, but in the morning, after shelling by the Notts Battery and observing preparatory movements of the mounted brigades against him, gave up and retraced his steps north. Fortune had favoured him, and opting for discretion in the end must have been indicative of weakening resolve. What, after all, was the use? The 4th Australian and the 5th Mounted Brigades were to pursue him, but their horses were too distressed for action and the move was cancelled.

The 3rd Light Horse Brigade, badly run down, was detached for a spell on the coast. The men had not had a wash for seventeen days and, having attended to that, slept, augmented their diet with the local brown bread, and swam. Their horses had been worked for 48 hours straight, without water.

FIFTEEN

Clearing the plain

Esdud, where Cox's 1st Brigade was encamped, was twenty miles northwards from Gaza, on the coast. The British forces could claim to have cleared the western or coastal part of the plain, but not its central, south-eastern part, where the Turks hung on in varying strength.

But now, 40 miles east of Esdud, lay Jerusalem, in the Judean Hills. The British thrust must veer towards it and scale the abrupt, rocky foothills of Judea on the other side of the narrowing plain.

However, first there was a detail to settle on the coast. The mouth of the Wady Sukereir, which lay three miles north of Esdud, had attractions: it seemed a good camping ground for mounted brigades, the beach was suitable for landing seaborne supplies and there was an expanse of fresh water ten feet deep, thirty yards wide and of greater length, a stone's throw inland. The Light Horsemen had not looked on so sweet a prospect since crossing the Suez Canal.

The 1st Brigade advanced on it from Esdud on the morning of the 11th. They were not expecting a walkover, but were surprised by the resistance: they were shelled heavily and suffered casualties. The 2nd Regiment rode up the left bank of the wady, crossed at a point where it curved sharply towards the sea, and came under heavy fire from Turks in the sandhills. The Light Horsemen knew how to fight in dunes and none better than

Colonel Bourne's 2nd Regiment, who had held off the Turkish attack all the first night of Romani. They moved forward confidently, almost easily, making expert use of cover. In a close rifle fight, the 2nd pushed the Turks from their higher ground, and before nightfall had secured a bridgehead commanding the wady's mouth.

The 1st Brigade then swung east, towards Burka. A brigade of the 52nd Scottish Lowlanders was to take Burka, with the 1st and 2nd Light Horse Regiments cooperating on their left. The infantry had the worst of all possible tasks — a frontal assault against entrenchments over upward-sloping, naked ground. The Light Horsemen were to support them with machine-gun fire, but had no other role.

The Lowlanders started forward steadily, then charged the first trench with the bayonet, crossed a hollow and charged up a long slope to the second. Their momentum, born of belief in themselves, was irresistible and they took the position with one relentless sweep. The performance invites comparison with Romani again, scene of a raw 52nd Division's initial failure, and shows a transformation due to their innate good qualities, and hard experience since.

The Turks counterattacked in the night and pushed the Scots from the right of their line, but were quickly driven off again. The counterattack might have indicated that the local enemy knew how serious the loss of Burka was, because it marked the deciding point from which the British could advance to Katra and beyond, and break the enemy's lines of communication, particularly rail, between Ramleh and Jerusalem.

The British were well placed now. Allenby had on his front line two infantry divisions at full strength and with the exception of the 3rd Light Horse and 7th Mounted Brigades, temporarily resting, all his mounted troops including the crack New Zealand Brigade and the Camels. Water supplies were expected to improve in the north. The enemy had launched 6000 of his best troops against the Australian Mounted Division at Summeil, with only further exhaustion and loss to himself.

The mounted divisions may have been exhausted, but they had the conditions and resources necessary for a quick recovery, whereas the fighting quality of the enemy continued to fall away. They had marched and fought beyond ordinary endurance and were ill-fed, ill-clothed and ravaged by malaria and dysentery. Superior British air forces now attacked them at will, with further severe damage to their materiel and morale.

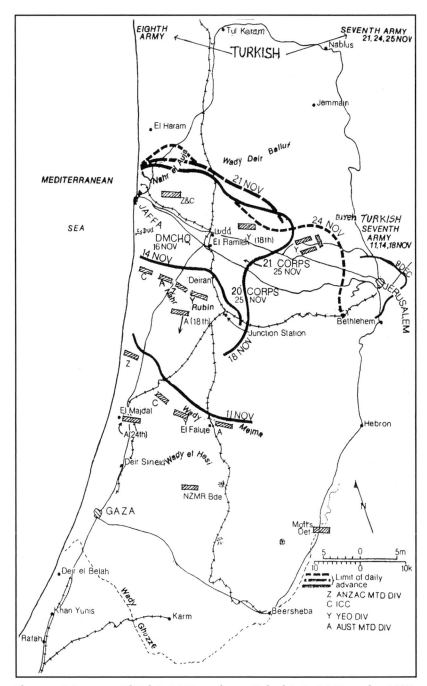

The pursuit in stages: El Faluje 11 November to Nahrel Auja, 21 November 1917.

On the next day, 12 November, while another brigade of the 52nd marched north, General Bulfin, the infantry corps commander, wheeled his 75th Division north-east, towards the most important railway centre of Junction Station, so-called because here, midway across the plain, the rail lines from Jaffa on the coast, Beersheba and Jerusalem all met. Allenby had planned for Chauvel's horsemen to take the station on 9 November, but was thwarted by lack of water. An infantry division needed only a third of a mounted division's water and the operation had to proceed on foot instead of at the trot. But a severe penalty would be paid for the lost three days, in fighting for Jerusalem.

The Yeomanry Division and a battalion of the Camels occupied the village of Yebna and Chaytor's New Zealand and 1st Light Horse Brigades moved inland towards Katra and El Mughar. Katra was a long mound surrounded by small fields and thickets of prickly pear cactus, familiar to the Turks from Gaza and ideal to defend. Near its mud-hut native village was a Jewish settlement of trim white houses with red-tiled roofs and well-kept orchards — for the troops, the first nostalgic reminder of their own home surroundings since leaving Cairo.

With the 75th Division advancing towards Junction Station, the 52nd attacked Katra and Mughar. The Turks defended stubbornly from the cactus until another inspired bayonet charge by the Lowlanders dislodged them from Katra, and they then slowly yielded its surrounding fields and gardens. Their losses here were terrible: 400 killed by machine-gun fire in a single field. The infantry then endeavoured to take Mughar village a mile north, over broken, difficult ground and a wady bed. The Turks, however, held them off with a nest of machine-guns in a plantation surrounded by cactus, just south of the settlement.

The Yeomanry Division was nearby and the 52nd asked for their help. General Barrow gave the task to the 6th Mounted Brigade, made up of the Bucks Hussars, the Berks and the Dorset Regiments, under Brigadier General C.A.C. Godwin, who was to become Chauvel's Chief-of-Staff on the last grand ride of the war to Damascus and Aleppo.

Godwin opted to gallop the Turks. The Dorsets were to take a hill a few hundred yards behind Mughar and the Bucks Hussars would aim for a ridge running between this hill and the settlement. The Berks Regiment was reserve. The other two regiments emerged from the wady bed with 3000 yards to go over level plain, then an upward slope to their objectives. They trotted forward under covering RHA (Royal Horse Artillery) battery and machine-gun fire, then at 1000 yards gave their eager horses rein. They galloped into streams of fire, shouting and brandishing flashing swords, but many fell. They gained the crest of a slope and the Turks immediately ahead surrendered. But on both flanks, enemy rifles and machine-guns poured in heavy fire and kept the issue in doubt. Captured enemy machine-guns were turned on the still free machine-gunners, two reserve squadrons of the Berks were brought up, and they went in dismounted, clearing the village.

The Dorsets on the left, attempting to dismount, lost many horses — while the Bucks Hussars, who stayed mounted and charged right home, lost few — but the enemy was beaten. The Yeomanry lost seventeen men and a grievous 265 horses, for the capture of 1100 Turks, two field guns and eighteen machine-guns.

A dashing mounted assault against modern fire power had won the day again, counter to doctrine, but nothing succeeds like success. The consideration of its merits as a shock tactic, however, had to be tempered by the weakened state of the enemy and the heavy losses suffered by one of the charging regiments.

The capture of Katra and Mughar cleared the way for the assault on Junction Station by the 75th and 52nd Divisions, and after a little resistance two armoured cars led the 52nd Division in on 14 November. This had assumed a degree of inevitability, but it was the heaviest of blows for the Turks. Their rail links in all directions were cut and, among other things, this prevented movement between their 7th Army at Jerusalem and the 8th Army north of Jaffa on the coast.

All eyes looked to Jerusalem — literally. The men could see those frowning hills in the east and fancied that every grey-stoned settlement they made out must be the Holy City. It lured them as pilgrims, if of somewhat varied reverence.

The infantry continued to move east, probing the passes that led up towards Jerusalem, while the mounted troops concentrated on the coast again and resumed their advance up the maritime plain. History was repeating itself: from the earliest wars — earlier here than anywhere — it was recorded that chariots and horsemen had fought on the plain and foot soldiers had fought in the hills.

The New Zealanders, along with Barrow's Yeomanry, had been held up at Beersheba and not until 14 November were they again able to enhance

ANZAC operations with their particular dauntless style. The ANZAC Mounted Division (less Ryrie's brigade) rode north that morning, Cox's 1st Brigade aiming for Ramleh and Meldrum's NZ Brigade aiming for the port of Jaffa, ten miles on.

The 1st Brigade was held up by a stubborn Turkish rearguard in the attractive Jewish village of Deiran, where there was abundant water with good pumps. The orchard country around Deiran consisted of olive and orange groves, almonds, vineyards and other fruit. It extended eight miles further on, through two more Jewish villages called Wady Hanein and Richon le Zion, and made up a fair and blessed prospect to those starved of anything like it for so long. But man was vile. While the Australians' horses were drinking, the Turks sniped at them and the brigade's RHA batteries were unable to silence the enemy.

While Cox's brigade was held up, they reported enemy troops crossing their front towards the New Zealanders, who were closing on Wady Hanein. Meldrum's brigade encountered machine-gun and rifle fire in their centre from these troops and the Wellington Regiment dashed forward and met them with the bayonet. They broke through the enemy line, killing twenty Turks and capturing two machine-guns. Then the Aucklands on the left encountered a strong body of infantry, with artillery fire from a battery in the direction of Richon. The Turkish fire steadily increased, and at 2.45 pm a force of 1500 troops advanced on the Auckland Regiment.

Prone, without cover, they shot well, but were too few and scattered. Lieutenant Colonel J.N. McCarroll signalled, asking for reinforcements, but only one squadron of the Wellingtons could reach them. The duel grew hotter and the Turks gained on them, then at 4 pm dashed forward with the bayonet and hand grenades. McCarroll had all his men, including batmen and cooks, in the firing line. The Turks got to within 50 yards when the Aucklands stood up and met them head-on with the bayonet. Being outnumbered was not exceptional to the ANZACs, but the way the young New Zealand farmers fought as the two lines clashed was, even for them. The Turks broke and fled, leaving 162 dead and many wounded, for 21 killed and 87 wounded New Zealanders.

This was the last effort the enemy made to save his Jaffa–Ramleh–Jerusalem communications. The next morning, the ANZACs rode on to Ramleh of the Tower of Forty Martyrs and Greek churches. A squadron of the 2nd found it deserted of troops and received an uninhibited welcome from both Christian and Arab citizens — the former as their deliverers, the latter, like sensible folk, accommodating their allegiance to the winning side. The 2nd Regiment rode on to Ludd, three miles north, rejoicing in the smiling countryside and its inviting Jewish enclaves, but watchful. Ludd was entered to another demonstration of welcome, this time conducted by an English-speaking Cook's Tours guide who assembled the notables of the village and called for three cheers for the British. They were given mightily.

However, Colonel C.H. Granville of the 2nd had other matters to attend to and took the regiment quickly clear of the revels: Lieutenant W.H. James, in charge of the forward screen, had reported that the Turks were streaming along the road further north. 'Get after them,' said the colonel.

James deployed two troops of twenty men each on either side of the road and got after them at the gallop. The Turks, straggling for miles along the road towards the German settlement of Wilhelmia, were infantry, well enough armed and with machine-guns, but barely took any notice as the galloping horsemen passed them. The two troops had lost formation, but were strung out according to the speed of their horses. Enemy artillery on the flank shelled both Australians and Turks, but after a three-mile gallop James reached the head of the column and the Light Horsemen pulled up. Then the Turks did respond with machine-guns and shrapnel at close range. However, the Australians were not to be deterred and took 297 prisoners, driving them back like so many cattle on the long paddock. One Australian troop leader was killed and six men were wounded.

While Cox was taking Ramleh and Ludd, the New Zealanders on the coast passed through the Jewish village of Richon le Zion, the main wine-growing centre of the district, and advanced towards Jaffa without serious opposition. The enemy had withdrawn across the Nahr Auja, a respectable-looking permanent stream, 30 feet wide, that reaches the Mediterranean a few miles north of Jaffa. On high ground, they dug in, apparently preparing to stand.

Allenby did not intend to occupy Jaffa at that stage and Brigadier General W. Meldrum was ordered to hold a line to the south of the city. However, on reconnaissance the next day, the Wellingtons seemed to find themselves drawn into an effusive welcome from Christian Syrians and other nationalities of the city, and as it was only a short walk to the water's edge they had a look down through the jumble of town buildings to the ancient, fascinating port. Jaffa was therefore occupied, but Chauvel hesitated for some hours before informing the Commander-in-Chief. It is not recorded that he objected, which must have been a deliverance. Old Jaffa is now surrounded by modern, bustling, sophisticated Tel Aviv.

Three more villages, including the German Wilhelmia a few miles inland, were occupied, and by 17 November the ANZACs held a front line 40 miles north of Gaza, running south-east from the coast to midway across the maritime plain.

As for the eastern front, after the British victories at Katra and Mughar, the Turks' 7th Army regrouped about Latron, in the Judean foothills. With the capture of all the main railway lines at Junction Station, the army now had to be supplied from the Jerusalem side, which imposed a great strain on the Turks and would only increase with the imminent wet weather. But they held a position of great natural advantages and had no need to dissipate their strength in movement.

The enemy's 8th Army had left a gap between the two armies when it retreated on the plains, a single but fatal flaw in the defence of Jerusalem. The Turks covered this by holding high ground on the hills of Shephelah, just to his south-west — as had the ancient hosts against the Crusaders and, further back, hosts beyond Biblical times. Tel Jazar, one of the defensive hills, contains the ruins of many successive civilisations.

From this height, the Turks stopped the advance of the 75th Infantry Division and, as at Mughar, the Yeomanry was brought into the fray. It happened that the task fell to Brigadier General Godwin's 6th Mounted Brigade again, who charged with the same indomitable spirit and overwhelming success. This was the third successive, and successful, charge by the Yeomanry since Beersheba. The Turks, always susceptible to shock tactics, shot wildly and deserted their posts. Over 400 enemy dead lay on the battlefield and 360 prisoners were taken, for 37 Yeomanry casualties. Tel Jazar had a good water supply, and with its capture this difficulty was practically at an end for Allenby.

The Australian Mounted Division, refreshed after its ordeal in the Summeil fighting and in unusual strength (it included the 2nd, 3rd and 4th Light Horse Brigades, the 5th and 7th Mounted Brigades and two armoured cars), was under the orders of Bulfin's 21 Corps at this stage and during 15 and 16 November made strong reconnaissances towards Amwas (Emmaus of the New Testament) immediately north-east of Latron. The country was rough for horses, however, and with the Turks doing what they did best, defending strong redoubts, the Australian Mounted did not penetrate far, although the village of El Kubab was taken. The 7th Regiment of Ryrie's 2nd Brigade took casualties from heavy shell fire. The brigade rejoined the ANZAC Division on the 17th.

The British had now outrun their communications, but Allenby considered there was still every prospect of taking Jerusalem by Christmas, before winter rain and mud immobilised him.

HISTORIANS COMPLAIN THAT THE LIGHT HORSEMEN LEFT MEAGRE PERSONAL RECORDS of their campaigning, including letters home. The reason is said to be that they were always going somewhere on horseback. The last thought of a trooper riding all night to a battle, then riding back, or riding on somewhere else, would have been to take writing materials for the edification of the folks at home. When he stopped, he slept.

There is a long gap in my father's letters, except for a brief note in September 1917 warning his family not to expect any letters for some time. He did manage to send a cable as reassurance of his continued unscathed existence, but the next letter was not written until December, when his regiment had at last stopped moving, after the first stage of the pursuit.

He covers the advance from Beersheba to Jaffa in five scrawled pages:

A whole lot has happened since my last letter, so much that I don't know how to begin, I made no notes at the time and am afraid I cannot give you a detailed account of operations.

It has been a long and hard business, though very interesting, as we got the Turks on the run and chased them over country strewn with their dead and wounded and abandoned guns and ammunition. The Regiment did well, getting a big haul of prisoners etc. General Allenby completely outfought the Turks in the way he handled his mounted troops.

First of all, he sent us to Beersheba, after that we went on the extreme right flank into the hills near Hebron, country that the Turks thought too rough for mounted troops to operate in. We fought there for about a week, then one night quickly pulled out and 2 nights later, put in an appearance at Tel el Sheria, in the centre of the line.

Had some rough-house there, and the next thing, we were on the extreme left, near Gaza. The Turks never knew where to expect us, in fact a captured German officer said as he patted one of our horses, 'You can thank these and General Allenby for your big win'.

Of the 7th Regiment's charge for the Hebron Road, he says:

At Beersheba, while charging a position at the gallop, we ran fair into the fire of a battery of guns and believe me, they poured the shells into us, but we got through, I think the gunners must have got excited at the sight of such a target so close. It was a great gallop, about 5 miles and exciting. No matter how tired the horses are, they always come up to the mark when there is a gallop to do, they like it and get very excited too.

I have come through as usual with a whole skin, though it was close a number of times. Was holding two horses when a shell burst right at the shoulder of one, sent him straight up in the air over my head, killed him of course, along with 3 others and a man, wounded two more chaps and left me without a scratch. The same sort of thing has happened to me many times, on Gallipoli and since.

The country here is beautiful, could not wish to see anything better. Lots of villages (Jewish) and hundreds of fine orange orchards full of fruit. We have been able to buy a bit of tucker, but the prices are too high.

He complains at length about prices, just like an aggrieved housewife. One box of matches sixpence, one beer bottle of honey six shillings, three bottles of 'home-made' wine one pound, and so on.

'Got a letter from a Miss Edith Brett of Sans Souci, she had bought a copy of our verses and wrote me such a nice letter. I am going to marry her.' Then one thought leading to another, 'I wish someone would put an end to this darned war, I want to go home ... I suppose one day we will be back. The third Christmas since we left will soon be here.'

It is a somewhat flat letter, considering the events it covers. I expect he was still run down and exhausted, his nerves strained, and while making allowance for hungry troops on hard tack without much money his irritation over the price of groceries was a symptom.

Riding lesson

We had a pretty chestnut mare with a silver mane and tail on our farmlet in the Hunter Valley. Aged eight, I used to bounce about on Silver, practising to be a Light Horseman. My father said she was a very rough ride, but I had no standard of comparison. The whole of his instructions to me were: 'Cross the reins in your left hand, the right hand's for your rifle or stockwhip. Not for hanging on with. Keep your heels down and your bottom down. The only time you let daylight in between you and the horse is when you're rising to the trot.'

He didn't seem to take much notice of my efforts, except when I had the obligatory falls. 'You have to have five before you can ride,' he would say, hoisting me up again.

He looked so natural on a horse that they were like a centaur together. I watched him narrowly for chinks of daylight and only ever saw one once, when he was coming up from the front gate on Silver at a hand gallop. I was quite shocked: he was in that tricky space where idols can overbalance.

'Dad!' I yelled. 'Daylight! You're letting daylight under you!'

Instantly, the offending butt was clamped down. When I grew up, I found that I could keep the daylight out well enough: I had inherited his long legs and small butt and could lock onto a saddle in the same way. Our family had 'good seats'.

On our place, there was an old disused windmill and a track leading from it over a bit of flat ground, then going up quite a steep rise on a slant, ending at a shed near the house. In the manner of horses, Silver loved to stretch out on that bit of track, pulling for her head. I mentioned this to Dad one day.

He was interested. 'What — fast?'

'Yes.'

'Galloping?'

'Yes, I think so.' I was not at all sure.

'Well, let's have a look.'

Oh, crumbs. I rode Silver down to the windmill and turned her. He stood a little way up the rise. I had never let Silver out fully, I had always put the brakes on.

She pounded up the track with me clinging on bareback. She charged the slope going faster than I had ever been. It was like flying and just as insecure, but I didn't dare grab her mane …

My hat flew off. Thank God!

I pulled up, turned round, got off and retrieved it.

Dad came up. 'I would have picked up your hat,' he said shortly. He was plainly annoyed and disappointed.

I thought later that I should have given him a hard glare, trotted back to the windmill and charged straight at him flat out. Alas, we always think of what we should have done too late. Sixty-odd years too late. All I could think of at the time was I'd never make a Light Horseman.

Now, after three more generations and writing this, I have a better understanding of what it was to be a soldier in that war, and also, to be a small boy. But the edges of our interaction have blurred and I am a lot less certain of the meaning of how we reacted on that occasion. It has become complicated.

SIXTEEN

To Jerusalem

In late 1917, the seasonal change in Palestine was abrupt as always and went from hot and dry to cold and wet on 19 November, with heavy rain, a gale and a huge drop in temperature. Troops without winter clothing and sufficient blankets — that is, most of the infantry, Yeomanry and Light Horse — suffered bitter misery until the supply trains following the front line caught up with them.

Both Light Horse divisions were on operations at the time: the Australian Mounted with the 75th, 52nd and 60th Infantry Divisions struggling up the Judean Hills towards Jerusalem and the ANZACs holding the coastal sector just north of Jaffa. As at Gaza–Beersheba, one of their objectives was to deceive the Turks as to where the main blow was falling.

Judea was a desolation of rocks and screes and bare stone hills. 'Long before its conquest by the blighting Turk, [it] had lost its bloom,' notes Gullett, 'and almost every trace of its rural glory has departed. The heavy rains of centuries had destroyed the little hillside garden terraces; tormented wadys, long uncontrolled, have swept the soil out of the narrow valleys. Judea, as it was first seen at close quarters by Allenby's army, was a rough, stony skeleton of a country, "the carcase of a land", a region where, even in the world-wide land-hunger of the twentieth century, no peasantry in crowded Europe would deem worthy of settlement.'

The 7th Turkish Army stood watchfully on its commanding heights. As the Holy City had always done, it drew invaders like a holy grail, the British perhaps more from moral and material motives than religious ones, though some spoke whimsically of avenging the previous British assault on it by King Richard in the winter of 1192, which had failed dismally. However, the British government of 1917 was most worried about damaging the holy place and being held to account for 'razing' or 'destroying' it, so told Allenby it must be taken, but without fighting in it. Fight *for*, but not *on*. Baffled or not, the Commander-in-Chief pressed on.

Latron, a settlement twelve miles west of Jerusalem, was at the centre of the mounted troops' first action. There was intelligence to suggest the Turks were evacuating Jerusalem and Chauvel ordered Barrow's Yeomanry Division to Bireh quickly, on the Jerusalem–Nablus road, to cut off their retreat. At the same time, Wilson's 3rd Light Horse Brigade was to outflank Latron from the north and north-east, while Grant's 4th Brigade was to assault it directly.

The lesson was learned again that horsemen fought on the Philistine Plain and foot soldiers fought in the Judean Hills. Wilson's 8th and 9th Regiments could not even ride on their approach, having frequently to lead their horses over steep and chaotic ground. They did eventually succeed in outflanking the Turks, but they were not retreating north and the endeavour was to little avail. The Yeomanry, too, were making little headway towards Bireh; and except for the camel-borne Hong Kong and Singapore Mountain Battery of the Sikhs, no mounted artillery could scale that country.

The same evening, the Light Horse brigades were pulled back. The Yeomanry continued on foot, however, using their horses to bring up supplies.

The Light Horse did not play an active part in the capture of Jerusalem, but Chauvel, appreciating its significance, arranged for the West Australian 10th Regiment to be attached to the 5th Mounted Brigade. That brigade was soon withdrawn, but the 10th remained, the only Australian troops in the direct attack. The home of Christendom, invested with world-wide and profound symbolism, was to be recaptured by Christians and it was fitting that Australia should be represented in such history in the making.

The infantry slogged uphill and on the 19th the weather turned on them. They wore twill shorts and tunics offering no protection against cold and rain. The one road from the plain became almost impassable, with hundreds of teamsters and motor lorries carrying the troops' supplies floundering in the mud. But there was no thought of failure from the high command down to the ranks: rather, the bad weather was a spur to getting the business over and the men went at it with new determination, gaining height after height with machine-gun, rifle and bayonet.

After three days, the 75th, made up of English and Indian troops, had gained much, but suffered two-thirds of its numbers in casualties and were reinforced by the Scottish 52nd. But Turkish resistance had stiffened and the two divisions were held up. There was a break in the weather and Allenby was able to bring up the 60th and 74th Divisions. The Turks still held, but their condition was becoming desperate. The balance was shifting slowly, but Jerusalem lived up to its reputation for grim and stubborn defence.

By this time on the coast, the ANZACs had established themselves in a line of strong posts three miles north of Jaffa on the south bank of the Nahr Auja, opposite the Turkish 8th Army, and the 54th (East Anglia) Infantry Division and Camel Brigade had marched up from the south to join them. Mounted patrols probed at all crossings of the Auja and ranged eastwards, but everywhere encountered sharp fire. The Turk meant to hold this ground.

Allenby decided to demonstrate in force on the coast, to prevent withdrawal of the 8th Army troops from the Plain of Sharon, as the country north of Jaffa was called, to reinforce the 7th Army at Jerusalem. Major General Chaytor gave the job of crossing the river and establishing a bridgehead on the north bank to the New Zealand Brigade. After vigorous shelling, the Canterbury Mounted Rifles crossed the Auja at its mouth, scattering a small party of Turks. The Wellingtons followed, capturing a bridge, and a battalion of infantry crossed by a mill at Jerisheh. At all points, the enemy was taken by surprise.

During the night, four companies of infantry and a squadron of Aucklands guarded engineers building a bridge to improve the Hadrah crossing. Before dawn, the Turks attacked the Aucklands in strength and forced them back on the infantry. The Canterburys came to their support, but the enemy was 1000 strong and the small combined force was heavily shelled. The infantry, followed by the Aucklands, had to withdraw from Hadrah to the south bank. Allenby's ruse was succeeding better than he might have wished.

The British and New Zealanders still held the posts at Sheikh Muannis and Jerisheh, but next morning the Turks attacked strongly again and won back all the north bank. The infantry withdrew across the Jerisheh bridge, followed by the New Zealanders who had covered their withdrawal. Some of them had to commandeer small boats and some had to swim, though these seasoned troops took it lightly, as something of an escapade.

Two days later, the Turks bombarded Bald Hill, held by a Camel battalion. The large Jewish settlement and repository of horse feed at Mulebbis, five miles east, having been patrolled by Ryrie's 2nd Brigade in the morning, was occupied by the enemy early in the afternoon. Ryrie's headquarters was shelled, killing a major of the Ayrshire Battery of Royal Horse Artillery. The Light Horsemen saw Turks creeping through an orchard towards the Camels, 1000 yards away: a troop of the 5th Light Horse caught these on the flank with Hotchkiss fire, but the movement was not checked and, under cover of their barrage, Turkish infantry closed with the Camels on Bald Hill, gained a foothold and by an astute enfilading movement secured the hill and two other Camel posts. This in turn made a post occupied by the 2nd Light Horse Brigade, called the 'Ypres Salient' after its Belgian namesake, untenable and all posts in this sector were then in enemy hands.

The Camels were ordered to retake Bald Hill after dark and although they regained their original posts with bayonet charges, General Smith assessed that Bald Hill would always be no-man's land because of its vulnerability to both sides and did not attack it — a judgment that was endorsed by Chaytor and Chauvel and later proved correct, to the satisfaction of the Camel Brigade, who had smarted under criticism for losing it.

With their Bald Hill attack, the Turks also assaulted the 54th Division at the German settlement of Wilhelmia. They suffered a reversal with heavy losses, but then crossed the Auja and dug in near the Hadrah bridge. The infantry raided this incursion at night and killed 50, but could not reclaim their original ground. The Turkish shelling continued throughout the night, but the ANZAC trenches were well dug and suffered little.

News of the fierce but piecemeal and apparently directionless Turkish offensive was well received by Allenby, who saw his left feint succeed again, pinning the 8th Army down on the coast while he prepared to launch the decisive stroke against the 7th Army in the hills. All he wanted of the ANZACs and 54th Infantry was to hold their ground.

His immediate need in Judea, however, was for the Australian Mounted Division (3rd and 4th Light Horse and 7th Mounted Brigades) to relieve Barrow's Yeomanry Division, which had been fighting hard on foot for a week, trying to secure the country northwards, towards Nablus. The three fresh brigades went into the line on the left of the 52nd (Lowland) Division, with the local objective of taking a dominating hill on which stood the village of El Burj. Chetwode's 20 Corps had relieved Bulfin's 21 Corps and the Australians came under their old leader and mentor again. They were to be engaged solely as infantry and sent their horses back to the plain.

After a week's spell they were refreshed, but much reduced in numbers from casualties and sickness and, except for a few lucky 'scroungers', still in light summer dress, like the infantry. Heavy rain fell on most days and the mountain cold was intense. Frostbite was a new hazard. There was no remedy, or safeguard against it. Trenches could not be dug in the rocky ground and defensive positions consisted of 'sangars', walls of loose rock which served as shelter from the wind as well as bullets. They had to be both manned and lived in. Most men had no blankets, not all had greatcoats and they slept in their saturated clothes behind the sangar, with a bivvy sheet thrown over the top of the wall and down over the head and shoulders.

It grew colder. A trooper of the 12th Regiment recalled to Ian Jones: 'Around 9 pm my feet would start to throb and about 11 pm the pain was almost unbearable and towards 2 am there was no feeling at all in the feet, they were hard and cold as stone, the pain next morning in getting some feeling back was just agony.'

But one of the battalions they relieved, the Royal Scots Fusiliers, evoked the Arab proverb of complaining about lack of shoes 'until I met a man who had no feet'. The Jocks were without tunics, in short khaki pants, and had one blanket between four men, no tobacco and very short rations. 'Our boys,' wrote a Light Horse officer, 'supplied them with matches and cigarettes and the "Dinkums", as they always called us, were very popular.'

On their first night of 29 November, the 3rd and 4th Brigade manned the line much under strength. The squadrons were so weak — two of the 8th Regiment numbered only 50 men each and consequently the gap between them was 200 yards — that General Hodgson committed the 4th

Brigade from reserve as well. This necessitated moving Wilson's 3rd Brigade half a mile left, into strange country. The Light Horsemen crouched behind their sangars and stared into a black void.

Soon after midnight, Major Walker of the 8th reported a movement close at hand, but could see nothing. Then the post was rushed by Turks in great strength. The men held their ground with grenades, rifles and bayonets but it was impossible to prevent the post from being enveloped around both flanks and Walker ordered a withdrawal. The first resistance had stopped the enemy for the moment, who were also unsighted in the dark, and the Australians fell back on Major A. Crawford's post, on higher ground and to the left rear, in good order. The two squadrons waited for the next assault and Crawford signalled brigade for assistance and artillery fire.

There was another dead-silent wait with strung nerves, staring into the darkness, then loud shouts of 'ALLAH' and 500 Turks charged up at Crawford's sangar. The troopers held fire until twenty yards range, then cut swathes through them with Hotchkiss and rifle fire, and grenades. The Turks threw bombs and came on bravely, evidently trying to get to grips in hand-to-hand fighting, with their advantage of greatly superior numbers. The Australians still held them when 50 Yeomanry of the Gloucester Regiment (attached to the 3rd Brigade in place of the 10th Light Horse) arrived, followed by some Royal Scots Fusiliers. The Turks retreated, but with Australian regiments on both flanks to cut them off, few survived their inspired assault. There were minimal British losses. These Turks were the best physical specimens the Australians had seen so far and it was learned afterwards that they were 'storm troops' from Galicia, specially trained by German officers.

It was a rough introduction to the fighting for Jerusalem and, had the Turks succeeded, the thrust towards Nablus would have been weakened and the left flank of the main advance on Jerusalem exposed. Such short, sharp little actions were not repeated, but constant sniping and shell fire continued. Each day brought good news of the advance on Jerusalem, however, and they had but to endure.

By the end of November, wheeled transport could no longer negotiate the broken-up road to the plain and the services of 2000 donkeys and thousands of camels were hastily organised. The sure-footed little donkeys carried loads as big as themselves and the lumbering camels scaled the steepest of tracks, their long thin legs slithering on mud and ice until gaining a purchase with their flat pads and, despite many falls, toiled up each night to the firing line. The lugubrious-looking beasts earned a new respect from the Light Horsemen, to whom they had seemed dull and vicious creatures compared with horses; and the despised 'Gyppos', who had habitually robbed them blind and deceived them, showed unsuspected courage and nobility as camel drivers. They were just barefoot boys clad only in cottons, but matched the troops in the line with their endurance.

There was a heart-rending scene on the track: a camel lay dead of exposure or exhaustion and his small Egyptian driver crouched dead at his side. The boy had seemed to have willed himself to die with his animal.

That winter, the Egyptian Labour Corps in their thousands worked on the Jaffa–Jerusalem road, rolling, carrying and setting stones, working against time to make it serviceable from end to end and able to carry supplies to Allenby's army in Jerusalem.

THE TURKISH OFFENSIVE ON THE COAST WENT ON WITH FIGHTING UP AND DOWN the Auja banks. Bald Hill was fought over again, neither side prevailing, as General Smith of the Camels had predicted.

The 2nd Brigade's front was on hill crests adjoining orchards, to which the enemy would creep to close quarters at night. On the night of 30 November, a detachment of the 7th Regiment under Major Nat Barton heard through some almond trees Turkish voices giving orders, then rifle fire opened on the post. Barton's party numbered only nineteen, with fifteen rifles and two Hotchkiss guns, but they were well placed and took severe toll of the Turks as they came uphill. Both Hotchkiss guns jammed, but the riflemen held on till daylight, when it was seen that the Turks had concentrated behind a cactus hedge. Light Horse posts on either side of the 7th's men then put down a barrage of Hotchkiss and rifle fire behind the enemy, while Barton engaged them again in the front. Thinking they were cut off, sandwiched between two hostile forces and facing destruction, the Turks raised a white flag and an officer walked down and took the surrender of 200 men.

Nat Barton did not bother to mention this trifle in his letters, though the official historian Henry Gullett devotes nearly a page to it. But Nat's mind in any case was soon to be completely occupied with other matters.

Trooper Brian Barton. BARTON FAMILY ARCHIVE

Nat Barton had two brothers: Brian, the oldest by five years, enlisted three weeks after Nat in 1914, in the 6th Light Horse Regiment. The third and youngest brother, Denis, also joined the 6th as soon as he came of age, in 1917. Nat and Brian sailed for Egypt in the same convoy though in different ships, and being in the same brigade were able to keep in contact. Nat's letters home usually contained news of Brian, and later, Denis.

Brian Templer Barton is not shown to full advantage in his photograph, sitting on a kitbag and doing something to what might be a Hotchkiss gun part. Standing straight, he was 6 feet 3 inches tall and in the words that come most readily to mind, 'every inch a soldier'. Nat's letters home relay the real affection Brian was held in by the 6th, whose members went out of their way to say so, and his photograph surely indicates an attractive and sunny disposition. Young brother Nat urged him from time to time to seek a commission and a mutual acquaintance in the Camel Corps once tried to arrange this at a time when the corps had vacancies through heavy casualties. But it did not happen: Brian evidently had the potential, but seems to have been one of those, not uncommon in the armed forces, who prefer for some reason to serve their time in the ranks.

The 6th Light Horse Regiment's War Diary records that on the night of 3 December 1917, C Squadron, under Captain D.C. Close, was ordered to attack Ypres Salient on Bald Hill. Gullett says: 'The salient was to be heavily bombarded for ten minutes, after which the barrage was to lift for ten minutes, while the Australians made their [dismounted] dash at the enemy, and to be put down again to cover their withdrawal'. The purpose of the attack was not to gain ground: it was a raid.

The War Diary said the party consisted of five officers and 100 men. They 'started from forward post at 1945, being held up at 1955 by our own barrage fire, which was dropping from 75 to 100 yards short of our objective'. Gullett continues: 'Unfortunately the lift after the first ten minutes was not complete, and many of the Australians, as they rushed forward from their advanced position in an orchard, were caught in the barrage'. Major Richardson, whose 7th Regiment was close by, observes the raid 'did not go well, owing chiefly to the faulty firing of one gun in the supporting battery, which dropped shrapnel right into the attacking squadron and held up its advance for two or three vital minutes'.

The casualties were 'Lieutenant Tooth killed, Lieutenant Dickson wounded, one other rank killed and 22 wounded in a few minutes, by their own guns'. The one other rank was Brian Barton.

The 6th's squadron did no less than what was expected of them: pressing home the attack into the enemy's trenches with the bayonet, killing twenty Turks and taking four prisoners. Then, bearing their own dead and wounded, the Australians returned to base within the ten allotted minutes for withdrawal.

The brief little clash exemplifies all that was best in the men. First, get the job done, then pick up the pieces. The nightmarish shock tactic: storm the enemy trenches in darkness, with the bayonet. Then against the clock, with a margin of minutes, collect and carry their own dead and wounded to safety before the barrage resumes. At any time, this would have required self-control, a cool head and every bit of their remaining strength, but in these shocking circumstances something approaching the superhuman would have been needed. What is left to them is grief, and by way of recognition, only the vicarious sharing of the wounded Lieutenant Dickson's Military Cross.

Nat was not able to investigate the location and burial of Brian's body until his regiment was relieved by the 4th Kings Own Scottish Borderers of the 52nd Division on 6 December, after that moving immediately to the Wady Hanein and, a week later, to sandhills near Esdud for a period of refitting and recuperation. Brian's remains had been buried and the 6th put up its own wooden cross at the site, which was later transferred to the burial plot at Nanima, the Barton family property at Wellington, NSW. But his remains were interred at Richon le Zion, and finally at the Ramleh Military Cemetery. Nat rode to Jaffa and through a Miss McConaghy, an English missionary living there, was able to get workmen and materials to put a concrete slab over Brian's original grave. He said after the war, 'I thought perhaps with such a solid business over his grave, they might leave him where he fell, but they removed him … to the cemetery at Ramleh, where he still lies'.

His grief was shared briefly with his mother by letter, before the regiment and the war moved on. He wrote: 'I went to early morning service this morning, it being Intercession Day and I doubt if I have ever felt more in need of help, however, we must all fight with the strength of ten now and may God be with us'. And, 'My poor mother! I feel for you with all the depth of my being, or perhaps with all the feelings which are not tarnished in me.'

On 9 December 1917, Jerusalem fell.

The successful attack did not come from the north and north-west — the Australian Mounted Division's sector — as originally envisaged, but from the south and south-west. By early December, Allenby had sufficient troops in position: the 10th (Irish) Division who relieved the 52nd Division, the lively 60th (Londoners), swinging along in summer uniforms with bare knees bandaged against the cold, and the 74th (Yeomanry), as well as a force known as (Major General) Mott's Detachment, made up of the 53rd (Welsh) Division and a regiment of cavalry, the Westminster Dragoons. Mott was advancing on Hebron from the south, but the town was so rich in religious historical associations that it was held sacred by all faiths — Christian, Jewish and Moslem — and fighting for it therefore had to be avoided. Mott felt his way cautiously towards it, waiting and hoping for the enemy to fall back.

To their astonishment, one of his patrols encountered two cars of the No. 7 Light Car Patrol, a British unit under a Lieutenant W.H.P. McKenzie, an adventurous New Zealander, coming south on the road from Hebron. In pursuit of a Syrian required by intelligence branch for interrogation, McKenzie had penetrated no-man's land ten miles north of Hebron at Solomon's Pools, and after many skirmishes with Turks was now retiring between the two armies without the Syrian, but with the information that Hebron, which he had just left, was deserted.

Mott marched forward at once, passed through Hebron, and on 6 December reached a position a few miles south of Bethlehem, where touch was made with the 10th Australian Light Horse Regiment under Lieutenant Colonel T.J. Todd. The West Australians had been employed on reconnaissance and road making and were as cold, wet and exhausted as everyone else, but still delighted with their representative role. Now they went forward with the infantry, forming a link between the 53rd and 60th Divisions.

On the eve of the final assault, the four British divisions were on their start lines from south round to west, ready to attack. Heavy rain fell all through the night. At 5.15 am on the 8th, after a barrage by all divisional artillery and other heavy guns, the whole line started forward steadily in rain, mist and darkness.

The Turks, wretched and fatalistic, managed to resist stoutly at some points, but inexorably were born back. It was nevertheless slow going, due more to natural defences than the enemy's: the steep and slippery climb by heavily laden troops in ceaseless rain and mist could not have been more cumbrous and by nightfall the attack had to be suspended while the line was re-formed and rebuilt. The 10th Light Horse and a regiment of Worcester Yeomanry were still in their sector, between the Londoners and the 53rd's Welshmen.

During the night, the Welsh battalions resumed their advance, found Bethlehem deserted by the foe and closed to two and a half miles south of Jerusalem. The Turkish 7th Army was going, already streaming northward. By 7 am on Sunday 9 December, the last Turkish soldier trudged through the city. They had lost Jerusalem, but saved their army. At sunrise, the mayor, with a white-flag escort of police, walked towards the British line and presented his formal letter of surrender to Major General Shea of the Londoners. It was the 24th time the city had changed hands.

General Shea, escorted by his muddy troops, went into the city to a demonstrative welcome by Christians and Jews, but the Arabs stood aloof, overweening, resentful. It was their city too, as one of the oldest and most sacred shrines in the world, the Mosque of Omar, bore witness. Gullett said: 'All the trouble that was to follow after the Armistice in the settlement of Arab claims was foreshadowed as General Shea drove through the streets of Jerusalem'. It could be added, all before as well, and very much to this day, all since.

The British divisions moved quickly around the city to secure it against possible Turkish counterattacks. There was resistance from a pocket of Turks on the Mount of Olives, put down by the Londoners with the bayonet, who then linked up with the 53rd to complete the encirclement.

The 10th Light Horse rode in in the afternoon, recoiling from the filthy state of the place — Turkish habits had not improved and Jerusalem, whatever else its attractions, had disgraceful drainage and sewerage — but also feasting their eyes on signs of civilisation, houses, shops, gardens, such as they had not seen for years. Through windows, a trooper saw a ball in progress, with people in full evening dress. But the men were too tired to do more than secure food, a billet and, if possible, a warm bed for the night: a rare luxury since leaving home three years ago. The horses munched and dozed in practically hedonistic Turkish cavalry stables and some of the men bedded down in the mangers. 'It seemed appropriate,' someone said dryly.

The Australian Mounted Division was not so fortunate, however, being still deployed in the freezing, wet hills with the 10th (Irish) Division, alert for a Turkish counterattack.

General Allenby made his entry on 11 December, on foot, through the side entrance to the Jaffa gate, with no bands playing or flags waving, almost as a pilgrim instead of a conqueror. The avoidance of triumphalism was in deliberate contrast to the German Emperor Wilhelm II's flamboyant visit in 1908, when melodramatic pomp and ceremony were used 'to impress the eastern mind'. Allenby did, however, have an honour guard representing all the troops of the campaign, some still in their mud-stained battle equipment, worn with pride. The 10th Light Horse and a New Zealand squadron were of course included.

SEVENTEEN

Winter camp and toehold in the Jordan

Greybeard octogenarian Arabs said they had never known a winter as bad as 1917–18. The interminable rain flooded the land and swept away bridges, roads and culverts. The roaring streams from the hills turned the plains into swamps, in which thousands of camels perished and horses sank to their bellies. The weather enforced a pause in the restless Allenby's operations — which, knowing that his troops had to recuperate from their harsh campaigning anyway, he must have recognised as serendipitous.

Before the worst of the weather set in, however, the British made one last advance for the year. The 52nd Division mounted a surprise attack across the Nahr Auja, dislodging the Turks from their defences and sweeping them back to ten miles north of Jaffa, abreast of the sea cliffs at Arsuf. The enemy had to revert to inferior defences inland and Jaffa was made safe as a port for landing supplies.

By late December, the British divisions north of Jerusalem held ground astride the Nablus road and on Boxing Day withstood a fierce Turkish attempt to retake Jerusalem. The Londoners and the Welshmen suffered badly, but again and again cut down waves of enemy rushing headlong at the sangars. The other British divisions (74th and 10th) then hit the Turks on their right, driving them back, and by the end of the month the British line was consolidated twelve miles north of Jerusalem.

The Australian Mounted Division still manned their sector in the ice-bound hills and had assisted with vigorous reconnaissance in these operations, but were not closely engaged. Their spartan discomfort was eased over Christmas by some token extra tobacco, sweets, shaving soap and toothpaste and it says much for their forlorn state that these small things were received with delight.

Colonel Bourchier of Beersheba fame, temporarily commanding the 4th Light Horse Brigade, wrote: 'My only covering was two bivvy sheets, with rain pouring through the holes and our clothes were wet through, blankets and all, day after day. And on top of this, all we were living on was bully beef and biscuits. It rained so hard on Christmas Day that we went without our dinner, such as it was, and all had a strong toddy of rum and went to bed in our clothes.'

Early in January 1918, the Australian Mounted Division was withdrawn to the old camp at Belah, just south of Gaza. It had been chosen originally because it was a good winter camp on well-drained sand, instead of mud. The division's horses, shin-sore, underweight and dejected, had missed above all rolling, and at Belah they rolled and rolled as if they would never stop. On the first night, after their evening feed, the stable pickets reported that every horse was down to it.

At Belah, the Australian Mounted were given preliminary instruction in using the sword, and from that time could operate as either cavalry or mounted infantry. They were further trained and equipped before the next big push.

The ANZAC Division had been withdrawn to the Jewish settlements of Richon le Zion and Wady Hanein, near Chauvel's Desert Mounted Corps Headquarters at Deiran, and all Light Horsemen were now out of the line. In December, they had voted in the second conscription referendum: a subject surely of great moment to them, but outwardly at least treated as just another thing to be done, like cleaning rusted stirrup irons and spurs. Colonel Richardson records one attitude in the ranks: 'if these cold footers won't come voluntarily, they should not be forced. Old hands have no wish to fight alongside — conscripts.'

If the big wet had to be endured, there was no better place in Palestine to do it than the Jewish settlements. An article in *Australia in Palestine* by

Major General Chaytor (right) with Brigadier General F.C. Cox of 1st Brigade, ANZAC Mounted Division, at Richon le Zion, Palestine. The ANZAC logo would be stylish today. AWM B00602

the pseudonymous 'Camp Follower' says the ANZACs developed lasting loyalties to the villages of Richon, Wady Hanein and Deiran, all about three miles from each other: the 1st Brigade and the New Zealanders favoured Richon, 'where the wine vaults are said to be the largest in the world', the 2nd Brigade stuck to 'modest little' Wady Hanein, while Deiran, the largest and 'with considerable social pretensions', was renowned for its pretty, dark-eyed and polyglot girls, from whom the troops attached to Desert Mounted Corps Headquarters had no wish to stray.

All the villages had biblical associations and ghostly traces of the Crusaders. Ion Idriess writes: 'What with Samson and the Israelites and Philistines, Abraham and Moses and Isaac and Australians and New Zealanders, not to mention the Yeomanry and Coeur de Lion, a man doesn't know whose dust he is riding in'. He said the horses liked the places: 'We can tell by their willing movement, by the quick ring of their hooves, that they think this land just fine'. In Wady Hanein there were tall mimosa hedges and white people greeted the troopers with 'Shalom! Shalom!' and 'an hour ago … we rode down a beautiful avenue of Australian gums'.

The 2nd Brigade was in Wady Hanein when Jerusalem fell. The Jews were beside themselves with joy. Their dream of a Jewish nation established once more in Palestine had had a huge fillip and they showered hospitality on the deliverers. Brigadier General Ryrie, the politician, moved them to tears with his speech of thanks — delivered in English, which they didn't speak. The village schoolmaster eulogised in Russian except for mention of 'Lord Cromwell', 'Mr Byron' and 'Sir Gladstone'. Camp Follower reported that the Light Horsemen's attempts at mutual understanding began with the mastery of 'Bread', 'Wine' and 'Darling' in all the languages of East and West.

These Jewish enclaves had been established by Lord Rothschild — one of whose nephews, Major Evelyn Rothschild, was killed in the Yeomanry charge at Mughar — and other wealthy Jews who had bought the land and negotiated the settlement of their disadvantaged people mainly from southern Russia, but some from Romania and Spain, even a few from British countries and America. They were farming and trading folk — and my father's complaints about overcharging were echoed, for instance by leave parties to Jerusalem, where the good Richon wine sold for less than where it was made.

The occupying Turks and the Arabs had harassed and pillaged these colonies, keeping the people cowed into timidity and in constant fear of ruin and extermination. But the Germans and Austrians, mindful of post-war reconstruction, 'were careful not to offend these foster-children, the special care and pride of great international Jewish financiers'. Gullett recorded that just seventeen years before the Holocaust: history moved quickly.

The British deliberations over Palestine at this time produced the Balfour Declaration. Arthur Balfour, British Foreign Secretary, wrote to Lord Rothschild on 2 November 1917: 'His Majesty's Government views with favour the establishment in Palestine of a national home for the Jewish people and will use their best endeavours to facilitate the achievement of this objective, it being clearly understood that nothing shall be done which may prejudice the civil and religious rights of existing non-Jewish communities in Palestine, or the rights and political status enjoyed by Jews in any other country'.

This clear and simple distillation of British policy was seen in terms of strategic advantage as much as philanthropy. The prominent Zionist Chaim Weizmann told Lord Cecil, Balfour's subordinate in the Foreign Office, that it would be a safeguard to the Suez Canal and Churchill promoted it in such terms right up to World War II. The Germans, having a march stolen on them, got together with the Turks to devise a scheme equally attractive to the Jews. This had support from German Jews and also the Young Turk

Talat Pasha for a time, but it did not develop and disappeared without trace on Allenby's conquest of Palestine and the establishment of the British mandate in 1918. British rule lasted until 1948 and the Balfour Declaration remains the cornerstone on which the modern state of Israel is founded.

One of the largest and most attractive of the foreign enclaves in Palestine was the German settlement of Wilhelmia, east of the others by about five miles. The mounted troops had visited it and their artillery had shelled it, and the 54th Infantry Division occupied it briefly. The men were, of course, wary of this little enemy patch.

The 5th Light Horse Regiment stopped for a meal there and were delighted to ride in down a beautiful avenue of Australian gums, 'with fine two-storeyed farm houses on either side, big stacks of hay everywhere, gardens, fowls and the atmosphere of perfect farming prosperity over all' according to Idriess. He is 'not at all surprised at the fine strapping girls. Where a healthy gum tree can grow, it is a certainty a good-looking girl will spring up.' The schoolhouse bell rang on the quarter-hour, which was 'such a bare-faced way of telling the German gunners we are coming. Dotted all over the place are snipers' cunningly concealed possies, each with its telltale heap of empty cartridges. At a house corner is a pile of shells where a machine-gun was turned on our troops as they advanced.'

All the young men, the women said, had long since enlisted, some fighting in France, others in Palestine. The women sold them brown bread, butter, honey, milk, fowls and sucking pigs, and hay for the horses, and at the same time 'scornfully and fearlessly they assured us that we will soon be driven back to Beersheba, out into the desert again, where the jackals will fight the vultures for our bones'.

'It is good for our eyes and strange to see the brown groups of contented horses shading among these healthy gums in this clean place.' However, the Australians were shelled: 'high explosive and earth spouted just in front of the houses … now comes another, another, another! Two of our signallers are down.'

The men believed that underground telephone lines in the cellars of these houses were connected to the Turkish lines and German batteries, and the women above ground, even German soldiers dressed as women, did the spotting for them. 'Also, their intelligence men can peep at us from the windows. The English would never allow their troops to enter houses. No wonder they call us fools.'

Soon after Wilhelmia, Idriess was in the line outside Jaffa and contracted 'Jaffa fever', which he likened to malaria, and seeking attention at sick parade was wounded, for the third time, by a shell burst. He was evacuated in fits and starts by sand cart, motor ambulance and train, from one clearing station and field hospital to another, arriving finally at Cairo.

His last diary entry was made on 2 January 1918: 'I am to be returned to Australia as unfit for further service. Thank heaven!'

THERE WAS NOW A SENSE THAT THE GREAT WAR WAS ENTERING ITS FINAL STAGES in both western and eastern theatres. Armistices were in fact signed with Turkey and Germany only twelve days apart in 1918 (31 October and 11 November), but while immutable factors in the victors' progress determined this, it owed something to good luck as well.

The total desertion of Russian troops to participate in the Russian Revolution in October 1917 freed a mass of German divisions that poured into France in preparation for a huge spring offensive. The French armies were still recovering from the mutinies of that year and the British armies had been weakened and exhausted by the hopeless Third Ypres struggle. Lloyd George, in abhorrence and despair at the carnage in Flanders, turned again to the Near East for some crumbs of brightness and hope, victories for Britain: in his best hopes, these would culminate in the taking of Aleppo and knocking Turkey out of the war.

Allenby had already insisted that there could be no major offensive before the ground was dry enough, in about February 1918. But the government, while looking to him for salvation, reckoned it could not afford to have seven British infantry divisions in Palestine and signalled that he should be prepared to lose some should expectations of the enemy's preparations for a ferocious spring offensive in Europe prove accurate. The pressures on Murray to reinforce France were now turning on Allenby.

The British in Palestine were uncomfortably aware that 20,000 Turkish troops were in the Jordan Valley, south of Amman. Allenby's left flank was secured by the sea, but the right was open to attack, and since the western supply route for the Turkish 7th Army had been denied to them, supplies were coming from the Land of Moab, across the Dead Sea by barge, then hauled up to the Jericho–Jerusalem road.

The next stage of Allenby's operations was therefore to secure this flank and stop the supply route by occupying the western side of the Jordan Valley, from the Dead Sea to the Wady Auja — one of the small streams trickling into the northern end of the Dead Sea and nothing to do with the Nahr Auja on the coast, except that in Allenby's plans his projected front line was sometimes referred to as 'the Line of the Two Aujas'.

Jericho was twenty miles north-east of Jerusalem via Talat ed Dumm — the Hill of Blood, a reference to its colour — on a well-metalled road that dropped gently at first. However, after Talat it zigzagged and swung in hairpin bends most precipitously down to the floor of the valley, though still a good German road, from 2000 feet above sea level to 1200 feet below it. The cliffs and the crags of iron-hard, red-brown rock on this route became familiar to the ANZACs and never failed to inspire them with awe and foreboding. Near Jericho, an astounding golden mass of rock rears up for 1000 feet: Jebel Kuruntul or the Mount of Temptation. Christ is said to have endured the 40 days in the wilderness here and Satan is supposed to have tempted Him with all worldly powers and pleasures. There are not many to be seen from this place.

On 18 February, the winter rains temporarily let up, and into this country marched the ANZAC Mounted Division (less the 2nd Brigade), on the right flank of the 53rd and 60th Infantry Divisions. The operation was under General Chetwode, but as Chauvel's ANZACs were taking part, he accompanied Chetwode up the Mount of Olives in Jerusalem to see the advance start.

The men were fresh and ready. They were approaching a philosophical journey too, such as Napoleon's Grand Army of the First Empire had made, wandering all over Europe for nearly twenty years, going where the battle led, uncomplaining, accepting the bad and making the most of the good, scarcely remembering any other life, and in time not hankering after one. The ANZACs had not arrived yet at such complete acceptance, but in time professionalism and fellowship could have supplanted longings for home and a routine, settled life in their thoughts. Now, they were looking forward to this next campaign, the fresh stimulus of new country and seeing ever more of this exordial and extraordinary world.

The Turks appeared to believe that if they could defend the Jericho road they would be safe, for the country on either side of it was a mess of narrow gorges, loose boulders and treacherous footing where a man could only stumble and a horse could only be led. They either overestimated the difficulties of the terrain, or reckoned without the agility of both the infantry and mounted troops, whose advances were made on a wide front. By early on the 20th, the infantry had taken Talat ed Dumm after brief but fierce fighting and the ANZACs, with the New Zealand Brigade leading, had found their way down through the wilderness of Judah and started a dismounted attack on two prominent hills five miles south of Talat. The country was indeed rough and the Aucklands and Wellingtons stumbled in single file along dark, narrow gorges or on foot tracks around the hillsides, under constant fire from machine-gun emplacements and artillery. The ANZACs had had to send their own badly needed wheeled guns down the Jericho road.

For some hours the advance was arrested, but at noon the infantry on the left of the New Zealanders won their way forward in terrain 'which seemed only accessible to fully equipped mountaineers'. They drove the Turks back on a Moslem hospice called Nebi Musa, where it was believed Moses was buried.

Both the Londoners from Talat ed Dumm and Cox's 1st Light Horse Brigade on the New Zealanders' right were now in reach of the valley floor, and soon after the New Zealanders took the two hills a troop of the 1st Light Horse Regiment, probing down a wady towards the Dead Sea, found it clear of the enemy and reached the level ground of the plain. Cox at once followed with his whole brigade and, unopposed, pushed out patrols northwards. Positions were secured for the night and plans made for a dawn combined assault on the enemy, converging from all quarters, west and south, and north and east, by all forces.

But the Turks, apprehensive that a brigade of horse roaming the valley could easily pen them in or cut off their retreat, evacuated Jericho during the night, stole away northward and across the Dead Sea. In the morning, a troop of the 8th Light Horse Regiment galloped into Jericho and Lieutenant W.C. Kelly signalled: 'Entered Jericho 0800. Captured twenty-three prisoners. Town now clear. Wounded in hospital. Plenty of water at running stream near town. Inhabitants report guns removed to east side of Jordan and are now near bridge.'

There was a minaret and a mosque in Jericho, but otherwise all romantic notions of it were dashed by the squalor of its straw and mud huts and the omnipresent and obnoxious leavings of the Turkish soldiery. Yet its traces of civilisation reach back for 12,000 years and it is even claimed to be the first known human settlement. In modern times, it has become the administrative centre for the Palestinian autonomous region of the West Bank.

From Jericho, Cox sent patrols north to the Wady Auja and east towards the Jordan River. Near the Auja, the Turks resisted for a time at the stone bridge across the Jordan, flowing swiftly from the Sea of Galilee to the Dead Sea. A squadron of New Zealanders rode on to Rujm el Bahr, a collection of little huts and a jetty at the north end of the Dead Sea that served as port for the barges towed from Moab with grain for the Turkish garrisons towards Jerusalem. A German towboat was at the jetty: the men mounted a machine-gun on it and put to sea, sank another boat, captured a third and forced a fourth aground. (Elyne Mitchell.)

That night, outposts watched and listened carefully for any Turkish movement to the east, but none was detected. The following day, the two mounted brigades (less the Auckland Regiment) were relieved by a garrison of infantry and marched back to their Jerusalem camps. In their expert judgment, it was 'not a bad little stunt'. They had suffered only three men killed and fourteen wounded, but the infantry, to whom most of the hill fighting fell, sustained many more casualties. Soon, small crosses would mark the graves of the Londoners along the Jerusalem–Jericho road.

The ANZACs had seen majestic, if sombre, country. The average rainfall in the Jordan Valley does not exceed five inches a year, but at that time the place was brilliant with wild flowers, and warm and sunny after the cold hills. All of it was of the utmost antiquity, alive with the ghosts of Romans, Jews and Arabs and all their works: Joshua and his trumpeters, Cleopatra and Herod, Sodom and Gomorrah, the Roman City of the Palms. Across the river, all along the frowning heights of Moab, the ancient goat tracks leading to the passes where Moses had seen the Promised Land and which his tribes ascended to colonise the East Bank country could still be seen. Southwards was Masada, where in AD 70 the Jews made their last stand against the Roman Flavius Silva. Nowhere in the world is the atmosphere so heavy with evocations of the past. Gullett sums it up with, 'The whole place is a sepulchre'.

On that first visit, the horses grazed and the men sunned themselves. Being of enquiring mind, they knew the valley was hot in summer, but not that they would spend the next summer in it, nor that this ordeal would nearly destroy them.

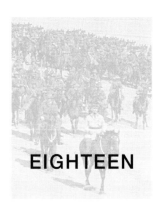

EIGHTEEN

'The roughest stunt': Amman

While Cox's 1st Brigade was in the Jordan Valley, Ryrie's 2nd Brigade was holding a section of the front line at Nalin, ten miles north of Jerusalem. The brigade linked up 20 and 21 Infantry Corps, the 7th Regiment of my father's in fact forming the connection.

He was a proud sergeant at last and had been sent to an NCOs school in Cairo during the lull in operations 'to get brushed up, as on active service one has very little ceremonial work and gets rusty. Am not looking forward to it except for the change and spell, will be away about 3 weeks.' He next writes from Nalin:

> We are having a pretty rough trot up in the hills holding part of the line. It is very cold and wet and the mud is about as thick in our dugouts as it is outside. We are high up in the world, living on the side of a young mountain down which the water roars at a great rate. The Turks are not close to us here and don't trouble us, thank heavens, the weather and mud are quite enough.
>
> Yes, as you say, the taking of Jerusalem was a great event, but I wasn't there, our work was from about the centre of the line to the left flank, which took us over to Jaffa. Have not seen Jerusalem yet, but hope to one day.

> Cannot write much this time, the rain is coming in and I'm too cold to sit still ...

The stoic Richardson does not mention the weather, but describes the rocky mountain country and its flora and fauna. There were wild flowers, poppies, anemones, even some wheat, 'which is looking well'. The poppies 'seemed to bear the Crusader's cross in black, on a red ground'. Gazelles roamed about. The energetic Lieutenant Colonel Onslow explored and kept his officers fit by co-opting them for strenuous walks.

The flow of reinforcements was thinning and Richardson, concerned about the men's fitness, returned to the conscription issue. The strain of recent operations had meant evacuations to hospital. In most cases these men rejoined the regiment after a few weeks and could carry on while conditions were not too severe. However:

> ... when hardships recommence, though struggling bravely, they would at last be compelled to go to hospital again. In this way, each regiment gradually acquired an increasing number of men who were not quite fit, men who appeared at intervals in the regiment, when ... they should have been shipped home to Australia without delay.
>
> But the slump in recruiting and the rejection of conscription were beginning to be felt and sick men in Palestine had to be kept with their regiments because healthy men in Australia would not see their plain duty.

The 2nd Brigade returned to their favourite bivouac at Wady Hanein early in March 1918, to find the old spirit of enterprise astir and speculation and rumour abounding. The plans were of course secret, but there is no disguising the signs from old hands.

Allenby's preoccupation with the Jordan Valley and beyond, to Gilead, had led him to conceive of an incursion in force to Amman, 30 miles east-north-east of Jericho, over the Mountains of Moab. The route was steep and difficult and the place well-defended, but the Commander-in-Chief was confident his troops could fight their way through it.

Emir Feisal, one of four sons of King Hussein, led Arab irregulars loyal to the pro-British Sherif of Mecca, who were operating along the Moab plateau, blowing up the Hejaz railway. This no longer exists, but was then the only reliable means of transport east of the Jordan. It ran north–south between Damascus and Mecca and therefore supplied all the enemy forces between these places, for a distance of 250 miles.

At Amman, called Philadelphia by Ptolemy II and the Ancient Greeks, the Hejaz railway went through a tunnel and over a long viaduct and the main object of the Amman raid was to blow these up, putting the railway out of action for the long term, perhaps even until the end of the war. The Arab irregulars of Feisal belonged to Allenby's command and he took a close interest in them, liaising frequently with their brilliant but wayward and untruthful mentor, Lieutenant Colonel T.E. Lawrence. With the help of attached British officers, Feisal's Arabs were breaking up the railway line with 'tulip' charges almost at will, but the Turkish and German engineers were repairing it just as easily and quickly.

Lawrence promised Allenby Arab support on this operation, which of course meant that the Sherifian leaders had to be informed of it. Not all the tribes' loyalties could be vouched for, however, particularly in the north, and it had to be assumed that the Turks were alerted. Certainly they defended Amman vigorously and, in the event, no Arabs turned up except small groups who swore loyalty, cadged food and ammunition from the British infantry during the action, and cleared out.

Allenby was also looking ahead. In his mind, he knew that when the time came, he would mount his next general offensive up the Plain of Sharon on the coast; therefore, as of old, it was strategically important to demonstrate all possible activity at the opposite end of the front: a major deception aspect of Trans-Jordan operations which was to lead to fighting in Gilead in March, April and May.

General Shea was given command of the Amman force. 'Shea's Group' consisted of his 60th London Division, the ANZAC Mounted Division and the Camel Brigade, a heavy and a mountain battery of artillery and, astoundingly, a brigade of armoured cars. The infantry had to force a crossing of the Jordan and hold it while a pontoon bridge was built, for the stone bridge at the place called Ghoraniye that Cox's brigade had reconnoitred had been blown up by the Turks. When the permanent replacement was built post-war, it was named Allenby Bridge.

The Jordan was in high flood with every inch of the way, including the precipitous goat tracks up the East Bank, sodden and boggy. Mounted operations looked out of the question and even on the high, flat tableland of Moab, around Amman, foot marching promised to be laborious and slow.

Chauvel was never enthusiastic about Trans-Jordan operations, mainly on logistical grounds. Neither was my father: 'Hope to go through Jerusalem and then further north. Am not looking forward to the business, it promises to be a pretty rough stunt with I think considerable fighting. We will be going through very rough country where the inhabitants, hill tribes, are hostile as well as the Turks. The country is worth seeing, but I wish we were seeing it under more pleasant conditions ... Think I told you I'm a troop sergeant now and a very busy one.'

His 2nd Brigade rode off from the Wady Hanein on 13 March, a rare and perfect spring day, even with larks singing. The young travellers were irrepressibly expectant: after months of stationary routine, they were off again — to see Jerusalem! If faith did not call to all of them, fame must have, and apart from the wrecked and despoiled Gaza it was to be the first big city they'd seen since Cairo.

They bivouacked for the night at Latron and the weather changed back to winter: strong winds, cold and heavy rain which fell all night, then incessantly for days. The plan had to be delayed and each hour lost increased its prospects of compromise. 'On St Patrick's Day,' my father wrote:

> we left Latron, the rain simply teemed still and we splashed along all day through mud and slush on the road to Jerusalem. Got our first glimpse of the old city about 5 pm, through mist and rain, rather pretty it looked, too. We rode through the new part of the city, spattered with mud from head to foot and dripping with water, yet the populace turned out in hundreds as we clattered through the streets. Out on the other side of town, we pitched our camp near the Mount of Olives and wet through, cold and muddy, stayed there three days. But all hands were able to have a good look round.

The three brigades of the ANZAC Mounted were now at Jerusalem, the Camel Brigade was at Bethlehem and the 60th Londoners were already concentrated in the Jordan Valley and in the hills around Jericho. All were within a night's march of crossing the Jordan, but it was in even higher flood, having risen seven feet in one night. The noisy, roiling torrent ruled out pontoon bridge-building and General Shea had to wait.

'I was deeply impressed with Jerusalem,' wrote Sergeant Baly. 'The Church of the Holy Sepulchre and the Sepulchre itself are inspiring to the highest degree and in these places, religion is carried out with such solemnity, profundity and whole-souledness it affords one considerable food for thought. In this wonderful old church, there was a service and Catholic procession and the singing was beautiful as it echoed through the great domes. We saw other places, the Mosque of Omar and the Jews' Wailing Place.'

What about the beer, Dad? He was never a pious man. But his generation was the last to profess absolute faith and practise strict observance, and lapses such as missing a Sunday service were frowned on. Crossing from Sinai into Palestine, a senior New Zealand officer stopped at a concrete border pillar, removed his hat and thanked God for letting him visit the Holy Land. My father does attribute his narrow escapes, such as holding horses that were killed and close shell bursts that left him untouched, to Providence.

Now, the cosmologists tell us that original nothing became everything in one meaningless cosmic explosion and everything is hurtling back to nothing again. Cold comfort for the churches. Yet people in peril for their lives still need to entreat some abiding safe conductor, however unknowable. In World War II it was said, 'There are no atheists in the fox-holes of New Guinea'.

At the first break in the weather, the 2nd Brigade moved further east to Talat ed Dumm, just above the Jordan Valley. 'Nine miles in front and below us, we could just see the river and to our right, the northern end of the Dead Sea, while immediately below to our left, was Jericho. Eighteen miles away, across the valley, we could see the escarpment on the east side, strongly held by the enemy … and there started the roughest bit of work we have been asked to do yet.'

The Desert Mounted Corps Bridging Train, an Australian and New Zealand engineering unit, was raised by Chauvel and trained in under three weeks. They could hardly have anticipated that their first job would be to bridge a flooded river flowing at seven knots, at night, under fire. But the Londoners had an even harder and more dangerous task: to swim the river and establish a defensive cordon on the far bank, behind which the sappers could work. A substantial Turkish infantry force had been observed abreast of the old Ghoraniye crossing.

At midnight on 21 March, selected swimmers from the Londoners entered the stream at several points, attempting to carry a line across the 50 or 60 yards to the far bank. They were fired on and all failed except one at Hajla, four miles south of Ghoraniye. The engineers, Londoners and Light Horseman got to work here, taking more lines across, and just after 1 am the first raft-load of 27 infantrymen landed opposite and deployed on ground covering the site. Sufficient infantrymen followed to afford protection and by 6 am construction of the pontoon bridge had started. The work went smoothly and the first span was across just over an hour later.

With daylight, the Turkish fire increased and the Londoners suffered many casualties, but were undeterred from getting a full battalion across by 8 am and another by noon. The bridgehead held while the work continued.

That night, the Auckland Mounted Rifles, who had been patrolling the valley since the occupation of Jericho in mid-February, led their horses over the first span. Then riding through the ring of Londoners, they extended the bridgehead and took the Turks in rear at Ghoraniye. They were already withdrawing and the Aucklands galloped them down and shot them at close range, clearing the area. More Londoners swam across here and another pontoon bridge was started.

Before nightfall on the 23rd, four bridges had been built at the two crossings and were ready to take the main force. Major General Chaytor marched his ANZACs and the Camel Brigade down from Talat ed Dumm and before morning the shod hooves of the division were clattering across. The night was fine and warm and, waiting their turn, the troopers relaxed on the ground, some sleeping, others boiling up for a brew.

The 6th Regiment led the 2nd Brigade over at the Hajla crossing. Three brigades of the 60th Division were already over and Cox's 1st Light Horse Brigade followed. Cox set off along the river northwards, seeking a track alleged to lead to the town of Es Salt twenty miles to the north on the Moab tableland. The brigade's task at this stage was to be left flank guard to the 60th Division and New Zealand Brigade in an attack on the town of Es Salt, while Ryrie's 2nd Brigade acted as right flank guard and was to secure Amman while the railway was blown up.

The 2nd Brigade advanced eastwards towards the frowning Mountains of Moab and Amman. At the foothills, they skirted bountiful crops of wheat in full ear, in agreeable contrast to the bare West Bank land. They also met, or were met by, some Hejaz Arabs.

They were big, hawk-faced, black-bearded, handsome fellows in coloured robes with jewelled daggers, of imposing physical grace and dignity, utterly unlike the scrawny scavengers of Sinai. They galloped up shouting, waving great curved swords and dangerously discharging finely-inlaid old rifles. To be welcomed by warlike Arabs promised well and the men responded sociably. But the Arab horses were for the most part emaciated and miserable, and here and there a wretched pony carried two strapping men. Harness was missing or held together with string, some saddles were ornate, others in tatters. They appeared to have no leader and when Ryrie's brigade interpreter questioned them, they all spoke in chorus.

Yet they were allies. They escorted Ryrie to their encampment in the foothills, and in a huge black goatskin tent insisted on plying him and his staff with coffee. The delay had to be suffered, but as might have been expected, these Arabs did not deliver on Lawrence's promise when it came to fighting. They did things spontaneously, not according to design or commitment. A British officer described them as 'good ten minute fighters', it seemed not so much from lack of courage but because all, or none, were leaders and they were devoid of any notion of concerted action. If their first wild rush at an enemy was unsuccessful, they went away. On this first acquaintance, Ryrie's ANZACs suspended judgment.

Like the tribes of Moses, Shea's Group were obliged to take goat tracks up the mountain because the Turks held all the roads. However, the tracks were much worse than current British intelligence had indicated. Ryrie's route was said to be fit for wheels, but after leaving the foothills it ascended steeply and wound abruptly round the beds of narrow, rocky wadys. Except for the Hong Kong and Singapore Mountain Battery, which carried its guns on camels, all artillery and limbers, including some carrying explosives for demolition of the railway, were in difficulties, and after four miles could not go any further: the track lay between rocks and measured less than their axle width across. Ryrie advised Chaytor that they must be left behind and, with some delay, the explosives were transferred to camels. What happened to the 'brigade of armoured cars', and whether it even materialised, is not known. Probably somebody thought better of it.

The advance resumed well after dark, with horsemen riding two abreast, but soon they were leading horses in single file through rocky defiles. By midnight the column was spread out over many miles with the Camels in rear. The advance, in unknown, enemy country and without their own properly deployed flank guards, was hesitant and apprehensive.

At 2 am on the 25th, the rain started again. My father wrote:

All that night and most of the next day the rain continued and the wind was bitterly cold. We had to keep going, walking most of the time, splashing through mud and water, climbing over rocks and dragging the poor old nags behind us. During halts, we simply lay down where we were in mud or pools of water and always in the pouring rain and slept like drunken men. We did ride in places where it was safe, but once in the saddle men could not keep awake and they got mixed up in wrong units. A horse, feeling no check on his reins, would quicken his pace and when the sleeping gentleman woke up, he was among strangers and far ahead of his own unit. Men became stupid from want of sleep and did and said silly things. Somebody told me quite clearly, but half awake and dreaming, that all my troops' packhorses had been stolen, an utterly impossible thing in the circumstances. Then I was dreaming myself of having a glorious feed of roast chicken before a big log fire. It was so real. Then I woke up.

The Camel Brigade in rear had an even worse climb. The men hauled and dragged at their mounts, the camels slipped and fell, and both struggled on in single file through gushing wadys and round the sides of hills on narrow ledges that would not have been attempted in daylight. General Smith said, 'The camels were carried up by the men'.

At 4 am the Light Horsemen reached the edge of the plateau at a locality noted on the map as Ain el Hekr, but otherwise of no apparent substance. Ryrie halted in a concealing gorge to wait for daylight. Dawn disclosed only his drenched and bedraggled men, two nights short of sleep, squatting in the mud and trying to light fires with the bundles of kindling they never travelled without, and heavy rain still falling. The head of the column was now within a few hours march of Amman but the Camels were still far below and the day had almost passed before all three of their battalions caught up.

Chaytor resumed the march with the 2nd Brigade and the Camels in the early evening. The going was flat at last, but the fertile land had been cultivated and the tread of animals over ploughed fields soon stirred it to the consistency of stew a foot deep. It was also sticky and, on foot, men not only sank in it to the knees but carried deposits on their boots. Any fast movement, mounted or dismounted, was out of the question. The temperature was below freezing again and heavy showers persisted.

The force was now close to Amman and the advance guard of the 7th Regiment moved cautiously. At every halt, men would drop off their horses and fall instantly asleep on clumps of wet bushes beside the track, or in the swamp. In the saddle, they were unable to stay awake and their mounts again got out of position.

At dawn, the column met the New Zealanders encamped a mile east of Ain es Sir. Their climb had been easier, but still too rough for guns and limbers. Chaytor's orders were to move on Amman as soon as his brigades were concentrated on the tableland. They now were, but had all been three nights without sleep and were in no condition to assault anything. He decided to delay the attack 24 hours and camped a little north of the New Zealanders. The rain stopped and the Light Horsemen rigged up their bivvies, dried their clothes and slept.

While the ANZACs were climbing the mountain, the 3rd Light Horse Regiment of Cox's 1st Brigade had ridden hard for the town of Es Salt, and with exceptional verve surprised it into submission without firing a shot. The regiment was then joined by the 60th Division, and the left flank was secured. The attack on Amman could proceed, but General Shea rightly doubted the capacity of the ANZAC Mounted to take it and ordered a brigade of the Londoners to march from Es Salt to Amman, to join Chaytor.

It was believed 4000 Turks defended Amman, together with German units of the Asia Korps. The place had some of the best preserved Roman ruins in the region, but unfortunately these lent themselves very well to defence, particularly the old Roman amphitheatre with three tiers of terraces overlooking the north and west approaches; and half a mile south of that was the conical Hill 3039, of commanding height. The target, the railway viaduct and tunnel complex to be demolished, lay two miles south of the town.

The plan of attack was to encircle the town with the New Zealand Brigade on the right, the Camel Brigade in the centre and the 2nd Light Horse Brigade on the left. They could put into the line fewer than 3000 rifles and the single light artillery battery to scale the mountain, the faithful Bing Boys of the Hong Kong and Singapore Mountain Battery. The 7th Regiment was particularly weak, having more than a squadron detached on various duties such as escorting the artillery back to the Jordan Valley floor and escorting the demolition parties.

Chaytor's brigades advanced. They could see neither the Turks nor the town because of intervening ridges and hills, and by now they had no confidence in their intelligence or maps. In the mire, their only mounted gait was a plod, robbing them of that precious mobility that had won them battle after battle.

The Turks, however, had a complete view of them. Their artillery had been registered on every possible approach and their machine-guns were placed to sweep every part of the front.

Gullett: 'As the brigades rode into range of the enemy's guns they were lightly shelled, but … it was clear the Turk was well satisfied with his position and disposed to let the raiders come to close quarters'. According to my father, those being shelled did not pass it off 'lightly':

> Two troops of us got into a hot corner right at the jump. We were riding over very boggy country and all at once came under heavy shell fire and had to get out. The horses could hardly carry us as they were sinking to their knees in the morass, so we had to dismount and lead them, but it was all we could do to get going ourselves, with the floundering, plunging horses, while the Jacko battery put them over us quick as they could load them. But thanks to the soft ground smothering their shell bursts, they didn't do much damage, except for killing a few horses and bringing on shell-shock in two or three men. We got under cover eventually, safe but exhausted.

The ANZACs reached the last crest and dismounted. The New Zealanders diverged to the right, the 1st (Australian) and 2nd (British) battalions of Camels, with their bigger, concentrated numbers, trudged towards the estimated position of the village, still not sighted because of intervening ridges. Ryrie's 6th and 7th Regiments left their horses a mile and a half from Amman and went forward on the Camels' left. It was, said Gullett, 'a striking picture of supreme courage engaged in a desperate and hopeless mission'.

The horses were left at the last ridge and the 6th and 7th Regiments advanced on foot down the boggy slope in extended order, on a front of about a mile. The mounted infantryman's spare and lonely formation must have been hard to bear that day. They covered three-quarters of a mile in a dread silence, then it came: on signal, the artillery, machine-guns and rifles of the enemy all roared out at once. They fell thickly, but squelched on until they estimated the village they still could not see should be about 600 yards ahead. The watching enemy corrected his range and stepped up the fire, forcing the leading men to ground for cover. The heavy losses continued. As they still had no targets a further advance would have invited annihilation and a retirement to comparative safety was ordered. My father:

> That afternoon, we advanced on foot with only rifles and machine-guns, against their artillery, machine-guns, rifles and bombs. We got a very warm reception, believe me, and they finally knocked us back … we retired with our wounded, leaving of course, the dead behind. Went back about half a mile to near our horses and held on there all night. We were just about played out with the hard journey through the mountains and the fatigue of the attack. The officers of my squadron had been wounded and we lost a good many other ranks, so there was only a thin line that night, it was horribly cold, and of course, no sleep again.

Nat Barton also wrote of that night and the following morning:

> … the horses went without tucker and the men had a tin of bully beef between four, to last them till late that night. However, we marched to the attack in the morning and were [in action] about 2 o'clock, I think. We met the hottest hole it has been our misfortune to strike so far and a counter attack [on both] flanks, drove us back. This squadron was second from the left and once the squadron on our left went back, we were exposed to solid fire from front and flank. I got hit through the knee first, but after lying for a minute, found I could use it, so got up and began to walk out further to try and see the Turks coming up on our left. I had gone ten yards before the second bullet came along, so lay there till a couple of men arrived, who carried me back till we got behind a little cover, where I was put on a stretcher and taken back behind the hill. The squadron had to retire a few hundred yards but managed it pretty right.

On this day, others fared as badly. The Brigade's machine-gun squadron under Captain Cain managed to reach an old stone house from which they

185

could cover the front of the advancing troopers, but the enemy's overwhelming fire still brought them up short. Further right, the British 2nd Battalion of Camels, with their greater numbers, made a gallant advance through a shrapnel barrage with perfect steadiness, but could not sustain it in the torrent of fire. The New Zealanders were also brought to a standstill in the roughest part of the approach. When the Turks suddenly counterattacked them, they fell back, but regained their ground before nightfall.

The 4th (Australian) Camel Battalion had been sent to blow up the railway line south of Amman. Some of the Wellington Regiment joined them, and during the night they destroyed some miles of track. At the same time, two squadrons of the 5th Light Horse (in reserve) were ordered to cut the line on the other, northern side of Amman. In darkness, they made straight for their main target, a two-span stone bridge, and blew it up, rejoining their regiment at dawn after a seven-hour march. Amman was now temporarily isolated, but it proved to be as invincible as ever.

The brigade of Londoners sent by General Shea from Es Salt arrived in the early morning of the 28th. There never was a more heartening sight, but they had marched through the bog all night and Chaytor, who had issued orders for an immediate mounted dash by the two horse brigades and a frontal assault by the Londoners, changed them to a general dismounted advance at 1 pm. The ground was still too soft for horses and the Londoners needed to collect themselves.

When they did advance, it was with such spirit and speed it seemed possible that they might break through. A trooper told Ian Jones: 'We saw them come out through the mud, their packs sodden from the rain, their big boots carrying pounds of the sticky soil of the land of Moab. We watched them go, wave after wave, now enshrouded in the smoke of the barrage, now emerging again, the thin lines still thinner, but the pace no slower and the direction unchanged.'

But the promise was short-lived. All the troops closed on Amman again in their half-circle, but they ran into the same wall of fire as before and the advance was blown away in sheer casualties.

On the extreme left, Ryrie's 6th and 7th Regiments still moved on in two lines, down a slope of barley. The 7th, just over 100 rifles strong, were checked at a steep ridge held by the Turks, behind stone sangars. More men fell and were taken out with great difficulty. Colonel Onslow of the 7th was directing both regiments: a squadron of the 6th, just 58 strong and without their severely wounded squadron major, had taken a piece of commanding ground 300 yards from the enemy line. Topography, if nothing else, favoured a further advance and Onslow ordered both the 6th's squadron and his own regiment forward again. Lieutenant Ridgway, now in command of the 6th squadron, represented that he was being heavily enfiladed from the left and strongly held in front, and the prospects of gaining more ground were small. The order was repeated, the 7th moved off and the 6th squadron made a heroic rush down the slope at the enemy. They were wiped out instantly by machine-guns and only one man, wounded in four places, rejoined the Australian line.

The 7th had likewise been stopped: Richardson lamented that artillery support could have easily put the enemy sangars out of business. But now the two regiments were in great danger and Onslow ordered a retirement of 500 yards, just as a bullet knocked a map out of his hand. 'Caught it this day hotter than ever,' says my father:

> they simply poured the machine-gun fire into us, we did not reach our objective and once more were compelled to pull back. I shall never forget that day, I was never more done in my life, carrying our casualties back through the bog a mile or more, with the Turks and Germans following us with their machine-guns. Five of us at the last were carrying a heavy man who had been badly wounded, the fatigue of it was awful, at times we could not take another step, so would put him down for a short spell, only to see the enemy coming and hear the spiteful hisses and pings of his bullets. But before evening, everybody was back to the horses more dead than alive and we set about making a rough firing line to hold that night.
>
> These two occasions are our first defeats in this whole campaign and that sensation is both new and disagreeable to us.

The 7th had sustained another 31 casualties, of whom only two were killed and all wounded except two were carried out. In the night more rain fell and the cruel teeth of frost put half an inch of ice on the swamp and gripped the men lying on the ground, staring into the blackness from their firing line.

Ingenious Turkish and German engineers repaired the stone bridge with timber and a trainload of enemy reinforcements arrived in Amman from the north next day. This dawned quiet in the line, providing opportunities for consultation and reassessment.

Two days of heavy fighting had resulted in no gain, only severe losses. There were reports of large enemy forces approaching Es Salt from the north, with the apparent intention of pushing Cox's brigade and the infantry out. If that should be successful, the enemy could then either swing east against Chaytor's force, or go down to the Dead Sea and trap the whole British force by sealing off their escape routes.

Other intelligence, however, suggested that the Turks were considering evacuating Amman. As intelligence had been faulty throughout the operation and these two reports ruled each other out, General Shea considered Chaytor should proceed. The New Zealand major general was far from admitting defeat himself and two more battalions of Londoners from Es Salt joined him. With this fresh strength, it was decided to attack again, but this time in darkness, on the night of the 29–30th.

All night and all day of the 29th, the enemy shelled the ANZAC and Londoners' positions. The Turks tried repeatedly to work round Ryrie's exposed left flank, showing their accurate appraisal of his serious losses and threadbare state. The 7th Regiment could put only 50 men in the firing line and the 2nd Brigade were forced to keep extending their line to counter the Turks' outflanking movements, until it became dangerously strung out.

Chaytor's staff planned the night attack and he briefed his brigade commanders. The plan rested on the premise that the enemy artillery and machine-guns would be rendered harmless in the dark, allowing the opposing forces to meet on even terms. The Turks seldom fought well at close quarters and the ANZACs, Camels and Londoners were by now familiar with the terrain.

The British were to keep their existing dispositions. The New Zealanders and the Camels were to take Hill 3039 and the Londoners were to aim at Amman village and the railway station. The 2nd Light Horse Brigade was too under-strength for another direct assault, but was to continue holding the left flank and, if it was not too late, distract the enemy by demonstrating a stronger presence than they in fact possessed. The plan had a fair chance of success. General Shea gave it his blessing and added: Amman must be taken.

The night of the attack was black, cold, wet and windy, heights of Moab weather at its worst. Anything was better than standing still and the suffering troops prayed for the order to move.

The appalling battle started again. As my father described it:

We had to advance a little and build up small stone sangars about a foot high and lie there all night. Nothing much happened except more rain and more cold and less sleep. All next day we stayed behind the little cover the stones offered and fought a duel with rifles and M.G.'s. We got the hottest fire I'd ever experienced. The lumps of lead sang and buzzed and hissed all day without ceasing. One of my good friends was killed, a sergeant from Rose Bay and we had other casualties. A Hun put some holes through the shoulder of my overcoat, but did not harm the wearer. They were trying to get round our left, and we had to keep them off. We stopped there again that night and by this time we were in a pretty bad state as the cold prevented sleep and tucker was running out.

At 2 am on the 30th the irregular half-circle with its many gaps occasioned by irregular terrain — and the absence of the 2nd Brigade — crept forward with bomb and bayonet. All went well for an hour, then the heavy fire resumed on the infantry's front and soon became general all along the line. The enemy was too alert, his guns were too well-sited and ranged, and surprise had gone too early.

The New Zealanders stole in behind Hill 3039 without detection, aiming to climb the disengaged side then rush the Turkish entrenchments downhill, from the crest. They did capture the higher trenches and at dawn compelled the surrender of a line of lower earthworks, but were strongly counterattacked, the Turks untypically charging to within 30 feet. The occupation of the hill remained only partial.

Only partial success attended the attacks of the Camels and Londoners in the centre. Neither lacked force, but both came under heavy enfilade fire. A small party of Camels did dash beyond the trenches and enter the village, as did some New Zealanders, but were driven out at once. The Londoners lost ground, took it back with the bayonet, but could go no further.

Chaytor found at daylight that his attacks had nowhere been decisive, and with the light, his troops were exposed to fearful punishment at close range. The New Zealanders were pinned down, the Camels and the Londoners prone and stalled. But the Germans and Turks, expertly entrenched and fully sighted again, at once reasserted their dominance of the battlefield. They increased their efforts to get round Ryrie's weak left flank; and if that crumbled, it could be rolled up and spell disaster for the entire British force.

With the morning well on, Shea at Es Salt asked Chaytor if he thought Amman could be taken that day. He replied in the emphatic negative and Shea ordered him to withdraw.

Soon after nightfall, a ticklish evacuation was accomplished without alerting the enemy and the battered and dejected column set out on the first stage, a fifteen-mile trek to Es Salt. There were motor ambulances at Es Salt, but they could not drive over the churned-up mud and the wounded were left with piteous alternatives: the torture of the jolting, gyrating camel cacolets with the camels skidding and slipping in the mud, or being tied head-down over a horse's rump, with their feet supported in nosebags slung over its back for stirrups, and hands tied under its flanks. Greatcoats for mattresses were freely given.

At Es Salt, they left Cox's 1st Brigade and the remaining Londoners holding off the Turks and set out on the easier route to the Jordan Valley via Ain es Sir and Shunet Nimrin, by which the New Zealanders had come up. The Light Horse rearguard was followed by about 500 Turks, who did not come within range. But the ANZACs overtook a most strange and heart-rending cavalcade of Christian and Armenian dwellers of the high country, running from the Turks in fear of retribution for this Christian army's attack on Moslems. Men, women and children in worse case than their own, carrying a few bundles, some barefoot, hurrying down the mountain in the freezing sleet and rain. They begged and cried for protection and help. Most ANZACs took a child, a woman or aged person up on their pommels. My father said that all reached the valley safely, where 'the authorities' took them over and fed them, then took them to a concentration camp behind the lines. The distressed human stream was still flowing when Cox's brigade came down the track a day later.

In the night, as the ANZACs passed through Ain es Sir, some fence-sitting Circassians thought they had better show preference for the Turkish victors and, at close range, fired a ragged volley into the Wellington

Regiment, hitting a dozen men. The New Zealanders, brooding over their first defeat in a matchless record and mourning their dead, were off their horses before the wounded men hit the ground and, rushing the Circassian houses, manhandled the amateur riflemen out, killing 36 of them on the spot. The column was not menaced again.

On 1 April, the Amman force reached the valley, followed by the Es Salt force the next day. 'Thank God it was warm,' said my father. 'We pulled the saddles off the horses and turned them loose. Since the night before we crossed the Jordan River, they had not had their saddles off for more than 24 hours all told, nor had one good square feed and of course, they had been as cold and wet as we were. They are marvellous creatures and we love 'em.'

Casualties for Amman were:

	MOUNTED DIVISION AND CAMEL BRIGADE	BRITISH INFANTRY
Killed	118	59
Wounded	551	347
Missing	55	70
Total for all		**1200**

Ryrie's brigade felt most keenly the apparent capture of young Lieutenant Ridgway of the 6th Regiment, for this ended the splendid record of not one Light Horse officer falling into enemy hands since crossing the Suez Canal. The Turks did not report his capture, however, and when in September the ANZACs returned to Amman and took it, 2nd Brigade officers conducted searches for Ridgway. His body was found where he had fallen at the head of his squadron. Pride struggled with sadness: the unique achievement was intact, but at too great a cost.

Nat Barton's war ended at Amman. The medical officer of the 5th Regiment made 'an excellent temporary job' of his wounds and, unusually, he found 'a couple of stages on the camel [cacolet] … really quite comfortable'. His young brother Denis of the 6th Regiment, unwounded, saw him at about this time, presumably before he set out.

He reached the field ambulance at Es Salt after midnight, was operated on next day and 'fixed up in a Thomas sling'. He then travelled in a sand cart for over six hours 'over frightfully rough roads' coming down the mountain and 'I must say I was about done by the end of the trip and was very pettish at being sent on at once in a motor ambulance'. He had had a companion in the sand cart with an abdominal wound who 'had an awful time but was very brave — he died the next morning, I believe'.

Nat was given a cup of cocoa and a whiskey and soda as inducement, felt better and 'had a comfortable ride in the ambulance' after all to another casualty clearing station, presumably in the Jordan Valley. From there, he went by three stages to Jerusalem, then in more fits and starts to Enab and Ludd. Here he was put on a train to El Arish, then Kantara and finally arrived in Cairo after ten days in all.

Nat was sufficiently recovered to be embarked for Australia on 12 July 1918.

Australians of the Camel Corps. 2ND/14TH L.H.REGT [QMI] MUSEUM ENOGGERA

NINETEEN

Allenby adjusts; fortunes of war in the Jordan

Allenby had been warned by the War Office in November 1917 about the anticipated spring offensive of Ludendorff on the Western Front, which according to the historian Basil Liddell Hart, 'in grandeur of scale, of awe and of destruction, surpassed any other in the World War'. One hundred and ninety-four German infantry divisions hurled themselves at the British on 21 March 1918, threatening irrecoverable defeat, and the wonder is that the War Office waited until the onslaught started before calling for reinforcements from Palestine.

Allenby was obliged to surrender two infantry divisions and the infantry strength of two more. They were the 52nd Lowlanders and the 74th (Yeomanry) Division to fight dismounted, together with another nine Yeomanry regiments. General Barrow's Yeomanry Division was therefore broken up within a year, but Indian cavalry, idle a long time in France, were sent to Barrow as replacements and, with one British regiment per brigade, became his 4th Cavalry Division. Allenby was also stripped of another ten British infantry battalions, but two good Indian infantry divisions were sent to Palestine from Mesopotamia. More Indian battalions filled up some remaining gaps, but these were very raw and needed training.

Eventually, there was a net gain in mounted troops, but again the Indian lancer regiments needed training. They were good horsemen, however, with their light build and thin legs, and moreover were mounted on Australian Walers, long supplied to the Indian Army. Chauvel's Desert Mounted Corps reconstituted itself as the 4th and 5th Cavalry Divisions, the Australian Mounted Division and the ANZAC Mounted Division.

The accretion over time of 100,000 Indian horse and foot formed a colourful addition to Allenby's force and were to earn their place in the firing line. There was also a French cavalry regiment of Spahis, excellent troops, with finely-bred and enduring Arab horses and Barbs from North Africa which, however, could not keep pace with the Walers of the Australian brigade to which they were attached. Later, Algerian Tirailleurs and Chasseurs d'Afrique, all good cavalrymen, arrived.

At the same time, the British naval and military air forces of the Royal Flying Corps were amalgamated to become the Royal Air Force and its Palestine Brigade was Allenby's to dispose of. It was made up of two wings divided into seven squadrons, one of which was Australian. The Bristol fighter aircraft maintained their superiority over the German machines and there was a 'giant' Handley-Page bomber, flown by ex-Light Horseman Captain Ross Smith, a modern marvel of its time that could carry sixteen 112 pound bombs and stay airborne for eight hours. Allenby's complete ascendency in the air war was assured.

But the vast reorganisation of his ground forces and their need for training dictated that his own projected spring offensive of 1918 be postponed to the autumn; and such training could best proceed if the Turks were kept occupied by his seasoned troops in the Jordan Valley, well away from his main concentrations west of Jerusalem. General Chaytor was given command of all Jordan Valley defences and the ANZACs bore the brunt of these operations and the ordeal of the summer months.

In the days soon after Amman, the enemy ventured in considerable numbers to eastwards of the Ghoraniye bridgehead, that is, on the East Bank, and extended upriver from Ghoraniye for about four miles. He was clearly more aggressive after his success at Amman and apparently seeking another test of strength. The ANZACs concentrated on building up their defences. The whitish clay of the bare ground they dug up was already dry and crumbling to choking dust, giving portent of trials to come, but when the work was finished the riflemen all had good, clear fields of fire.

The mud hills peculiar to the valley overlooked exposed flats and gave good protection, but the line securing the Wady Auja, the valley's permanent supply of good water, extended north for some miles and the defensive posts on these hills were scattered and not connected up. The Wady Nimrin, a clear and sparkling little stream, also traversed the mud floor in a narrow cut and meandered into the Jordan just north of Ghoraniye.

Cox's 1st Brigade covered the East Bank and approaches, while the Camel Brigade and the 6th and 7th Light Horse Regiments covered the West Bank. Musallabeh, a rough hump of mud 400 yards long and 200 wide, marked the northern extremity of the defended ground on the West Bank, with the 1st Battalion of Camels (Australian) dug in on top of it.

Before dawn on 11 April, the Turks attacked at both places. At Ghoraniye, the 1st Brigade's regiments plus the 5th Light Horse of the 2nd Brigade were entrenched on either side of the Wady Nimrin and the Turks advanced right up its bed. Daylight disclosed successive lines of infantry about 1000 strong, pressing forward. Colonel Bourne's 2nd Light Horse Regiment was at the centre of the defence and astride both banks of the wady, and so fought the engagement right through, with support from other regiments on either side, as opportunity offered.

Bourne reserved his fire until the Turks were within 100 yards of his barbed wire, then felled them at close range. By 6 am, two 60-pounders and three Royal Horse Artillery batteries had joined in, but though they suffered wholesale casualties, the Turks were stiffened by German officers and would not give up. The day became very hot and so effective was the Australian fire that the Turks, pinned under the banks of the wady and tantalised by its cold, clear water trickling past, were unable to reach it except at the risk of being shot. Several attempts ended this way before they gave up.

Brigadier General Cox sent the 3rd Regiment out to ride round the Turks in an attempt to envelop them, but their ranks reached right back to the foothills and the endeavour was not practicable. However, under cover of night, the enemy withdrew, leaving 150 dead and 500 wounded on the ground. The 2nd also took 90 prisoners, for the loss of six killed and seventeen wounded.

The simultaneous attack on Musallabeh began with a heavy artillery barrage on the hill, while enemy infantry crept up the wadys running down its sides in darkness. At 5 am the barrage was lifted and the Turks rushed the Australians from concealment, within grenade-throwing range.

The Camels' only zone of effective fire was from the forward slope of the big knoll, and as soon as they showed themselves above cover they were shot at. An intricate battle of wits, as much as bullets, was waged for three hours. So close were the Turks that when the Camels ran out of ammunition they threw stones at them. At 8 am the attack died away, but it was renewed again hotly in the late afternoon. By this time, however, a British company from the No. 2 Battalion had joined the Australians and the Turkish attack was abandoned at nightfall, at the cost of 170 dead for seventeen of the Camels.

Steadiness, good fire discipline and straight shooting had won both encounters, which were just such sharp little exercises as the Australians needed to eradicate the lingering and bitter aftertaste of Amman. The actions also demonstrated the correctness of Allenby's hypothesis that, if the water of Auja and Nimrin was denied to the enemy, he could not stay in the Jordan Valley.

There were already Indian troops in the firing line and Richardson says that, after Musallabeh, the 7th Regiment was relieved by the Hyderabad Lancers. As well, the 1st Light Horse Brigade was reinforced by a battalion of Alwar infantry. The Indians were quick and eager learners and delighted to be in a hot climate again after France. In the line, they had a keener eye for movement than their mentors, but at night the white men could better identify any movement by sounds.

After their failures in the valley, the Turks built up an infantry force of 5000 at Shunet Nimrin, about five miles up the ascending route to Es Salt. The Arabs continued to importune the British for more action east of the Jordan and it seemed possible that, if Es Salt could be taken as quickly and cleanly as it had been before by Chauvel's mounted troops, the Turkish force at Nimrin could be sandwiched, then attacked from the valley floor and annihilated or captured, with all its guns. As well, if the British could hold the Amman–Es Salt country until the Arabs arrived from the south, the Turks would be denied a good harvest, just then maturing in Gilead.

Allenby decided to make such an attempt in mid-May. Chauvel was appointed to command it and hastily established his headquarters in the wilderness near Talat ed Dumm. His force was to consist of the ANZAC and Australian Mounted Divisions, a brigade of Yeomanry, two regiments of Indian cavalry, Shea's Londoners, an Indian infantry brigade and a good deal of artillery, including a siege battery. Hodgson's Australian Mounted Division was on the coast and marched across Judea to the Jordan Valley. It was their first acquaintance with the place and Major Jack Davies gives his impressions to his wife:

> We are camped about 1 mile from Jericho and three from the place in the river where our Lord was baptised. Lots of places of interest hereabouts, though I don't think I care to live here long. The northern end of the Dead Sea is visible from where I sit. It looks very beautiful in the moonlight, we don't know anything about our plans for the future ...
>
> They say the Jordan Valley is a terrible place, being 1,200 feet below sea level of the Mediterranean, but today has not been so terrible so far, though ... the dust here is nothing to what it will be in a week.
>
> Jim, as I told you, had a spill, I have heard nothing since, but Colonel Farr told me he was quite all right and walked nearly 1,000 yards after he got out of the plane which was smashed beyond redemption, he reckoned he'd be OK and flying again in a couple of days.
>
> Must stop now, darling, will write again when I get a table fixed up, love ever your Jack.

Jim was Mildred's brother, Lieutenant James Traill, originally of the 1st Light Horse Regiment, then at Gallipoli a divisional signaller, later still of the Camel Corps, and from October 1917 observer with No. 1 Squadron, Australian Flying Corps. Traill, along with two other pilots and observers of the squadron, was awarded the Distinguished Flying Cross for shooting down four enemy aircraft on 23 September 1918. The German pilots were attacking Arab partisans near Deraa: Lawrence appealed to Allenby, the Australian aircraft were dispatched and from that time the enemy aircraft were not seen again.

By mid-April, operational plans were complete and all forces were assembled. On 18 April, a feint was made at Shunet Nimrin. The ANZAC

Mounted Division rode out from the Ghoraniye bridgehead and made a strong demonstration against Turkish defences there and in the foothills on either side. The object of this, according to Allenby's orders, was 'to inflict losses on the enemy and to convey the impression that we are about to advance again to Amman'. To lend more credence to the feint, an infantry brigade was marched across the plain and all available artillery fired on the foothills. The Turks, resisting the ANZACs stoutly and from trenches, inflicted more losses than they received. Towards nightfall, all troops were withdrawn.

This move was inexplicable. Allenby did indeed 'convey the impression that we are about to advance to Amman', and the Turks thereupon did everything possible to stop him. Shunet Nimrin became a hive of activity with reinforcements pouring in and fortifications made, then when all was ready they settled down to wait. Allenby could hardly have dealt a greater blow to Chauvel's chances of success. What was in his mind, only he knew: such records as survive indicate only that Chauvel didn't like the operation. It has been speculated that Allenby had not yet made up his mind to launch a second incursion into Gilead and even that he contemplated something different — which might then have given point to the feint, as deception. But what happened next indicated that this could not have been so.

On 23 April, emissaries from the high-powered Beni Sakr tribe of Arabs, who held the country south of Amman, claimed to have 7000 fighting irregulars concentrated at Madeba, twenty miles south-west of Amman and east of the Dead Sea. They proposed a joint expedition to Moab, in which the Beni Sakr would advance northwards at the same time and link up with the British troops on the Moab plateau between Amman and Es Salt. They would also cross and secure the Ain es Sir track, which Ryrie's 2nd Brigade and the Camels had struggled up so desperately towards Amman. But the Arabs said their time was limited because their grazing at Madeba was nearly exhausted and the operation had to be mounted before 4 May.

Allenby was attracted to this combined operation and, to suit the Beni Sakr, brought his operation forward to the end of April. How seriously he took the Arabs may possibly be judged by the fact that there appears to be no British official record of their proposal and Lawrence, as well as other British officers who might have been concerned, were ignorant of it. It seems to have stayed on the 'old boy' net. A fancy comes to mind of the Commander-in-Chief saying to himself with a slight muscular reflex which in others would be realised as a smile, 'Well and good — if it happens'.

In some confusion and uncertainty, the die was cast.

My father wrote on Jericho's Jordan Hotel notepaper that he was not living there, unfortunately, but had souvenired the paper and was enclosing a letter written some time ago which he had not had a chance to forward (his long account of the Battle of Amman). He added:

Es Salt town with the road to Amman at right. 2ND/14TH L.H.REGT [QMI] MUSEUM ENOGGERA

Have got a bit of news which may please you, I have been awarded a small decoration, the DCM, for our last bit of fighting in the hills east of the Jordan, see enclosed.

There were a couple of others won in the regiment and I believe the fellows were invested with their colours yesterday, I was not present as I am temporarily on a detached job so when this is finished and I rejoin the regiment, mine will be forthcoming …

One little request, when writing to me now, please omit the tail to my name, don't make much out of little by putting DCM when addressing envelopes, that is only swank.

Fond son Jack

Later: Am uncertain now whether my medal is DCM or MM, of the two, I fancy the former.

Later still, MM.

TWENTY

The Es Salt raid

In the event, Allenby's orders for the operation were ambitious. They directed Chauvel, having consolidated his hold on the Moab plateau from Es Salt to the Jordan River (at Jisr ed Damieh) and established control of the country to the south of Amman as far as Madeba, to 'at once prepare for operations northwards, with a view to advancing rapidly on Deraa'. Deraa was 80 miles further on, even a few miles north of the Sea of Galilee. The Commander-in-Chief said bold and rapid marches must be made and that it was 'probable that during these operations, considerable help may be counted upon from the Arabs and the closest touch must be maintained with them'.

Allenby has been criticised for such ambitious thinking, but with his troops being sucked into the Western Front and reeling under the German offensive, his mind was on a global plane and trying to devise a scheme that could knock Turkey out of the war. With Deraa captured, it would be another short step to Damascus, then Aleppo and the ultimate possibilities. But Chauvel had to produce the ways and means, and at the final conferences had the plan at least broken down into components, each dealing with some objectives. In this way, conditions would be implicit, such as if and when the line Jisr ed Damieh–Es Salt–Amman is consolidated, and so on. One thing at a time.

The incursion to Amman was always called a 'raid', with that word's connotation of withdrawal afterwards. The Es Salt incursion of 1918 had 'raid' thrust upon it in the history books. There had not been any intention to withdraw, but rather to open up a large and ambitious front. The German General Liman von Sanders fought it for the enemy and gave it a chapter called 'The Second Battle of the Jordan' in his memoirs.

Chauvel's tactical plan was the simplest he could make to cover complex terrain and contingencies. Shea's 60th Infantry Division was to make the frontal assault on Shunet Nimrin at first light on 30 April. At the same time, Grant's 4th Brigade of the Australian Mounted Division were to gallop up the East Bank from the Ghoraniye crossing straight to Damieh, to prevent the Turks using the Damieh crossing to reinforce Nimrin.

Wilson's 3rd Brigade of the Australian Mounted were to follow Grant closely, to assist in capturing Damieh if necessary, then to take the Damieh–Es Salt track and ride with all speed to occupy Es Salt. The 5th Mounted (Yeomanry) Brigade, following Wilson, was also to strike at Es Salt, but via the lower Umm esh Shert track. Having won the town, General Hodgson was to send a mounted force down the main road to Shunet Nimrin, to sandwich the Turks between the Australians and Londoners and cut off their retreat.

The first move was made on the night of 29–30 April. The 7th Regiment of the ANZAC Mounted Division, with a squadron of Hyderabad Lancers, a machine-gun section, a battalion of Patiala infantry and eight guns of the Royal Horse Artillery, all under Colonel Onslow, were to feint at Turkish positions to the south of the Londoners' line and east of the Hajla crossing. Onslow's force attacked in the early hours and if the amount of smoke, noise and dust generated was a measure of whether it drew the Turks' attention away from the main assaults, namely the Londoners on Shunet Nimrin and the 4th Brigade's gallop up the river flat to Damieh, it must have had some success.

The rest of the ANZAC Mounted were to follow the Yeomanry Brigade to the Umm esh Shert–Es Salt track junction and Onslow was to rejoin the ANZACs there after his feint.

When the Australian mounted troops clattered across the familiar pontoon bridge at Ghoraniye and out through the British perimeter, they passed by the Londoners drawn up in fours, waiting to move on Shunet Nimrin. It was one of those 'poor bloody infantry' moments. Ian Jones, in his book *The Australian Light Horse*, quotes a trooper: 'We smothered and half-choked them with the fine white clay dust of the valley. There were no exchanges of greeting. We rode by in silence. But we were thinking hard and we thought, although our gallop on the plain under the Turkish guns at dawn would be no joy ride, we were lucky not to be those little Cockney infantrymen.'

Just before dawn, with the 4th Regiment leading, Grant's brigade set off along the Jordan flat. As dawn broke, they heard a burst of bombing on their right, followed by machine-gun fire, then the noise built into the continuous cacophony of small arms fire. The Londoners were at it. They had achieved complete surprise with silent rushes, but the Turks were awake and ready soon enough, in their excellent defences. The Londoners were trying to get to close quarters, but taking severe casualties in their attempts.

Grant had fifteen miles to go to Damieh, on a river flat offering no serious physical obstacles. The brigade was quickly extended in artillery formation, on a wide front. A landmark known as Red Hill lay alongside the route, three miles beyond the Umm esh Shert track junction, where encroaching foothills from both sides narrowed the plain.

Grant increased the pace to the trot, but at once the enemy gunners on Red Hill, alerted by the uproar at Nimrin, detected him and shrapnel started bursting over the scattered squadrons. Instantly, they went up to the gallop and each troop and individual drew further apart until there seemed to be no longer any formation. These horses had made the charge at Beersheba and, with who knows what memories and prompts stirring, became excited and fought for their heads. Nose bags, bundles of feed and rations, firewood, quart pots, spare bandoliers and assorted canteen stores bounced and pounded on their bodies until even the most expert knots gave way and the 4th's passage was strewn with every kind of Light Horseman's possession. However, the effectiveness of galloping horses through shell fire was proved again: over about five miles, only six men were killed and seventeen wounded. Grant's horse was one of the first killed, but he was able to remount at once. The men christened this section 'Igorree Flat', after a corruption of the Arabic term for hurry up.

The Damieh–Es Salt track was reached and crossed. By then, the shell fire had been turned on Wilson's following 3rd Brigade and the 4th reined up near their objective, the Damieh bridge, in miraculously good order again. Grant pushed out his regiments towards the river and the bridge and waited anxiously for news of their progress.

The regiments found the country rougher, with higher mounds and deeper gullies than on the valley floor, which worked against forming the best sort of line; and gathering Turkish resistance was holding them off the bridge itself. Trying to get round the Turks but only 900 strong dismounted, they had to spread thinly over eight miles and were forced to check a mile and a half from the river. There they were not in sight of the bridge and could not have resisted enemy troops crossing from the west; and they were exposed on both flanks.

But in essentials, Grant had gained his objectives, and considered he was in a position to resist all but an overwhelming enemy advance. Brigadier General Wilson's 3rd Brigade arrived at 6.30 am as planned, the two leaders conferred and Grant gave his assessment that he did not need the 3rd's assistance. Wilson departed to negotiate the sharply ascending and difficult track to Es Salt, according to his orders.

Grant had been allotted all three batteries of his division's artillery and they fired at Damieh bridge, but at extreme range and without effect. The day wore on without much development, except that the regimental leaders became increasingly aware that their vulnerable, fragmented line was not going to change for the better; rather, if the Turks concentrated and drove forward they could easily overcome the Australians, especially on the left. Grant himself was now uneasy. The gravest potential threat came from the dominating Red Hill, behind which, it was learned later, the Turks were throwing another pontoon crossing over the Jordan.

Late in the afternoon, Chauvel drove up to see Grant. The brigadier canvassed the threats to his situation. At the base of Red Hill, he had two Light Horse squadrons, but the largest gap of all stretched from them to Bailey's 11th Regiment, three miles distant. Grant asked for another regiment to cover this gap and Chauvel appreciated the danger, but after referring back to his headquarters said no more troops could be spared.

Why this was problematical is hard to see. The huge concentration of the ANZAC Mounted Division and the 5th Mounted (Yeomanry) Brigade was three miles south astride the Umm esh Shert track, ready to support the Londoners' left if possible and waiting to advance on Es Salt. It would have seemed not inconvenient to have sent a regiment to Grant's aid —

especially since the ANZACs were under the orders of the Australian Mounted at the time.

On his departure, Chauvel took Grant's brigade under his direct control. Outposts in the line having reported increasing movement of enemy troops, he ordered Grant to withdraw his northernmost posts to concentrate about the Damieh–Es Salt track, until attacked. And he added Grant was not to 'compromise' himself holding the track.

During the night, it was discovered that the Turks had completed their new pontoon crossing behind Red Hill, exposing Grant more surely to attack: but while his horsemen could retire east if necessary, his three batteries of artillery were now in rocky, chaotic ground and had no apparent way east, or south, out of danger.

Wilson's 3rd Brigade meanwhile suffered the vicissitudes of climbing the Moab plateau en route to Es Salt. The track rose sharply and the men had to lead their horses in single file as the ANZACs had done. Wheeled transport was out of the question again, but the Bing Boys' six guns of the Hong Kong and Singapore Mountain Battery, packed on 360 camels with all their ammunition, stuck to them.

Gullett says that the 3rd Brigade's ride on Es Salt was 'one of the cleanest and most decisive pieces of Light Horse work in the campaign'. After the climb, mounted progress on the plateau became easy. The ground was firm and the weather fine. The route lay through burgeoning crops of wheat, vines in tender leaf and wild flowers. Horses snatched green mouthfuls along the way.

The brigade rode on serenely for seven miles, then the screen encountered a troop of enemy cavalry. A brush at close quarters resulted in the shooting and capture of some, but others escaped and, a little further on, the alerted Turks were discovered in strength. They were manning some sangars on a high ridge to the left and more were seen on two hills close to the ridge.

Wilson was out of touch with his division, but his signallers had intercepted a radio message from Chauvel to Hodgson saying that Es Salt must be taken that night. The 3rd's advance had been delayed by the slow climbing of the camels and it was now late in the afternoon.

The brigade attacked all three positions. A determined dismounted assault broke the Turks' hold on the right-hand hill and the Light

Horsemen soon had cross-fire pouring into the sangars from it. Another assault on the other hill carried it, with the assistance of the Hong Kong and Singapore Battery. Three of their guns then bombarded the sangar, and a bayonet charge by the 9th Regiment culminated in hand-to-hand fighting behind the stone shelters where some enemy, including German officers and men, fought to a grisly finish.

Wilson had had the 8th Regiment formed up and standing by for a mounted charge on the town. As soon as he was confident that the two hills and the sangar were securely held, he signalled the 8th by dipping his lance with its red brigade pennant. Purposefully, the 8th trotted forward.

By the time they reached Es Salt they were at a full gallop, and without pause rode headlong into the place. The horses scrabbled and scraped round twisted streets on cobbles worn smooth over centuries and there was an uproar of hoofbeats, shouting and shooting as astonished Turks and Germans were shot down or capitulated. The invaders swarmed all around the town, only drawing rein when they met another troop coming the other way. A German officer said they 'galloped their horses where no-one else would have ridden at all'. In a matter of moments, the 8th had overridden and captured 200 enemy and large quantities of war material. The Turks were moved to announce by way of an intercepted message: 'Es Salt has been captured by the reckless and dashing gallantry of the Australian cavalry'.

Superlatives about the Light Horse, like advertising, may wear thin with repetition, but none had greater integrity than those propounded by the enemy.

Colonel Olden, in his history of the 10th Light Horse Regiment, which was following hard on the heels of the 8th, says that night in Es Salt was 'the weirdest and most uncanny that it had ever been the lot of the regiment to experience'. The town was in darkness, illuminated only by the moon through a bank of clouds, but showing the dead, stripped by the Bedouins, lying on the cobbles. The silence was broken by the howling of dogs and the groans of the wounded and an occasional gunshot — a native 'settling a long-standing grievance with his neighbour'.

At that long day's end, Chauvel had checks and balances to weigh. Wilson had gained Es Salt and the Yeomanry Brigade, having advanced along the Umm esh Shert track, were due to arrive there the next morning. Wilson was expected to continue his march another seven miles towards

Amman, but the two squadrons of the 10th he dispatched were strongly held a mile short of this objective.

The infantry assault on Shunet Nimrin had failed. With all their spirit and initial surprise, Shea's men could not surmount a piece of naked plain behind which over 4000 of the enemy had them in their sights from steep escarpments. Again and again on the first day and those that followed, the Londoners sacrificed themselves for nothing. It was Second Gaza re-visited. 'The Turks sat in their redoubts and shot the division to pieces,' wrote Cyril Falls. Overwhelming numbers and a strong flanking movement could have prevailed, but as it was, the only prospect of victory was to take the Turks in rear from the Moab plateau — as had been provided for in the plan. But early attempts by Shea to use the ANZAC Mounted Division for this had been defeated by the chaotic terrain of such a descent and well-entrenched Turks.

Grant's task of holding Damieh was vital to any improvement, but how long could he last?

Only the Arabs could make a difference. Where were they?

Instead of securing the Ain es Sir track and going northwards to join the troops as promised, they held back until the stalemate of the Shunet Nimrin battle seemed in prospect. After the initial failure to seize the first objective, and without waiting for the outcome at Es Salt, they broke camp at Madeba and drifted away. Chauvel, of course, did not know and hoped still for some show of strength, if not much else.

Instead, on the morning of 1 May, disaster struck. A small force of Light Horse and Camels, the latter operating on the West Bank, had deployed at daylight with the aim of seizing the Damieh bridge. They were deflected from this by the sight of large Turkish concentrations across the river, beyond the reach of Grant's artillery. Enemy cavalry were also sighted to the north.

Grant had only 900 rifles. At 6.30 am, he and both regimental commanders surveyed their positions from a hilltop near brigade headquarters. Both Colonels Cameron and Bourchier believed the enemy had strongly reinforced his bridgehead overnight and that, if he attacked determinedly, their long, thin Light Horse lines could offer no effective resistance. Grant decided to pull their lines in a few more miles southward, the better to concentrate on the Damieh–Es Salt track.

Just as the three officers walked down from the hill, the storm, so long in coming, broke. Ian Jones says:

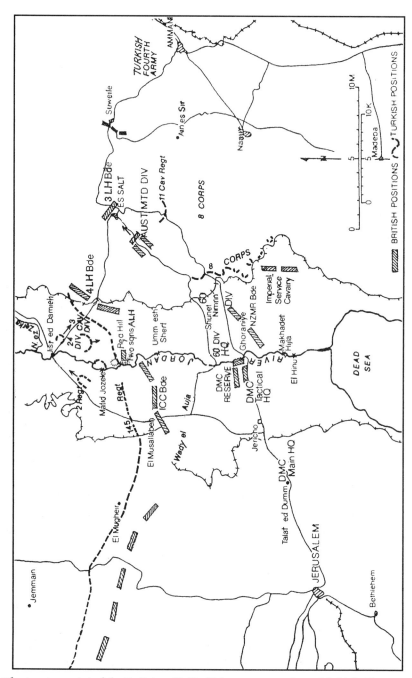

The turning point of the Es Salt raid: Turkish counterattack on 4th Light Horse Brigade at 8 am, 1 May 1918.

Soon after 7 am, there was an explosion of machine-gun and rifle fire from the clay hills flanking the Jordan and a huge line of Turkish infantry moved out into the open on a 7,000 metre front. They advanced with parade ground precision, about 10 metres apart, in unusual dark grey or blue uniforms and wearing German-style steel helmets. A second line followed, then a third and a fourth. Grant's artillery opened fire and blew gaps in the line. But men from a following line moved up to fill each gap, with almost eerie discipline. By now another five lines had emerged — nine waves of Yilderim storm troops — about 6,000 men in all. Turkish horse artillery batteries galloped out into the open, the waves of infantry started to run and enemy cavalry speared out on the Light Horsemen's right flank.

'Yilderim' is Turkish for lightning. The Yilderim Army Group had been formed in mid-1917 with the aim of recapturing Baghdad, then under British control. It was assisted and augmented by the Germans and, though untested in battle, had acquired the reputation of elite and highly-trained shock troops. When the Baghdad ambitions receded in the light of continuing enemy reverses, the Turks started to commit their Yilderim troops to the Palestine fighting.

They had happened upon Grant. Wave after wave of infantry made bold frontal attacks, more infantry smashed down on the open right flank and their cavalry detoured into the hills, trying to cut in behind the Australians. The brigade must retire, the only question being, could they do so in good order? At 8 am, the Turks, having worked out Grant's weakest spot, struck south for the gap between the Australian left and Red Hill. Another force crossed the new pontoon bridge to attack the two weak Light Horse squadrons still deployed there, unable to influence their destiny and now fighting for their lives.

In half an hour, the enemy, having advanced down the river flat, were closing on the Es Salt track. Grant's artillery and machine-guns mauled them at ever shorter range, checking the advance for an hour, but all the while the Turks were building up fresh battalions for renewed assaults. At 10 am, the two squadrons at Red Hill were overwhelmed and swept south, still intact and with their machine-guns still enfilading the enemy force coming down the river flat.

Then the Australian right was forced back onto the Es Salt track and, according to Gullett, 'Disorder was now showing in Grant's command'. The enemy was so close that contact between different sections in the line could not be maintained and, according to a Trooper G.T. Birkbeck, whose account is quoted by Bill Gammage in *The Broken Years*, some of the 4th Brigade got the order, 'every man for himself', became demoralised and left the guns without escorts or horses. Order must have been restored quickly, however.

But the guns were in great peril. The enemy were closing on their left and on their front. The ground was suitable for artillery only towards the river and then south, but this meant marching into the Turks' heaviest concentrations and certain destruction. Grant had to order one battery to withdraw eastwards and with struggling teams and much manhandling all except one of these guns, which overturned, reached safety. The other two batteries continued firing fiercely until 1130, when the whole brigade with its limbers were ordered to retire. The limber teams were promptly shot down and the limbers had to be abandoned. It was clear that the two remaining batteries had also to be abandoned along with the Damieh–Es Salt track. Grant gave the despairing order and took the 4th and 12th Regiments into the hills.

He could still have defended the guns from the hills, but left them because he faced a disaster infinitely greater than the loss of two artillery batteries: the Turks' advance between Red Hill and his left was now rapidly approaching the track leading from Umm esh Shert to Es Salt and, as it had turned out, this now was the only escape route for all four of the mounted brigades on Gilead. Seized of this stark fact, the two regiments must force march south and grab the Shert track before the enemy reached it; and Bailey's 11th Regiment, still on the river flat, had to resist the Turks' advance until it was done.

Gullett describes the retreat-turned-to-advance of the 4th and 12th: 'many little columns of led horses in single file were picking their way along the side of steep ranges. All ridges and gorges ran east and west; the route of the horsemen was south ... It was a grim race between the Turks marching on the level plain and the men leading their horses on the heights.'

Ian Jones quotes Trooper Alf Hird on the struggle over these sharp limestone ridges: 'I shall never forget the horror of that ride, slipping, sliding, crawling from ledge to ledge. A slip and a horse would topple over and fall for perhaps a hundred feet. At times, we had to force them to drop from ledge to ledge like goats. Here and there, one would miss a ledge and that would be the end of that particular horse.'

On the flat, the 11th Regiment fought delaying actions, dismounting to form a firing line until outflanked or forced back, then galloping south to a new position, dismounting and fighting again. This kind of fighting normally progressed by one regiment or squadron passing through another in 'lay backs', with each unit covering the other in turn, but the 11th had no such luxury because it was fighting on its whole front. Finally, it was driven to a position in the foothills east of Red Hill — and there, men of the 4th Regiment began to converge on the 11th's right flank and to reinforce the firing line. A comparatively strong position became established and the enemy was checked. To the immense relief of all who had struggled through this nightmarish retreat with its unthinkable consequences, the Shert track was saved.

The War Diary of the 12th Regiment covers the fighting of 1–3 May on one page, averaging just seven entries per day. On 1 May, it reads:

> 0730 Enemy were observed in large bodies on the side of the
>   Jordan River.
> 0830 Enemy attack develops. C Squadron ordered to reinforce left
>   flank, A Squadron find escort for machine-guns.
> 0930 B Squadron commenced to withdraw to hills in rear under
>   heavy fire.
> 1400 Regiment withdraws to a line 7 miles south.
> 1800 Night outpost line established. Defences built and dug in.

The commander of B Squadron, Jack Davies, wrote to his wife after Es Salt:

> I am well and have got a whole skin ... was not at the start, as you know if you got my letter written from Jerusalem; only arrived on the field about 1000 [on 1 May] since then its been stoush, rearguard dig then withdrawal by night ... we got back here [Jordan Valley] at 3 am this morning [4 May] and very glad too, we were in a pretty hot spot for about four days with a real good chance of the Division going to Constantinople ... we are resting at present, we had 20 casualties and

were most fortunate, the 11th and 4th [Regiments] are much worse off. Don't worry, darling, Providence thought fit to pull us out of that hole and we must be thankful.

What detached duty delayed Jack Davies' arrival at the front on 1 May is unknown, but he preserved a report of his activities on that day in the family archive. It is a dense, tense narrative, not easy to follow, but it is worth reproducing in part for its dramatic character and depiction of the urgency with which he and all about him tried to avert the looming calamity as they dealt with continuing and rapid changes for the worse. When Davies arrived, his regiment was already embarked on the dreadful flanking march south through the limestone crags, to establish a last-ditch defence of the Umm esh Shert track before the Turks seized it, and Davies operated independently for most of the day:

'At 1030, in company with four other ranks, proceeding to join 12th Light Horse. I met two motor cyclist Despatch Riders who informed me that the 4th Light Horse Brigade was in danger of being cut off.'

The despatch riders were looking for a signal station where they could clear traffic to Divisional Corps Headquarters. Davies showed the way, then:

I ordered Mr Bennett [possibly a senior NCO] to follow … them with a message to Div Corps from me, warning that the 4th L H Bde was in difficulty: they had endeavoured to get a priority message through while I was at the signal station, which was interrupted by bad insulation.

[Then] I met an armoured car returning with 2 officers, one wounded, [who] was getting ammunition. He informed me that another armoured car had been lost, falling into a gully.

Pushing on [further west] for half a mile, I met a wounded man riding who reported enemy within 200 yards from the foothills, when he left about one hour before. Another half mile in the direction of foothills, I met a section [four men] at 1100. I ordered these men to join my own [section] under Sergeant MacLean, [who I told] to keep to a low stony ridge and gully. The enemy was at this time advancing east along a gully, 80 yards from a stony knob held by [another] troop under Sergeant McInnes.

I then ordered MacLean to prepare to withdraw to a hill … 200 yards in rear overlooking the position he then occupied; and I would go up the hill and collect any available rifles [to cover] his withdrawal, as I could see horsemen riding south along it, 4–500 yards from MacLean.

Before reaching the riflemen, I saw General Grant and reported to him that MacLean would be withdrawing. [But] the Gunners told me he must hold on at all costs and that I was to [organise the supply] of all available ammunition.

I immediately galloped back to MacLean and ordered him back [to his original position], then … I met Mr Francis with a section of MacLean's troop. Francis had gone to see [report to?] General Grant. I immediately indicated the position they would have to take up down the hill.

I next met Massie coming down with 30 rifles and sent him to assist the guns in [map reference]. Seeing another body of horsemen further up the hill, I went [to them] to collect all available rifles, but found they were artillerymen without rifles, who had had to abandon their gun. I suggested to the officer in charge that he might be able to assist in extracting a gun which had overturned in a wady below … This officer took his team towards the gun.

I got to the firing line about [illegible]. Four machine guns, Massie and a Field Regiment [artillery] were in action at about [map reference].

Seeing another squadron on my right, I proceeded … to their position. Found some of B Squadron on the immediate left of the Machine Gun Section, with 2 troops of A to the right of them, and 1 and 4 Troop on right of [illegible]. Brigade HQ on top of stony knob.

I reported to Bde HQ these dispositions … On returning to the 12th Regiment, the 4th Regiment having withdrawn, I received orders for the 12th for withdrawal to take place in the order, Machine Guns, A, C, B Squadrons.

I withdrew … B Squadron in accordance with these orders to a position on Black Hill [map reference].

At 1800 … 11th Regiment took over this line, my squadron and remainder of Regiment took up a position in a wady … facing north-west [map reference].

The brigade held these positions until General Chaytor arrived with reinforcements.

Brigidier General W. Grant, 4th Brigade commander, Australian Mounted Division.

Chaytor had so far not taken part in the Es Salt action: except for a New Zealand regiment and two of Yeomanry, his brigades were under the commands of Shea and Hodgson. When Chauvel, whose telephone communication with Grant was cut, learned of the extreme gravity of the 4th Brigade's situation, he ordered Chaytor to take over the defence of the Jordan Valley from the north. Riding at once up the river flat with his three regiments and some armoured cars, Chaytor joined Grant in the position just east of Red Hill. The Light Horsemen were holding their ground at that stage, but Chaytor selected a better spot further south about a mile short of the Umm esh Shert track, to which all troops retired. They were strong enough now to hold on, and although the Turks followed the withdrawal they did not renew their assault that day. Chaytor's front was improved by vigorous trench-digging and sangar-building during the night.

Although Grant's casualties, apart from the deaths of horses, were only two killed and 51 wounded, his deliverance was marred by the loss of the nine guns — the only ones under control of Australian troops to be lost in the whole of World War I. The issue lingered: the British Army was uncompromising about saving guns and the War Office raised it with Allenby. He was critical of Grant's dispositions, saying the 'retreat was ably conducted, but the original plan of defence was faulty'. It was the old weakness of the left flank again. Allenby also blamed Chauvel for not stressing this danger to Grant adequately, and he conveyed his views to both officers. Grant's frustration at having asked precisely for another regiment to strengthen his left flank may be imagined, but he was also at fault in declining help from Wilson's brigade at the outset.

When 1 May ended, another assault by the Londoners on Shunet Nimrin had made no headway and Shea's force was reduced by a Yeomanry regiment and the Leicester Battery of artillery — both sent to join Chaytor. The Turks resumed their offensive on that front, increasing the pressure on the Shert track, while other Yilderim battalions surged up the Damieh–Es Salt track.

But news of the repulse at Damieh had not yet reached the British field commanders at Es Salt. General P.J.V. Kelly's 5th Mounted Brigade arrived there that morning to a good deal of light-hearted coarseness from Wilson's men, because the 5th had come arrayed for battle, unaware that the Australians had taken the place twelve hours earlier.

Following the 5th, the ANZACs reached the town and Ryrie's 2nd Light Horse Brigade was straightaway ordered by General Hodgson to capture Hill 2900, four miles due east. Ryrie found the hill unoccupied, and from there was well placed to close the Ain es Sir route to Amman, in case of a Turkish retreat from Nimrin in that direction.

Cox's 1st Brigade was deployed on the Shert track, to block any Turks escaping northward from Nimrin.

At last, the concentration of forces enabled General Hodgson to send the 5th Yeomanry down the main road to Nimrin, to attack the Turks in rear — the immediate object of taking Es Salt in the first place.

But it was all a mirage. Hodgson was still ignorant of the enemy break-through at Damieh. He believed his entrapment of the Turks to be complete.

Early in the afternoon, Wilson was directed to support Ryrie towards Hill 2900 and dispatched the 8th Regiment, leaving only two troops (40 men) of the 10th in reserve. Es Salt was unguarded from the west. Only then came news of the loss of the Damieh–Es Salt track and the enemy marching up on it in strength. Instantly, Hodgson's plans collapsed.

215

The two troops of the 10th were rushed out along the Damieh track, Ryrie was recalled to Es Salt and ordered to join the rear attack on Nimrin after the Yeomanry were held up some way short of the halfway point. Hodgson's words were, 'The road must be opened today'. Ryrie and Kelly conferred and decided that the Yeomanry should seize some high ground on their left and cover Ryrie's advance down the road. Cox's 1st Brigade were exhorted to get as far from Es Salt as possible down the Shert track, and hold it.

But in the face of enemy resistance at all points and the dislocating pinnacles and gorges of the country, little progress had been made by nightfall. The invaders were suddenly on the defensive, and during the night the Turks kept the pressure up. Wilson tried to encircle Es Salt with his 8th and 9th Regiments and part of the 10th, to guard against attack from any side by forces from both Damieh and Amman. But his manpower would only stretch so far.

The Turks had now to win very little ground in order to isolate the four mounted brigades in the hills. But Chauvel had not given up hope. He ordered Shea to renew his assault, and Hodgson to march every possible man down the main road to Nimrin the next morning.

At 2 am on 2 May, the Londoners resumed their self-immolation at Nimrin. The despairing business would have broken the spirit of lesser troops long ago, and this time they even made slight gains, but after two hours of bitter fighting they were again driven off.

With daylight, the 2nd Light Horse Brigade and the Yeomanry were still stalled on their descent towards Nimrin on the Es Salt road. Outflanking, mounted or dismounted, was impossible in the terrain: Kelly's Yeomanry were fighting on a front of little more than the road itself, and Ryrie's regiments could not get past them.

During the night, the Turkish threat from Amman took shape and Hodgson withdrew Ryrie's 7th Regiment from the Nimrin expedition to reinforce Wilson's thin line around Es Salt. Back went the regiment to the town for the third time. At 8 pm, the enemy attacked Colonel Todd's sector, held by composite squadrons of the 8th and 10th. In heavy mist, they charged to within twenty yards of the Australians, but were held off by Hotchkiss and rifle fire. Two more attacks were made, with similar results, then at first light the defenders leapt from cover and swept the Turks back with bombs and bayonets. They retired about 1000 yards and did not

Light Horse and British Yeomanry mingle in Es Salt on 2 May 1918. The Yeomanry arrived ready for battle to find the 8th Light Horse Regiment had stormed the place 12 hours earlier. AWM B00065

approach again that day. Their casualties were believed to have exceeded 1000 killed and wounded, while Australian losses were trifling.

In the late morning, Brigadiers General Ryrie and Kelly advised Hodgson that the country towards Nimrin 'was so difficult that they could not hope to reach their objectives much before dark' and they recommended that the attack be stopped.

Hodgson ordered them to continue.

Ryrie and Kelly repeated their advice and recommendation.

Hodgson again ordered them forward. However, a short time later, learning that the enemy was concentrating again on the Amman road, he proposed to Chauvel that both brigades be withdrawn for the defence of Es Salt.

This meant abandonment of the plan's prime objective, the seizure of Shunet Nimrin. Chauvel was not yet prepared to do it and said the two brigades must press on to Nimrin. But later, he agreed to sending the 5th Regiment to the immediate defence of Es Salt. That left Kelly's Yeomanry with only one regiment of Light Horse (6th) remaining, and between them they had no chance of moving on. Hodgson had nothing to offer him now, except the advice that he should not retire before dark.

It was three days since the mounted troops had crossed the Jordan and no supplies had reached them. Orders to live off the country were issued and the natives' cattle and produce were requisitioned by way of written

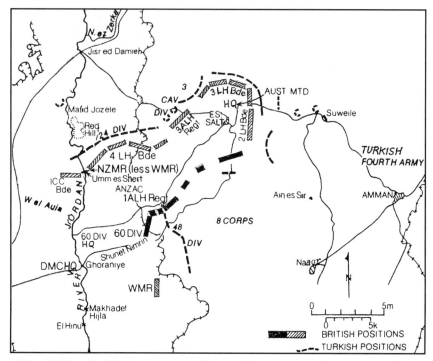

The withdrawal of the Desert Mounted Corps from Trans-Jordan, 1–4 May 1918.

orders from the British government. The horses found good grazing in the crops and Es Salt contained stores which, together with fat beef cattle, made enough to feed all hands.

There were two more attacks on the Es Salt defences: one outnumbered section gave ground, compelling a readjustment of the line. Then a force of 3000 enemy was detected advancing from Damieh. Hodgson had committed all his reserves, including batmen and cooks, and half the horse holders were in the firing line, leaving the rest handling eight horses each. The Londoners, though reinforced with a fresh brigade, failed again at Nimrin. The Yeomanry had at last been forced to abandon its rearward thrust and Chaytor's regiments were being fired on by increasing enemy around the Umm esh Shert escape track.

Not only had the entire enterprise failed, but the mounted brigades on Gilead faced terminal defeat. The Turks were ever-resurgent. Ammunition was running low, stores, especially medical stores, were short and no-one had slept for four days. Allenby drove down from Jerusalem to Chauvel's forward headquarters near Jericho. He listened quietly and could only acknowledge the facts. 'I can't lose half my mounted troops,' he said, and consented to a withdrawal. The orders went out at 4 pm on 3 May.

To deceive the enemy at all points, Hodgson's withdrawal would demand good discipline and alertness from troops sapped of vitality by four days of climbing and fighting in the ranges. The strain on the rearguards was the most severe, but they kept up the appearance of presence and pressure on the Turks while the main body assembled and moved off down the mountainside. Every wounded man who could sit up was put on his horse, but the worst cases had to make the descent in camel cacolets — on a track considered too rough for camels to climb with supplies. Many camels fell. One with two wounded rolled over and over downhill. One man was found in the darkness, but the other, whose arm had just been amputated in the Es Salt hospital, appeared in the Jordan Valley next morning riding a donkey.

Again, the retreat sparked panic in the Christian inhabitants of Es Salt. Hundreds more fled in a state of frenzy, snatching up what they could carry, and the horsemen had once more to take up these moaning, crying refugees stumbling down the goat track towards deliverance. That their terror was only too warranted was understood.

The 4th Brigade with Chaytor's men, still astride the Umm esh Shert escape route, held off enemy encroachments on three sides while the refugees and the rest of their own division went past, followed by the ANZAC Mounted and the Yeomanry. Both the 4th and 3rd Brigades had repulsed attacks to the last minute, then had the wry satisfaction of observing Turkish assaults on their positions after they had gone. When all had passed, the 4th followed down to the valley floor and the rearguard crossed the river to the West Bank just before midnight of the 4th. 'I have never seen a large body of men more exhausted than these were after that baksheesh Es Salt stunt,' said Trooper 'Chook' Fowler to Ian Jones. 'Most of the men were too exhausted to erect a sun shelter and were found [next morning] sleeping in the very hot sun.'

The Light Horse had lost 50 killed, 278 wounded and 37 missing, while Shea's infantry casualties were 1116. As usual, enemy losses were believed to be much greater, including 1000 prisoners brought down the track. But this did not offset an escape from disaster by the narrowest margin.

A.J. Hill further illuminates the workings of the Commander-in-Chief's mind through this 'raid'. Speaking of it, Chauvel used the word 'failure' to Allenby and he snapped back, 'Failure be damned! It has been a great success!' adding that he would explain later. Already, he had determined to launch his next all-out offence on the coast and to keep the attention of the enemy fixed on the wrong flank. He had done that at Amman and Es Salt and would keep it up all summer by activity in the Jordan Valley. But otherwise, the 'success' of Trans-Jordan operations was manifestly in the eye of the beholder. When his plans for the final offensive were revealed, they must surely have come as no surprise to Chauvel.

TWENTY-ONE

Jordan summer and Abu Tellul

'Summer' and 'valley' are romantic, poetic words. 'How Green was My Valley.' 'But come ye back when summer's in the meadow.' 'The Last Rose of Summer.' They conjure to the English, and those not English-born though with the legacy of language, smiling pastorals and long, expansive days after a pinched, constraining winter.

In the Jordan Valley, it was the summer that constrained. Both sides of the rocky gorge frowned down from 4000 feet, 1300 of which were below sea-level. One statistic claimed the Jordan poured 6,000,000 tons of water into the Dead Sea daily, all of which was lost by evaporation. The thick air, with its burden of moisture that never fell, imposed itself insidiously on people, like soft, formless fetters, and did not stir except when some trick mismatch in pressure spawned a willy-willy: a black and shrieking thing that spun through the camps and tossed tents and trappings high in the sky. The temperature backed and filled around 100 degrees, varying little from week to week or from day to night, except when it shot to 130 degrees. The grey-white dust, powdery and cement-like, rose with every footfall and the mobile army whipped it up into a ragged, almost unbreathable pall hanging overall. The dust turned everything a repulsive putty colour. A rider could not see another half a horse's length away in it.

The ANZAC Mounted Division spent the entire summer of 1918 in the Jordan Valley, apart from brief rotations in the uplands. The Australian Mounted Division spent nearly as long, and British and Indian cavalry and infantry spent varying periods with them, defending the Jordan's West Bank hinterland. Except for the sedentary and cloistered monks of the Greek monastery high on the golden rock face of the Mount of Temptation, no human beings stayed in that valley over summer, the Arabs warned.

Chauvel's troops had left on the Es Salt raid in the last week of April, when the sun was already hot. When they returned from the bracing heights five days later, the full summer regimen had taken hold. Vegetable and animal life had disappeared, except for hyenas cackling maniacally at night, snakes, immense black and hairy spiders, centipedes, flies and six-inch long scorpions whose thorny carapaces clicked when they crawled through the tents, attracted by warm flesh. Some men wrapped themselves in blankets and suffered the heat and sweat rather than the bites and stings. These were most painful and usually turned septic, but could be treated adequately. However, the medical corps' scrupulous anti-malarial measures could never prevail over mosquitos airborne from enemy territory and in time, with powers of resistance sapped, the ranks succumbed to this disease in hundreds. Other maladies such as 'sand-fly fever' and 'five-day fever' were prevalent and stomach disorders were universal. Rations came regularly, but nothing was appetising: the bread crumbled to dry chaff, the bully beef swam in its fat and oil.

In this hellish place, the men turned to with picks and shovels to fortify their positions. The enemy still held Gilead down to the foothills and had access to all the East Bank land up to the bridgeheads: Ghoraniye and two others further downriver. And on the opposite bank, they could attack in strength from the north at any time. Many miles of trenches were dug in the choking dust, and stone sangars were built at the foot of the escarpment. Tracks were cleared and roads made for transport coming down from Jerusalem and Talat ed Dumm, where Chauvel established his headquarters.

The only saving feature of the valley was water. The Jordan water was slightly muddy and smelt unpleasantly of its high mineral content, but it was drinkable and of course had value beyond appraisal for recreation.

Packhorses crossing the Wady Auja, Jordan valley, 1918. Indian troops in the foreground. 2ND/14TH L.H.REGT [QMI] MUSEUM ENOGGERA

Always there were horses being bathed in it and off-duty men in the stream, floating on its dense suspended minerals. Effort was required to submerge.

Those in the firing line had to be content with warm water in bottles on their watch, but troops moving on the river flat were always in touch with running water. The pure mountain springs of Gilead delivered it through the Wady Nimrin, while the Auja and others flowed from the Jericho side. The Jordan contained edible fish, too well fed to be caught except by the forbidden expenditure of ammunition such as Mills bombs. But if done discreetly and the catch disposed of judiciously, no questions needed arise.

The valley had to be held. The road from Amman and the other routes down from Moab giving access to the East Bank bridgeheads continued to threaten Allenby's flank. As a deception bonus, the Turks had come to believe that wherever the Desert Mounted Corps were, there the British would strike. Chauvel later made available to his biographer a note of the discussions he had had with Allenby:

> He practically gave me the option of withdrawing from the actual valley if I thought it better, but told me that if I did so, I would have to retake the bridgeheads over the Jordan before the autumn advance. I considered I would lose more lives retaking the valley than I would through sickness in holding it and, furthermore, there was neither room nor water for large bodies of cavalry in the jumble of hills overlooking the southern end of the valley and the climate was precious little better. I told him I considered it better to hold the valley. He agreed and I was instructed to do so.

Chauvel kept himself informed of the status quo and the troops' conditions by visiting brigades in the line and inspecting them often on relief. Allenby also visited them, and on one occasion reacted with volcanic fury to the sight of Light Horsemen riding in shorts. They had reverted to Gallipoli summer dress, or undress, of hat, infantry shorts and boots, because their thick breeches and leggings were intolerable in such temperatures — one day reaching 131 degrees. But The Bull had already issued orders forbidding riding in shorts and fulminated, firing off an edict that any officer whose men offended would be 'severely dealt with'. They reverted to the heavy riding kit and sweaty saturation without a change of clothes. In time and after representations, Allenby permitted the wearing of loose khaki slacks. There had been a few cases of blood poisoning through bare legs rubbing horses' flanks in the unhealthy conditions and the C-in-C said he was not only concerned by the 'unsoldierly dress and bearing' — read Australian loose-jointedness and easy posture — but more importantly, prevention of disease.

From both sides of the river, the enemy kept up artillery fire on the British advanced positions and headquarters and the troops needed to be as alert and alive as on any other deployment. At night, they patrolled mounted in no-man's land. It was nervy work, probing at the enemy carefully until they drew fire. There were frequent brushes with Turkish cavalry and they captured parties of Turks trying to slip down to the Jordan for water. Allenby's hold on all the wadys since the first occupation was paying off.

Gullett mentions the Wady Kumran (now spelt Qumran) anent the capture of Jericho, and in a letter my father refers to ancient ruins in that vicinity. It is not surprising that these ANZACs, Indians and Englishmen trekked back and forth without discovering a particular cave, since nobody

Brigadier General G.M. Macarthur Onslow (seated centre) and staff, 5th Brigade, Australian Mounted Division. 'No man rode harder and straighter in action' (Gullett). AWM B00384

did for 2000 years. But just the possibility that one of them might for some reason have entered that cave and stumbled on the Dead Sea Scrolls is a thing to wonder at.

At this time, the Camel Corps was broken up. The animals had proved their worth in the desert, but in hilly, arable country they were outmarched by horses and, as the Trans-Jordan incursions showed, tended to retard operations. The Australians of the Camel Brigade were given horses, and after retraining became the 14th and 15th Light Horse Regiments. To these were added a composite French regiment of Spahis and Chasseurs d'Afrique, the whole becoming the 5th Australian Light Horse Brigade. Colonel Onslow of the 7th Regiment, a descendent of John Macarthur, went to the new brigade as brigadier general and Major Richardson was promoted to command the 7th. Onslow had an excellent reputation. Gullett remarks on his 'very shrewd sense of ground' and says he was 'by instinct a dashing leader of horse. No man rode harder or straighter in action.' He had won for the 7th their position of honour as vanguard when the ANZACs advanced. The French colonials were good cavalrymen, but their Arab greys were slower than the Walers, and black men in red and blue uniforms on grey horses were conspicuous when the need might be for concealment.

Concurrently, regiments of Jodhpur and Mysore Lancers and Poonah Horse became the new British 5th Cavalry Division under General H.J.M. Macandrew, a doughty Scot.

Chauvel now commanded four divisions, breaking down into 12 brigades, or 36 regiments. Of these, 14 were Australian, 13 Indian, 5 British, 3 New Zealand and 1 French: in all, 30,000 mounted men. They were the largest body of cavalry ever and they would soon embark on the greatest cavalry feat of all time.

Allenby's army had become a most motley horde. In addition to the cavalry mixture, there were South African artillery, Rarotongan boatmen, Egyptian camel drivers and Labour Corps, and Italian, West Indian and Jewish infantry.

In the Jordan Valley, the summer dragged on. The troops were rotated to Solomon's Pools and other upland places for spells of cooler weather. My father mentions such an expedition in early June when they struck winter conditions crossing the Mount of Olives, rougher weather still in Bethlehem and a driving mountain mist when they arrived at Solomon's Pools, huddled in greatcoats.

Solomon's Pools were built by either King Herod the Great or King Solomon himself, it is not clear which, but it is certain that they supplied Jerusalem with water from 37 BC through aqueducts. The men could swim in the reservoirs — always with a sentry posted to shoot water snakes — and take short leave in Jerusalem and Bethlehem. The new CO, Colonel Richardson, ever solicitous of the men's health, thought it was not the best possible place for R and R, because the horses' water supply was some miles away and the men were occupied too much in watering them when they should have been resting. To him, every hour was precious.

After this spell, my father wrote from the valley:

... the flies used to drive us mad, but now there are hardly any left, the heat has killed them. Next month is to be the worst, I believe, I can't see how our horses are going to stand it. Several have died from snake-bite. We have to camp with our horses in the wady beds and hollows to get cover from the shell fire and down here, of course the heat intensifies and if there is any moving air up top, we don't get it. The horses have cut the place up so it is a heap of fine dust ankle deep, we must be full of it inside.

The reinforcements can't stand it, they last about a week and off they go to hospital. The old hands stick it out, nothing short of a bullet will put them in hospital. The new chaps go down ... and are not much help to us ... some of them have hearts like chickens. One man with three years' service is worth half a dozen of them. Am in good health myself, don't seem able to get sick at all.

The strain was showing. It was not like my father to be so disparaging of anyone, and if the green reinforcements' constitutions could not stand the shock of the infernal place it was through no fault of theirs. But they would have further strained the old hands, and their short-handed troop sergeant, charged with finding men for trench-digging, patrolling, pickets, the firing line, stables and other commitments in rotation.

Abu Tellul is a ridge jutting boldly into the Jordan Valley on the West Bank, just north of the Wady Auja. The British did not fortify this ridge, but made a series of separate defence posts on mud hills stretching almost in a circle round it, though with a gap to the north. The next series of defended mud hills upriver were those at Musallabeh, where the Camel Brigade had repulsed a fierce Turkish attack in April, after the Amman defeat. Allenby called Musallabeh 'the Camels' Hump'.

This river flat was like no other, because of its peculiar mud or clay hills, rearing abruptly from the floor. Some could be defended well, such as the massive ones of the Ghoraniye bridgehead, from where the troops could survey all the land eastwards, towards the Turkish concentrations in the Moab foothills; and from the commanding summits of the Musallabeh hills, cool, straight shooting had won the day. Usually, a troop of about twenty men manned the posts. Thirty or so posts made up the wide circle around Abu Tellul.

The Wady Auja was the principal water supply for the Jordan Valley force and the mud hills in its vicinity were all strongly fortified. Possession of the harsh and stony ridge of Abu Tellul itself was the real key to defending the water, but it was too close to the water supply to be in the firing line. While the Auja was fought over, the water would be inaccessible. Defence of the water, therefore, was in the hands of those manning the posts on Tellul's western side.

By mid-July, the posts were dug, some were reinforced with stone sangars, and barbed wire was laid on and between them. Each post had its store of food and water, in petrol tins and empty beer bottles. They could communicate through their local brigade headquarters, but to a limited extent only with each other through line-of-sight.

Chauvel, Chaytor and their staffs spent much time inspecting the posts and, although satisfied that they were as well placed as possible, had misgivings, based on dead ground between them through which an enemy might advance. There were large gaps in the effective fields of fire of machine-guns and rifles that could not be filled and insufficient artillery to block the enemy by barrage. They noted these things and were troubled.

Yet the British historian Cyril Falls comments, after the successful defence of Abu Tellul by the ANZACs' 1st Light Horse Brigade: 'The correctness of the defence tactics of holding posts wired all around and disregarding what happened on the flanks, even in the rear, was proved up to the hilt'.

Think again, Chauvel might have responded. The 'correctness' of the defence depended on the troops. Being surrounded is never desirable. The defence succeeded in this case because the men would not give up. But it is true that in such confined, close fighting the advantage can shift from one side to the other almost by accident.

Brigadier General 'Fighting Charlie' Cox's 1st Brigade of ANZACs relieved Grant's 4th Brigade at Abu Tellul, having been in camp near Bethlehem. That was the only spell Cox's men had enjoyed since February, and all hands were extremely jaded. Heavy wastage and the diminishing trickle of reinforcements had left them well below strength. On relief, the 4th Brigade were kept a few miles south of the Auja, as a general reserve.

From June into July, the men, including the regiment in reserve, worked by night on the posts, completing the wiring, digging and building sangars. But sleep by day was impossible in temperatures of up to 128 degrees in the shade. Such a pernicious cycle of deprivation could only be borne by troops of great mental stamina, whatever their physical condition.

There was a build-up of enemy fire on Abu Tellul into the first half of July, along with increased enemy troop movements and other activity. The shell fire did little damage to the posts, but inflicted severe casualties in the horse lines along the Auja.

An attack appeared imminent. In view of the gaps in their defences, the Light Horsemens' sober appreciation was that they could hold out for at least some hours, until the reserves were brought up and deployed. After that ...

Colonel G.J. Bell of the 3rd Regiment was asked if he thought a determined attack could be stopped by the posts.

'No, they are bound to come through,' he said.

Then what of the post's fate?

'The posts will stand, unless they are withdrawn ... or completely destroyed. Since we landed on the peninsula, I have never known a single instance of Light Horse troops, whether under officers or non-commissioned officers, having given up a position they were ordered to hold.'

After a searing day on 13 July, the men were starting to enjoy a beer ration cooled in the Auja when enemy night patrols were heard close to the Australian wire. At midnight, a report from Musallabeh said enemy were massing in strength in front of the two most north-western posts, named Vale and View. British artillery was called in and the enemy's guns replied. When the guns ceased at 2 am, the Australians heard orders shouted in German. Ninety minutes later, 1000 enemy fell on Vale. Against such odds, the garrison of twenty men could only be wiped out and Colonel Bourne of the 2nd Regiment ordered their withdrawal. This troop, of Bell's regiment, confirmed that the attackers were Germans.

Germans! The 1st Brigade had not yet fought Asia Korps riflemen, only artillery. The Germans were the 'real' enemy. The contest took on an extra fillip of competition and interest.

The Germans swarmed past Vale post along the ravines on either side. Bourne was already withdrawing his headquarters and found himself in a fighting retreat. He swung eastwards onto the slopes of Abu Tellul, firing at the enemy on his heels.

Simultaneously, the Germans assaulted the garrison at Musallabeh. Cutting through the barbed wire, they bombed the Australians out of one post, but a spirited counterattack led by Sergeant J.E. Carlyon drove them back. There were four posts on Musallabeh and the Light Horsemen held them through the night, but the enemy infiltrated south and east of the Musallabeh posts and spread out like a tide. Some were on Abu Tellul's northern slopes and others on a feature called The Bluff. Three posts, Vyse, View and Vaux, were attacked furiously but the garrisons beat off wave after wave. The Germans committed two battalions and a company of Jager (light infantry) storm troops to this action.

The Bluff and a neighbouring post on Tellul were manned by one troop each. Two more posts were occupied by Colonel Bourne's regimental staff and a handful of men who happened to be there on details. Bourne's orders were to hold on at all costs and these isolated parties obeyed to the letter. On The Bluff, the young commander was badly wounded but continued to direct the fight with just three men left alive and unwounded: and this remnant was still on their ground when the battle ended. The neighbouring post fell 'at all costs' — every man was a casualty.

West of Tellul, two more posts were fiercely attacked. A collection of batmen, grooms, signallers and two young regimental staff officers were all that stood between the Germans and the British artillery batteries 200 yards in rear. One of these posts was lost and Bourne withdrew the other, along with his own, to a prepared trench just below a crest. Here, the Germans showed against the dawn sky as they came on and made good targets. For over an hour, Bourne's group held them off.

Cox at brigade headquarters was in touch with General Chaytor, and both were seized of the dangerous situation. Chaytor ordered Grant to send one 4th Brigade regiment forward to Cox forthwith, and to bring the rest of his brigade to immediate readiness. Colonel Granville's 1st Regiment galloped up to Cox's position.

Frederick Charles Cox, 55, was the most intuitive of the original ANZAC leaders, relying on inner counsels for decisive intervention. Gullett: 'Standing well over six feet, handsome and well-proportioned, Cox looks what he is, a very spirited cavalryman. He is by intuition a master of cavalry rather than a leader of mounted riflemen. He is in action a man of instant intuitive resolve and swift, tempestuous action ... in more than one crisis, [he] took hold of his force ... and turned a critical fight into sudden complete victory.' He had done exactly that with his Nelsonian treatment of Chauvel's signal to withdraw at Magdhaba: 'Take that damned thing away and let me see it for the first time in half an hour'. Some of his contemporaries thought he had more than his share of luck and feared he would one day sustain a bad failure, but his record stood over four years of fighting.

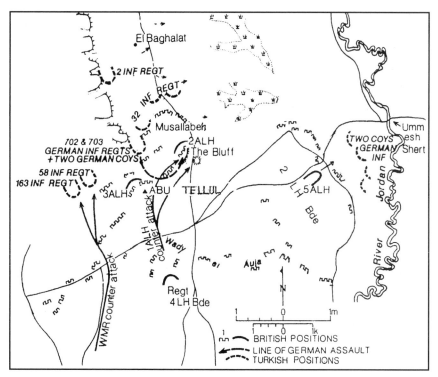

The action at Abu Tellul, 14 July 1918.

231

So it was at Abu Tellul. With daylight, as soon as Cox could confirm there were Light Horse posts still standing in rear of the Germans, overrun but intact and fighting, he said to Colonel Granville: 'Get to them, Granny'. Only that, with no thought of the odds of 450 men against, he knew, well over 1000 (in fact there were 2300). No planning or appreciating, just the lightning flash of conviction that it would be done.

Granville's men were waiting with their horses. They knew the rugged country well and knew how hard pressed the 2nd and 3rd Regiments would be. They cantered upriver, dismounted and retired the horses out of range. Then Major F.V. Weir went forward to join Bourne, leaving one squadron in reserve. At that time, just after dawn, Bourne's right was coming under renewed pressure and the desperate defenders rejoiced to see the deliverers flop down beside them.

Saving Bourne's position was one thing, a counter-stroke to rescue the encircled posts ahead was another. Weir ordered one squadron to fix bayonets and led them, roaring and blustering with the steel, over the crest. Scattered and surprised, the Germans offered some resistance initially, then broke, individuals fleeing down the gully. But as they ran, they crossed the fire zones of Vyse and Musallabeh posts on their right and View and Vaux on their left. Trapped and confounded, they 'ran about like a lot of mad rabbits', according to one of the Australians.

Abu Tellul was delivered, but the surrounded posts of View and Vaux and the post on a rocky outcrop called The Bluff were fighting yet. Granville took his reserve squadron east of these positions, then doubled back on them, but his advance was checked by shell fire. Weir's squadron was again called on with the bayonet. After artillery counter fire from the Notts Battery, the squadron cleared The Bluff with another charge, taking over 100 prisoners.

The German initial attack was marked by their characteristic discipline and vigour, but from the moment they were flanked by Vaux and View, they deteriorated. Trying to scale Abu Tellul, they were fired on directly from the back. But the biggest factor in their defeat was thirst. They had drunk what was left in their bottles by early morning. Now, with the temperature climbing rapidly to 120 degrees, they were approaching a state of collapse by 8 am and an hour later it was all over. The fighting stopped, Australian water bottles were produced and the prisoners taken to Jericho for transport to Jerusalem. They were treated with such consideration and sympathy that when the trucks set out that evening, they gave three cheers for their captors. That is, those still standing did: some of the poor fellows had stumbled on the brigade's beer supply and drunk themselves insensible.

Abu Tellul was no 'great' battle, but it had lasting significance. It was the last time the enemy challenged the British hold on the Jordan, or any other territory, for the rest of the war. It was the first time British troops had engaged Germans per se in the theatre and the morale of both combatants was affected: the victors most positively and the vanquished dismally. Turkish troops were present in the early stages and some were captured, but the Germans blamed their defeat on the Turks' desertion: a division of Turkish troops were supposed to have advanced with them on both flanks, and had they done so it would have been a very different battle and, possibly, result. A contemporary theory was that the Turks, long resentful of German harrying from the rear while they faced the bullets, deliberately pulled back to let the German infantry suffer, as they had done, thanklessly, for years.

That morning at 5 am, two more German battalions threatened the Australians three miles east of Abu Tellul, from near the river bank. Here the 2nd Brigade of ANZACs held Star, Salt, Shell and Scrap posts. They initiated an artillery duel with the enemy, after which he showed no disposition to come to close quarters. The 2nd Brigade, and the 5th Light Horse Regiment in particular, did, however: they were intent on teaching these Germans a lesson, and indeed took matters so lightly they seemed almost to be showing off. A party of nearly 200 of the 5th crept forward to within twenty yards of the enemy, then on discovery, opened fire. Before the Germans had recovered their senses, the Australians had seized fifteen prisoners and departed. At 8 am, two hours later, the same officer, Lieutenant J.D. Macansh of the 5th, went forward again with just twenty men to within bombing distance, then charged the Germans with bombs and bayonets, this time killing 25, wounding 30 and capturing 30. The rest fled to their wire entanglements 1000 yards in rear.

Down south at Ghoraniye and the Dead Sea, a force of Turkish infantry marched towards a ford at El Henu. Indian cavalry held this sector and welcomed their initiation to independent action. The Jodhpur and Mysore Lancers galloped out from the ford, while the Sherwood Rangers and Poonah Horse moved out from Ghoraniye. The Indian

A Light Horse supply column in the Jordan valley. Turkish prisoners at upper left.
2ND/14TH L.H.REGT [QMI] MUSEUM ENOGGERA

regiments crashed into the Turks, killing 90 with lances and capturing another 90.

Again, these brief skirmishes had morale effects beyond their scale and scope. Enemy dead numbered 105 and 25 wounded were rescued from inside the Light Horse posts. Four hundred and twenty-five prisoners, of whom 388 were German, were taken. Australian casualties were 23 killed and 46 wounded.

At the war's end, the Light Horsemen were told quarantine regulations could not be relaxed for their horses. They could not be repatriated to Australia and were to be sold locally.

However, the men witnessed daily the mistreatment of animals throughout the region and a groundswell of protest swept through the ranks. The army compromised: those horses fit and young enough would be given to Indian cavalry regiments and the rest would be shot. According to Ian Jones, the rejects were picketed in olive groves at Tripoli, Syria, given a last nosebag and shot by special squads of marksmen. They were shorn of manes and tails for saleable horsehair, their shoes were salvaged and their skins were cured and sold.

Australia in Palestine included an illustrated poem, 'The Horses Stay Behind', by 'Trooper Bluegum':

In days to come we'll wander west across the range again;
We'll hear the bush birds singing in the green trees after rain.
We'll canter through the Mitchell grass and breast the bracing wind:
But we'll have other horses. Our horses stay behind.

Around the fire at night we'll yarn about old Sinai;
We'll fight our battles o'er again; and as the days go by
There'll be old mates to greet us. The bush girls will be kind.
Still our thoughts will often wander to the horses left behind.

I don't think I could stand the thought of my old fancy hack
Just crawling round old Cairo with a Gyppo on his back.
Perhaps some English tourist out in Palestine may find
My broken-hearted Waler with a wooden plough behind.

No; I think I'd better shoot him and tell a little lie: –
'He floundered in a wombat hole and then lay down to die.'
Maybe I'll get court-martialled; but I'm damned if I'm inclined
To go back to Australia and leave my horse behind.

'Trooper Bluegum' was the pen name of Major Oliver Hogue, originally of the Camel Brigade, then the 14th Light Horse Regiment. He died of illness on 3 March 1919, and it may be that he did not leave his horse behind by more than a heartbeat after all, for on or about that day all horses were disposed of.

TWENTY-TWO

The magisterial stratagem

Allenby's plan for ending the war included deceptions that mirrored those practised at Gaza–Beersheba nearly a year earlier and its greatest wonder is that the Turks and Germans, in particular the able Prussian General Liman von Sanders, allowed themselves to be wrongfooted again. The scale of the deception was much bigger and plausibility more difficult to carry off, but the Commander-in-Chief kept a throttling hold on security and what might now be called the roll-out. Nothing of the stupendous sleight-of-hand leaked.

He confided in his corps commanders, Generals Bulfin, Chetwode and Chauvel, at various meetings through August 1918, but he did not brief the regimental commanders and brigadiers taking part until two or three days before the jump-off. The Australian Mounted Division, who were to advance 50 miles on the first day–night ride along with Generals Barrow's and Macandrew's 4th and 5th Cavalry Divisions, were briefed two days beforehand on 17 September. General Hodgson spoke to them without notes. Nothing was issued in writing and what individual officers jotted down for their own use was later collected and destroyed.

That the enemy was expecting an offensive in the interval between the summer heat and the November rains was beyond doubt, but von Sanders was unable to fall in with the notion that, because every indication pointed to an advance out of the Jordan Valley, the British must really be planning to break through on the coast, at the other end of his 50 miles of front. The nature of the country anyway dictated that the bulk of his forces should be concentrated about the heights of Samaria, rising just north of Nablus, because this formidable obstacle commanded the Plain of Esdraelon immediately westwards, which connected to the coastal north–south strip called the Plain of Sharon — the obvious and only cavalry route should the British break through on the coast. But Samaria was also about equidistant from the Jordan Valley (twenty-odd miles), should the British advance on that flank, as the enemy believed they would.

Allenby produced a design so bold, swift and decisive, and yet so meticulous in its inter-linking detail, that it would keep the enemy off balance for long enough to gain a foothold on his flank on the first day, 50 miles to the north of his own starting point. Then, the mounted troops must keep up their momentum to spin a half-circle net round the central enemy stronghold, by consolidating on the Plains of Sharon and Esdraelon and extending to the Jordan Valley at Beisan, well north of General Chaytor's ANZAC ground and only twenty miles from the Sea of Galilee. This was the tallest part of the order, but Allenby was firm in his faith that it could be done. Any hold-up or missed connection, however, could consign the operation at once to the sort of stationary and grinding attrition of the old Gaza–Beersheba line after that failure to take the town with the first blow.

It was a courageous, majestic gamble, but with nothing left to chance but chance itself. The Commander-in-Chief believed in his rehabilitated army, retrained, fit, rehearsed and ready to go after the long summer, and they believed in him. They thought they could do it, and they did.

His staff ran the program of deception as if the notional operations and events would take place, at the correct intervals and with due allowance for phantom movements, support and logistics. The buying of large quantities of horse forage by Lawrence's Arabs with British gold, on the Moab plateau, for 'many horses coming through', was done when it would have been done if it was true, and the buyers themselves believed it. An officers' club in Jerusalem was ostentatiously emptied, sentry boxes were placed at the entrance, military telephone lines installed, and a rumour that Allenby was moving his headquarters from the coast to this place was floated. The Arabs east of Jordan prepared for a sham attack on Amman, establishing a base, reconnoitring and cutting the railway between Amman and Damascus. They may well have believed the attack would happen. Dummy wireless messages from Desert Mounted Corps were transmitted from the Jordan, long after Chauvel had moved his HQ west. A 'race meeting' for D-Day, 19 September, was advertised on the coast, a track prepared and tents erected.

When the Australian Mounted Division climbed out of the Jordan Valley in early August, they did not know it was to be for the last time, and only the prospect of returning to the Jordan's hardships seemed to lie ahead. But their orders were changed. They marched secretly and joyfully, by night, right across the front and concealed themselves in the olive and orange groves of Ludd. Here they encountered the stir and buzz of new enterprise and joined it, first with the issue of, and final instruction in, cavalry swords. To the horses' saddles were attached long leather rifle buckets on the offside and a sword frog on the nearside. Mounted, the troopers felt a strange freedom without the weight of the .303 rifle they had carried on their backs for so long. One former trooper told Ian Jones he had 'felt unarmed. As though I was heading off on a muster. I never thought I'd miss that bloody weight on my back.'

The Australian Mounted were now dual-purpose cavalry and mounted infantry. They became so at their own request, after their experience of the Beersheba charge. The ANZAC Mounted Division, however, opted to remain as they were.

The ANZACs stayed in the Jordan Valley. If it seemed brutal to keep these men there, who alone bore the scars of the entire three years' fighting and were growing weaker and sicker as the late summer temperatures soared ever higher through September, they were less fit than the other mounted troops for the strenuous campaign ahead. And by cruel paradox, they could be relied on to stick it out in the Jordan better than most. Then when the moment came in the great plan for Allenby's right flank to advance, they would summon their last remaining strength, scale the Heights of Abraham yet again, take Amman and Es Salt for the third and final time and clear the enemy from the Moab plateau.

From mid-summer, when their resistance had fallen away, malaria in the Jordan force became epidemic. My father was a victim. He wrote on 4 August:

The fourth anniversary of the war finds me in hospital again, with malaria. I got it about 10 days ago in the Jordan Valley where it is very prevalent. Have had rather a bad time but am on the mend now. I am in hospital at Gaza, will no doubt go on to Cairo or Port Said when I get a bit stronger …

We were attacked by Germans in the valley, but they got a knock back and we took swarms of prisoners. Up to now, we have been the attackers and they have sat back and waited for us, but this time things were reversed and they made a mess of it. They only had one water bottle each for all day and a night.

I don't suppose I'll be back with the Regiment for some time now, so you can regard me as quite safe for a while. I believe I was shortly to be sent back to Egypt to train for a commission, but this will of course upset things. However, am not going to worry about it till I am quite fit again, would rather be well than swell. Things will be better for me if it comes off, a troop officer doesn't do much work, the poor old sergeant does it and it's me that knows it, eh what?

Apart from their own evacuations from sickness, the ANZACs watched the Jordan force slip away regiment by regiment, brigade by brigade. Infantry and cavalry, British, Australians and Indians all left. The ANZACs scratched their heads ruefully. Strange orders were given and strange things happened. Columns of British infantry marched back again from Talat, raised the dust by marching and counter-marching all day about the valley, and when night came were trucked back up to Talat, only to repeat the performance the next day.

The ANZACs pitched acres of empty tents and made 15,000 dummy horses out of canvas, old blankets and greatcoats stuffed with straw to fill the empty horse lines. They were propped up on sticks and had straw tails. The men spurred their own mounts about the ground, dragging bushes and branches behind them to raise ever more dust of simulated cavalry movements, and at night lit the loneliest of camp fires.

They did not have it all on their own, however, and at various times welcomed two battalions of British West Indians, two Jewish battalions raised in England and a brigade of Indian infantry. These spread the load, but being untried, were unknown quantities when it came to fighting.

Neither Allenby nor his corps commanders wanted to trust Lawrence's Arabs with operational responsibilities after the disappointments of the Trans-Jordan campaign, but in one particular they had no option. The important rail junction of Deraa, 30 miles east of the Jordan River and 60 from the British start line, was too far away to be secured on the first day's advance, yet this was essential to prevent Turkish reinforcements pouring south. The Arabs were tasked and, with the support of some British armoured cars and a detachment of Ghurkhas, moved resolutely on the place and by 16 September had destroyed a railway bridge and sections of the main lines to the south, north and west of Deraa.

The Palestine Brigade of the RAF, six British squadrons and No. 1 Squadron of the Australian Flying Corps, rose to such a pitch of efficiency that, while in one week of June 100 enemy aircraft appeared over British lines, by August the weekly average was eighteen. During August and September, fifteen enemy aircraft were shot down, all falling to Australians. Ross Smith's lumbering Handley-Page made 150 bombing raids up to the armistice with Turkey on 31 October. Without the air forces' total mastery of the sky, Allenby could not have concentrated his force of approximately 35,000 infantry, 25,000 cavalry and 384 guns in secret.

Opposing the British concentration were just 8000 enemy and 120 guns, but these were able to be reinforced immediately. The British could not reinforce so readily, and had von Sanders known of this audacious forerunner of Blitzkrieg he would have been confident the cavalry would soon outrun their supplies and have to live off the parched land.

Water was the most intractable problem for the British. Cyril Falls notes that 7000 camels with fantasses were ready to carry it to the fighting men, but at their own pace; the Desert Mounted Corps were issued with engines and pumps in the hope that they could use wells en route; and the records of the Palestine Exploration Society were searched for evidence of ancient water supplies that might be rehabilitated in the ground ahead.

By sunset on 18 September, all was in readiness.

All ranks knew this offensive portended a scale of conflict to dwarf anything in their experience, and that the stakes of ultimate victory or defeat would guarantee its ferocity. Cyril Falls calls his book on the subject *Armageddon 1918*, and not only because there happened to be fighting around Megiddo, the place of the former fabled conflict. The individual's final moments before the start were given to introspection, prayer and the last letter home.

Jack Davies' letter to his wife touches dutifully and tenderly on the prospect of his own death. The record he left suggests that he never took pains to write well, but scrawled spontaneously and almost at the pace of his thoughts. His letter to Mildred is the more true and poignant for it.

September 18th 1918

My Darling Mill,

This may be the last opportunity I shall get of writing to you for some time.

Whatever happens now old darling, don't let yourself be worried, this should prove a very interesting campaign, so no doubt there is a hard time in front of us, there is no reason to be anything but confident of the result, of course it is all in the hand of Providence, but one thing is certain, Johnny Turk is going to be very busy for a few days.

Now old darling what I am going to write about now is just in case of possibly my not coming out of this; in course of time it might so happen that you'd think of marrying again and if such were the case, I would only wish that you should do so. The only thing to be considered would be whether the chap was really good enough for you. Not that I reckon I'm any blooming paragon of virtue, but I know how fond we are of each other and I know I treat you properly, which might not be the case with another man, there is also the certainty of my children and a third thing to be considered is the monetary side of the thing, should anything happen to me the Estate would continue to pay you ... income to bring up the children and provide them with education ...

Jack writes of trustees and various family assets and properties, concluding this part with:

... you've been used to having what you want in the way of money and I don't like to think of you being reduced in any way.

You must not let this worry you at all because I don't for one minute feel I won't come out of this. I go into it absolutely confident and trusting in God to bring me out all right.

He mentions having seen Jim Traill, Mildred's airman brother, two nights ago and he was 'well and cheerful as usual'.

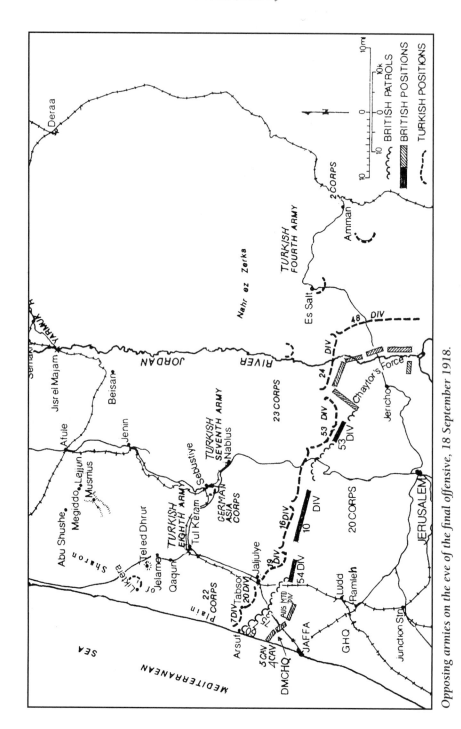

Opposing armies on the eve of the final offensive, 18 September 1918.

I must stop now Darling, there are endless things to do … everyone is quite enthusiastic about this show, it promises wonderful developments if all goes well. As before I go trusting in God and thinking of you and the children and looking forward to my next leave (to Cairo.) One long big kiss and a kiss for Jay, Lloyd and Barbara, cheerio old thing good - bye-e-e-e-e.

Jack Davies did not go with his own regiment, but all the way to Damascus was attached to the British and Indian 5th Cavalry Division as liaison officer for the Australian Mounted Division.

The night of 18 September was fine and still. The Light Horsemen loaded their horses with the standard three days' rations, water bottle and spare bandolier round the neck, mounted and joined the long queue making for the start line. There, they silently dismounted and half-slept by their horses' heads — as they were to do, but less frequently if at all, for the next fortnight. The horses' tail switching, the stamp of a hoof or, above all, whinnying and snorting kept the men half-conscious lest the sound should carry over the unknown divide.

That night, an Indian sergeant, a Moslem, deserted to the Turks. When appraised of this, the small need-to-know circle restrained their inclination to change anything. It was too late, and too late for the enemy. The man certainly knew of the imminent attack up the Plain of Sharon, but would Liman von Sanders trust him? He could be persuaded that the Indian was just a British ruse, especially in view of the Arab attack on the railway at Deraa three days earlier. The German did dismiss the fellow — and ordered a German battalion from the coast to reinforce Deraa. The luck of the British held.

With the first flush of dawn on the 19th, the guns erupted and General Bulfin's 21 Corps went forward. Their first task was to punch a hole in the defences through which the cavalry could stream.

The battalions made a swift, clean advance upon the enemy trenches just a mile distant and engaged the Turks before they were fully alert. Some patchy and sporadic resistance inflicted losses on them as they crossed open flats towards defended sand ridges, but their momentum did not falter. They gained the trenches and the reserve trenches beyond with bomb and bayonet, and the Turks broke and fled. The Turkish line on the

Plain of Sharon and foothills was shattered in such good time and style as exceeded all British hopes.

By 7 am, the mounted men were picking their way through the enemy's broken trenches, and half an hour later rode through Shea's 60th Division on the coast, to shouts of greeting and encouragement from old comrades-in-arms, then quickened the pace. In the order from seaward of Barrow's 5th Cavalry Division, Macandrew's 4th Cavalry Division and then, slightly rearward, Hodgson's Australians, they went to an extended trot and then with flank guards galloping wide, lances flashing and pennants streaming, the huge body of horsemen spilled over the Plain of Sharon like the flood of a bursting dam.

The Great Ride had begun.

TWENTY-THREE

The Sleepless Fortnight: first 2000 square miles

Of the many poems about horses written by one-time Major A.B. (Banjo) Paterson, commander of the Light Horse Remount Depot at Heliopolis (and cousin of Nat Barton), one is called 'Do They Know?'. In part, it goes:

> *Though the sweat on the ears*
> *Gathers cold, and they sob with distress*
> *As they roll up the track,*
> *They know just as well their success*
> *As the man on their back.*

Paterson was writing about racehorses, not war horses, but celebrating the nature of all horses.

On the Plain of Sharon, they knew. Exuberance passed from rider to horse, yet another, deeper meaning came from horse to horse. The great company of them were going somewhere fast, to do something, together. They snatched at their bits and tossed their heads, making light of the 250-pound load, in some cases 280, in which the man's only concession to comfort was one blanket and that doubling as a saddlecloth: camping and

245

waterproof equipment were left behind. These horses were far from the peak of fitness, especially the Walers that had endured the Jordan Valley summer, but in The Banjo's words, they 'ran true to their breed.'

Day One: 19–20 September

The three cavalry divisions had some discretion with regard to objectives, but in general they were to take the important railway communication junction of El Afule and Nazareth on the first day, then Beisan, 80 miles distant, the day after. But they were to move only in consultation with the 60th and 7th Infantry Divisions, for if either the infantry or cavalry drives faltered, the plan to corral the enemy between them would fail.

The 5th Cavalry Division ran just a mile or so inland and, curving slightly to the right, by nightfall were approaching a pass at Abu Shushe, gateway into the Plain of Esdraelon between Samaria and the Carmel Range. At the same time, Barrow's 4th Division, running parallel five miles east, were advancing on the Musmus Pass into Esdraelon. So far, the fast and furious thrust had gone famously for twenty-odd miles.

The Australian Mounted Division was on Barrow's heels but in reserve, except for the newly promoted Brigadier General Onslow's 5th Light Horse Brigade, which was attached to Chetwode's 21 Corps for the first phase of operations. Onslow's task was close to his heart and promised a brilliant launch to his senior cavalryman's career: to advance from the infantry line at the start and strike at Tul Keram, a somewhat forbidding bluff rising out of the eastern foothills of the plain, from which the Turks might interdict the British horsemen and oppose the infantry. Onslow was then to continue into the hills of Samaria across the main avenue of enemy retreat, and cut the railway line between Nablus and Jenin.

The 5th Brigade slipped through the infantry lines on the right of Chetwode's 7th Division of Indians and galloped forward, quickly clearing the infantry fighting. By midday, they had reached the plain immediately in front of Tul Keram and swung north-east around it, into the foothills. A squadron of Africans from Onslow's French Colonial regiment made a spectacular debut by galloping down and capturing an Austrian artillery battery. At the same time, Tul Keram village was heavily bombed by British aircraft. The place was already crowded with refugees from the fighting to the south and the bursting bombs and the sudden appearance of Onslow's men redoubled the panic and confusion: a howling host of thousands fled eastwards after a large column of retreating Turks.

Leaving Tul Keram to be occupied by the 60th Division, the 5th deployed on either side of all this distressed humanity and, threading their way through the refugees, rode the Turkish column down. They surrendered en masse, just as British and Australian aircraft, patrolling for such a target, bombed and machine-gunned them, catching vehicles and teams in a narrow defile. By 6 pm, Onslow had 2000 prisoners and fifteen guns. Then part of the French regiment took off again after more Turks moving north: it was a long chase, but the French Colonials brought back hundreds more prisoners late at night.

Onslow's orders were to proceed with all dispatch to Ajjeh, in the hills, where he was to cut the railway line between Nablus and Jenin. But it was 2 am before his brigade could be reassembled and he could not make up time, owing to the extremely rough and trackless country. At 7 am, two squadrons of the 14th Light Horse Regiment reached the railway and broke it up, but the brigade was now strung out over fifteen miles, so he decided to reassemble the regiments at Tul Keram again before setting out for Jenin, as ordered. This took all the remaining daylight hours of the 20th, by which time he was redirected to Nablus.

The 4th and 5th Cavalry Divisions had seen virtually nothing of the enemy since starting out, but they approached the entrances to the two passes over the Carmel Range with due caution. Both were high, narrow and rocky defiles, difficult for cavalry under the best conditions, but now darkness had fallen.

Then Barrow's screen rode down a Turkish officer who gave information that an enemy infantry force, with machine-guns, had been ordered to march from El Afule to block the Musmus Pass. Barrow could hesitate no longer and his leading brigade entered it in the dark, followed by the whole 4th Division. Macandrew's 5th Division followed his lead and negotiated the pass at Abu Shushe, both cavalry divisions emerging on the Plain of Esdraelon in the early morning.

The 4th Division debouched at Megiddo, soaked in blood from the most ancient times and mythological site of the final battle between the Forces of Good and the Forces of Evil. The 4th Division's passage was not without contretemps, however, which resulted in Barrow sacking on the spot his 10th Brigade commander, Brigadier General R.G.H. Howard-Vyse, a Royal Horse Guards officer whose previous appointment was as Chauvel's Chief-of-Staff. Nicknamed 'The Wombat', he had enjoyed a long and warm association with the Australians. According to A.J. Hill, Chauvel himself, driving up to the passes to see his divisions safely through them, encountered Howard-Vyse riding back alone. Chauvel was distressed at his misfortune. But, as leading brigade, the 10th had missed the entrance to the Musmus Pass in the dark: got lost, in plain words, and caused a delay of two hours. It was every kind of bad luck, but it could have cost lives, a defeat, the ruin of the whole plan. Barrow went looking for the 10th personally, with his own Chief-of-Staff, who happened to be Australian (Lieutenant Colonel W.J. Foster) in what he described as 'the worst 15 minutes of my life.' He was desperately concerned that the division could be trapped in the defile by the reported approaching Turkish force.

In the end, Barrow used the 12th Brigade to lead his men through the pass — and just in time. The battalion of Turks arrived as his vanguard of Indian 2nd Lancers emerged. They immediately galloped the Turks down, crashed through them from one side, then crashed through again from the other, with the lances. They killed 46 and rounded up 470 prisoners.

Barrow wheeled right to march on El Afule, while Macandrew went straight across the rich plain northwards, through overgrown weeds and grasses killed by the summer. But Macandrew's 14th Cavalry Brigade passed within sight of El Afule en route and took it with little resistance, saving Barrow the trouble. Nazareth now lay just seven miles further north and Macandrew's 13th Brigade under Brigadier General Kelly headed for it.

Liman von Sanders was at Nazareth. He was aware of the breach in his right flank by Chauvel's cavalry, but apparently not of the extent of the disaster, nor of the rapid advance of the mounted troops since. At 4.30 am the Gloucester Hussars and Indians of the 13th Brigade trotted up the road to what Gullett calls 'the little saucer on the heights of Galilee which contains the bright town of modern Nazareth' and surprised a German motor convoy of about 70 vehicles. These were severely dealt with, the drivers shot and vehicles run off the road into deep gorges. Then, still unchallenged, the brigade clattered into the town, capturing officers and officials in their beds at the Hotel Germania.

But 200 yards from von Sanders' headquarters, some German troops resisted strongly, enabling the enemy C-in-C to scramble in his pyjamas to a French orphanage in the rear of his HQ.

Chauvel drove up the Nazareth road, impatient for news of the town's capture. A distant car approaching turned out to be a Mercedes — von Sanders' car! For a minute, Chauvel thought the German general had been captured, but Macandrew stepped out to make his report.

Brigadier General Kelly had taken 1200 prisoners and valuable booty and documents, but had slowed his advance to search villages and weakened his already exhausted troops by dropping squadrons off to guard points along the way. Consequently, he was not quick enough, or strong enough, to throw a cordon round Nazareth and seal the road to Tiberias along which von Sanders escaped. When Allenby eventually studied all the reports, he removed Kelly from his command — the second such casualty for the day. Kelly's accomplishments included fluent Arabic, and he had an excellent operational record as a colonel in some African colonial uprisings of 1916. The Bull's judgment was considered, made after the event, but it seemed harsh to historian Cyril Falls and, later, to Chauvel's Australian biographer, A.J. Hill.

Day Two: 20–21 September

The 4th Cavalry Division drove on from El Afule towards Beisan, with detachments guarding both flanks against attacks from Haifa on the coast and Samaria town to the south, both equidistant. In the night, a column of Turks from Haifa, attempting to march to Tiberias via Nazareth, had been surprised by the Indian 18th Lancer Regiment galloping through them with their lances, killing some and capturing 300. How could they have stood up to these ruthless tribesmen on thundering horses with their fearful medieval skewers, at night? The simple, demoralised Turks quailed before bayonet charges. The Indians' light, thin frames were to their advantage on horseback; they were expert riders and had superior night vision.

The road was clear down the Valley of Jezreel, the going was good, Beisan was occupied and the road north-west to Samaria sealed by late afternoon. The huge gamble had paid off: the net had been precisely cast about the enemy's general headquarters at Nazareth and the 7th and 8th Turkish Armies, from the coast to the Jordan. Only the bridge across the Jordan at Damieh and some minor fords on the river remained open to the enemy, and the ANZAC Mounted Division would soon account for these.

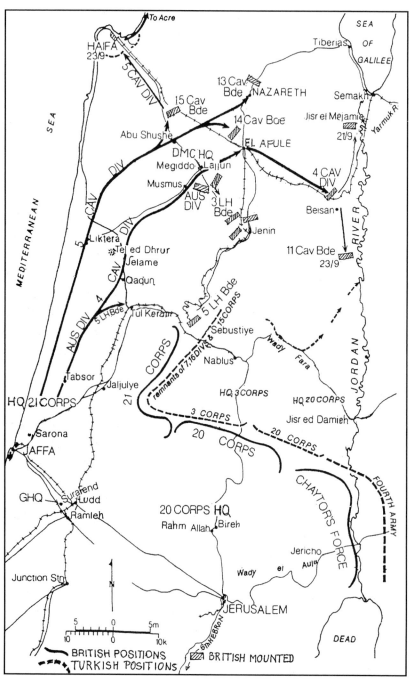

Gains on days One to Four of the Sleepless Fortnight, ending 23 September 1918.

The 4th Cavalry Division had covered 80 miles in 34 hours without off-saddling, and the 5th only 15 miles less. They had outdistanced their own transport by 50 miles and were on emergency rations. Yet only 26 horses foundered in the almost forced march conditions and still-intense heat of a lingering summer: small clouds of condensation formed over the massed, sweating horses as they went. Some territorial mounted units' reputations were nothing to boast about, but this was a superb cavalry feat, made possible by the troops' resolve and horsemastery. And it was just the beginning.

But what of the Australians? Together with the New Zealanders, they had led every mounted advance since the Suez Canal and were keenly disappointed to be bringing up the rear of this one. However, they had to expect to be in reserve at some time, and it is reasonable to conjecture that Chauvel may have wanted them particularly to be the freshest of his three divisions when the Turks recovered sufficiently to strike back. In any case, the detached 5th Brigade of Onslow's was in the thick of it and Chauvel, having established the new Desert Mounted Corps headquarters at Megiddo, needed occupation troops to protect it. He designated Grant's 4th Light Horse Brigade for the job: a brigade of Macandrew's at Nazareth watched over El Afule, while both brigades guarded against a Turkish move from Haifa.

Of the Australian Mounted Division, that left only Brigadier General Wilson's 3rd Light Horse Brigade free for action. It soon came.

The runaway advance of Chetwode's infantry divisions into the foothills near Tul Keram and Samaria had bent back the Turkish front line away from the coast so that it turned sharply north, towards Jenin. Ten thousand defeated Turks retreated on this line, making a despairing effort to reach the town, about ten miles away, before the British seized it. At Megiddo, Chauvel was nine miles away and he dispatched Wilson's 3rd Light Horse Brigade to deal with them. The 3rd had of course ridden its 50 miles the day before, but set off five minutes after the order, with every man impatient for action.

This was unerringly what Allenby had intended: for the infantry to drive the enemy into the waiting arms of the cavalry. What the C-in-C did in his private moments is unknown, but it is difficult not to think of him dancing for joy.

At the halfway point, the 9th Regiment rode down an enemy outpost. Alternately trotting and cantering, the brigade made good time, approaching

Jenin just before sunset. They needed daylight. The next enemy they saw were a body of Turks encamped in olive groves north-east of the town. The Light Horsemen attacked instantly: a troop with drawn swords galloped into the camp and the Turks fell over themselves surrendering. Three more troops joined the first and within minutes had secured 1800 prisoners, including a force of Germans and 400 of their animals.

Trying to beat the fading light, Wilson pressed on to Jenin with just his vanguard, swept round the town and closed the roads leading out north and east. (Compare with Kelly's capture of Nazareth: Wilson's order of priorities was effective.) The 9th and 10th Regiments, having collected their prisoners, then caught up with Wilson in a rush. Bewildered, exhausted and demoralised Turks were everywhere surrendering. However, the Australians were fired on from the town's houses by the machine-guns of a German rearguard: a machine-gun duel ensued and soon these Germans surrendered to the 3rd Australian Machine-Gun Squadron, attached to Wilson's brigade.

It was now dark. Wilson ordered the 10th Regiment to deploy on the Nazareth road, with two machine-guns. These crews, under Lieutenant R.R.W. Patterson, were taking up their station when they suddenly came upon a strong enemy column moving on Jenin from the south. Patterson had only 23 men, and while he cast about for a way to handle this Trooper George suggested they might bluff the Turks into surrender. Patterson, still from concealment, fired bursts from his machine-guns over their heads. As the enemy started to deploy and take cover, Patterson shouted at them to surrender and rode forward alone.

In the lead, a German nursing sister who spoke English was marching with some German officers. Patterson announced that he was at the head of a large force and repeated his demand. The woman translated to the officers, and after a brief parley this column of 2800 troops and four guns surrendered to 23 Australians.

Wilson's tally amounted to 8000 prisoners including hundreds of Germans, five guns, two aircraft, a wagon loaded with gold and silver coins, crates of champagne and miscellaneous booty too vast and varied to be inventoried. But the captors spent a ticklish night: some of the bolder prisoners resented having been bluffed into surrender by this handful of men and there were mutterings in groups, black looks and fierce gestures. All night the Light Horsemen rode through them with drawn swords.

General Hodgson's 4th Light Horse Brigade was despatched from Megiddo to assist with the prisoners and they were marched off in the morning under proper guard.

An ammunition dump had been fired by the enemy, and by its light at dawn the Arabs swarmed in from all quarters in a frenzy of looting, shouting 'Arab! Arab!' as if the identification served as entitlement. Whenever the armies left such centres as Jenin and El Afule, these scavenging hordes converged on them, on donkeys, camels and on foot. The women staggered under huge loads, while the vain, proud and unencumbered men watched and directed.

The prisoners were in a wretched state and moaning the familiar 'moya! moya!' (water! water!) as they went. Many Turks had dysentery, some wore makeshift sandals instead of boots. While the Light Horsemen had triumphed with their usual audacity, the Turks were too sick, malnourished and demoralised to offer much resistance. Only the Germans did so.

Day Three: 21–22 September

On this early morning, the detached 5th Light Horse Brigade of Onslow was marching on Nablus, as ordered. The route was south-easterly from Tul Keram and through the Vale of Barley for seven miles. Three troops of the Hertfordshire Yeomanry joined the brigade and they made contact with infantry of Chetwode's 7th Division advancing from the south-west.

The Vale of Barley narrows as it climbs into the stony Samarian hills and parties of Turks with machine-guns fired on the 5th Brigade from the defiles. Onslow sent dismounted men forward and wide on either flank and, taken in rear, these Turks surrendered. With the 14th Light Horse Regiment leading, the advance on Nablus was resumed, but again the regiment was fired on from the town. This was just a street or two of old buildings huddled along the south bank of the Wady esh Shair: the 14th rode fast along the north bank and, leaving Nablus on their right, penetrated to Jacob's Well, three miles further on.

Outflanked, Nablus fell to the French regiment, to the usual demonstrations of allegiance to the conquerors — of whatever side. The Turkish troops had abandoned it for the surrounding country and the civic leaders formally surrendered the place to Onslow. The 5th then collected about 900 of the former garrison in the hinterland.

Onslow was ordered to resume the pursuit to Beisan and then, in the fluid and fast-altering priorities of the offensive, redirected to Jenin and to rejoin the Australian Mounted Division. The road to Jenin branched off about ten miles to the rear and, shepherding their prisoners, the brigade backtracked.

In the last two days, the Turkish 7th and 8th Armies had fought the six infantry divisions of Chetwode and Bulfin, sometimes stoutly, but had been rolled back into the foothills of the Plain of Sharon. From the Tul Keram heights, the commanders had seen with the naked eye not only the strength and scale of the British infantry assault, and their own broken ranks in flight to the foothills, but also the great horde of British cavalry galloping across their front, regiment after regiment with pennants flying and swords and lances flashing, towards the passes of Esdraelon. They knew now that they could not recover and the order to retreat to Jenin was given.

It was to be the Turkish High Command's last coherent order. The British blow had been so overwhelming, the air attacks and the harassment by Onslow's brigade so unnerving, and the implications of the British cavalry movement so demoralising that within hours they had lost all vestiges of control and the retreat was a rout. 'A great army machine, complete and working smoothly, had as by an earthquake, been sundered and flung down in ruins,' wrote Gullett.

The head of this shattered procession was laid hold of by Wilson at Jenin. Now, Onslow advanced on its tail. This became a matter of driving before him those scattered remnants along the western side of the Samarian Range, picking up more prisoners as he went. On his way to rejoin the Australian Mounted, Onslow could have reflected that his new and makeshift brigade of converted cameleers and French colonials had measured up to Light Horse standards very well. Some cultural divides needed bridging with the French, who in the absence of such staples as wine and coffee were inclined to loot foodstuffs as of right and with the sanction of their officers. But such things would be settled in time.

There still remained one way of escape for the Turks, by mountain tracks leading north-east towards Beisan, then directly eastwards to the Jordan River crossings still in Turkish hands. This route soon became strewn with all that was left of the Turkish armies.

British and Australian aircraft had roamed the skies at will since before the offensive and had all Turkish movements covered. The Australian squadron was charged with all airborne reconnaissance for the British Army and were first to fly off each morning on target selection. Early on the 21st, flying low over Samaria, they observed a huge body of enemy troops and transports moving north-east, along defiles and wady beds, towards Beisan. The airmen signalled by wireless to all the aerodromes where other squadrons waited, bombed up and ready for the day's work.

Within the hour, the slaughter began. The troops had massed as they entered the narrow gorge of the Wady Fara and the British and Australian bombers dived. They smashed up the leading vehicles and blocked the gorge. Then strafing and bombing up and down the chaotic jumble of motor and horse-drawn transport, artillery pieces and thousands of troops surging back and forth like a tide with no outlet, they proved the terrible power of the aircraft. There had not been such a major and dramatic demonstration of this kind so far in warfare and the ground attack role was to become a stock-in-trade of all air forces.

As one flight ran out of ammunition, its place was taken by another while the first returned to base to re-arm. Most aircrews flew four sorties in one day. Just one small detachment escaped the onslaught on a half-concealed side track, but when it reached Beisan it fell into the waiting arms of Barrow's Yeomanry and Indians. In less than five miles of road, the airmen accounted for 87 guns, 55 trucks and 916 other vehicles, while the human casualties were inestimable.

With this attack, all threats to the 4th Cavalry Division at Beisan melted away. Now, Chaytor's ANZACs could advance out of the Jordan Valley.

Meanwhile, Chauvel moved on the major coastal centre of Haifa. Air reconnaissance reported it was already evacuated, so he sent a detachment of armoured cars and No. 7 Light Car Patrol, under the Desert Mounted Corps' artillery commander, Brigadier General A.D'A. King of the Indian Army.

Alas, the air force might have shone in its ground attack role, but it was not perfect. The little column was fired on nearing Haifa. However, King pressed on until a mile and a half away, when he came under heavy shrapnel fire again. Armoured cars were hit and King's touring car was destroyed. After a hectic and strenuous twenty minutes of turning the cars around under fire on a track crossed by deep drains and ditches, the expedition withdrew.

The next day, Chauvel ordered Macandrew's 5th Cavalry Division to take the place and the Indians made short work of it, galloping into the town after being held up for a few hours by machine-gun and artillery fire. At the same time, the 13th Cavalry Brigade took Acre, a few miles to the north. Nearly 300 more prisoners were added to the bag.

Chauvel now held the country from Beisan to Acre. The 7th and 8th Turkish Armies had been destroyed, few enemy troops remained further north between Nazareth and Damascus, and an advance to Deraa, across the Jordan and 40 miles further east, was practicable. The British horses were rested and well fed after their double marathons of the 19th and 20th and the men, though still sleepless, were fit enough to go on. And they could appreciate as well as any staff officer that they were well on the way to winning the war.

At the end of this crowded day, Jack Davies wrote to his wife from El Afule, with the 5th Cavalry Division:

My Darling Mill,

I hope you got my last letter written just before we left our last fixed camp, since then we've done nothing much but move, I don't think I'd better say too much yet as regards what's happened, but everyone you see here is going around with a grin from ear to ear. It has been a most wonderful show and if I am not mistaken, will be written down in history as one of the world's decisive victories, both in point of results and the extraordinary speed at which it was all carried out …This has been a generals' battle and mighty well they did their job too, quite a luxurious affair, we've been out four nights, I have shaved every day and had two baths, so a chap can't want much more.

I certainly did not want much more in the way of riding. I got about 60 miles in including about 12 over sand in 20 hours (i.e. 4 hour's spell during the first 24 hours). I am quite all right and so are all our regiment as far as I know, though I have not been with them at all yet, am working on a special job with another division. I have arranged with Les Willsallen for you to wire Mrs Les that he has been working with me and is all right, don't worry any more now. I saw Jim [Traill] day before yesterday; he was all right, no-one has seen a Hun plane off the ground this time, with one exception: he [the Hun] landed here by mistake yesterday, not knowing we were here and so he did not go away again. Fondest love from Jack.

P.S. if you see old Arnott [Colonel J.M., commanded 7th Light Horse at Gallipoli, then 10th Light Horse, then Commandant ANZAC forces in Egypt until 1919], you can tell him I rode his old horse very nearly but not quite to a standstill, but he has had a couple of easy days and is quite fit again. Love to children and your dear old self, ever your loving Jack.

On the same day, Davies wrote to his CO, Colonel D. Cameron of the 12th Light Horse:

My Dear Colonel,

I am sending one of the men back as his horse is too done to carry him on to Haifa. I had an idea my job would have finished on arrival here … [but after various enquiries Davies is told to remain with the 5th Division] so now I'm off to Haifa in the morning (that is if the fleas don't eat me tonight.)

This has been a wonderful stunt and I have had an opportunity of seeing the Divisional Commander on the loose at the head of his Division. Div. HQ consisted of the General Officer Commanding and his General Staff Officer, with the leading Brigade, the rest were nowhere within six miles most of the way … he's some goer is General Macandrew. I don't know whether we've been any use to the [Australian Mounted] Division, but we have got some messages back … Prisoners to date 22,000 (15,000 to Desert Corp.) Nablus fallen of course. Charles was at El Damieh today.

The whole show has come as some surprise, yesterday two carloads of Hun Staff Officers came into Beisan, to be greeted … by General Barrow. This has been a great generals' battle. They … conceived the idea so well there was not much for anyone else to do … that sort will do me, anyhow I feel a bit guilty leaving you to clean up all the filth and debris, but hope … I'll be able to see the GOC handle his division … what I have seen so far a tremendous object lesson, though certainly not in any book. Talk of Advance Guard, it was Division in Column single file. Hills all round.

Yours sincerely,

Jack Davies.

TWENTY-FOUR

The Sleepless Fortnight: the ANZACs break out

The ANZACs in the Jordan Valley saw flashes light up half the western sky in the early morning of 19 September. Their hearts leapt, not with wild surmise, but with certainty: they needed no telling to recognise the reflected light of Allenby's 384 guns in their preliminary bombardment on the coast. The advance was on! Half-sick, grim and weary men dragging themselves about routine tasks in the white hot dust, they recaptured some lightness of step, heedfulness and a positive inclination. How soon could they go?

Not until Major General Chaytor was convinced that the Turks were pulling out. There was not much point now in stepping up the fighting, however effectively, when the Turkish 4th Army opposing him were in such desperate straits after the collapse of the 7th and 8th Armies around Samaria that they must decide any time soon to break contact with Chaytor, fall back on Es Salt and Amman, then retreat to Damascus.

Allenby's orders to Chaytor were to be ready at any moment to take the offensive, 'to prevent the enemy withdrawing troops to reinforce other parts of the line … [and to] use every endeavour to protect the right flank of 20 Corps' when it advanced on the 19th. When the Turks did reduce their strength in the valley, he was to retake the old Damieh bridge across the Jordan, scene of tragedy and loss, then recovery and escape for Grant's 4th Light Horse Brigade in the Es Salt raid. Chaytor would then retrace his steps east to Es Salt and Amman again, where he was to cooperate with the Arabs. This instruction might have raised eyebrows, but all these aims were achieved to the letter, as was the rest of Allenby's plan. In this respect, it was practically unique in military history.

Chaytor continued his probing of the enemy line in the valley, seeking clear evidence that he was pulling out. On and after the 19th, the probing gathered intensity, resulting in fire fights and considerable small-scale action. Colonel C.D. Fuller led his 6th Light Horse Regiment, the 5th and a battalion of Patialas on a convincing deception against Kabr Mujahid, approaching the Turkish-held foothills of Moab. At the same time, Brigadier General W. Meldrum's New Zealanders reconnoitred boldly enemy earthworks on the West Bank, ten miles upriver.

Meldrum ordered a battalion of the British West Indies Regiment to take a height in the vicinity and these troops exceeded all expectations with a dashing advance, digging in and holding on under shell fire, then at first light on 20th charging with the bayonet and taking the feature. The critical ANZACs were impressed and admitted them to fellowship. There had been doubts about these insouciant, fun-loving blacks' performance in battle, but they embraced it with the same exuberance and drive as they did life in general. One battalion took Grant Hill, and later the other took Chalk Ridge.

The two Jewish battalions, known as 38th and 39th Royal Fusiliers, were under similar scrutiny but suffered by comparison. They were deployed in the easternmost defence posts that ringed Abu Tellul, but when ordered to advance against Turkish trenches they wilted before machine-gun fire and let their attack fade away. They would achieve little in the campaign.

With the stunning successes of 20 September, both sides in the Jordan became more active. It was now urgent for the British to seize the Damieh crossing before the fugitives from Samaria, Esdraelon and Jezreel reached it, and for the Turks to prevent them. Turkish artillery stepped up attacks on all the Jordan bridgeheads but the New Zealanders continued to dislodge them from points further upriver towards Damieh, and established a new line only three miles south of the bridge. On the East Bank, the 2nd Light Horse Brigade found the enemy were still firmly entrenched in the Moab foothills.

The probing night patrols continued. For another night, nothing changed, but early on the 22nd, the inevitable was confirmed. A troop of the 6th Light Horse Regiment heard the scrape and rumble of wagon wheels going away on the East Bank and at 4.30 am one of the Jewish battalions on the West Bank, seeing no sign of life in the Turkish trenches ahead, went forward and reached the Umm es Shert track. Then reports of the Turks' retirement came in thick and fast and the chase was on.

Meldrum's New Zealanders and the West Indies battalions went all out for the Damieh bridge and at 5 am the Auckland Regiment reached the Damieh–Nablus road, while the Wellingtons seized El Makhruk. Here they encountered the first destitute and exhausted fugitives from Samaria and the Wellingtons promptly seized 700 of them. A squadron of the Aucklands riding for the bridge cut through another column of retreating Turks, but then were counterattacked strongly and had to give ground. Colonel J.N. McCarroll's Aucklands, a squadron of Canterburys and a company of West Indians attacked again and established themselves 500 yards from the enemy. This force then went forward dismounted with the bayonet, drove the Turks from their ground and gained the bridge. It was undamaged.

This action was only a trifle in the annals of the ANZACs, though McCarroll added his own praise of the West Indians' 'keenness and great style', but its significance was immense. Now nothing could save the Turkish 4th Army.

But there was still a gap in the new front line from the Damieh bridge to Beisan twenty miles further north, out of reach of standing patrols from Beisan. Enemy remnants heading west were getting through it to cross the river, then making for Deraa. It was surveilled adequately by the RAF, although Allenby has been criticised by Cyril Falls for this one 'mistake' in an otherwise perfect operation. Mistakes have adverse consequences, but there were none: Chauvel promptly ordered the 4th Cavalry Division at Beisan to close the gap and Barrow dispatched a brigade for the job (11th). Soon, fighting for the fords, this brigade had collected another 5000 prisoners including a Turkish divisional commander and the problem disappeared. The line never was continuous: Chaytor's Force dealt in

ABOVE: *1st Brigade of ANZACs ford the Jordan River, taking the Umm esh Shert track to Amman on day four of the Sleepless Fortnight.*
BELOW: *On day six the ANZAC Division fire their last shot of the war in the last Battle of Amman. Here, 2nd Brigade troops oversee some of their 4500 prisoners.*
2ND/14TH L.H.REGT [QMI] MUSEUM ENOGGERA

isolation with the Turks in Gilead, while the other three cavalry divisions swept on northwards to the Sea of Galilee and Damascus.

Day Four: 22–23 September

Chaytor's Force began to move at night on the 22nd, and before dawn had shaken off the dust of the Jordan Valley for the last time. All the enemy rearguards fled up the tracks to Gilead. The 7th Light Horse Regiment took Kabr Mujahid, then the 6th led the three regiments of Ryrie's 2nd Brigade up the Ain es Sir track towards Amman. The 2nd, with its bitter memories of Amman, must surely have gone with vengeful anticipation of this sweetest of all victories, but Richardson contents himself with them 'following the long trail up the mountains of Moab for the third and last occasion … but under less disagreeable conditions than on the two former well remembered occasions'.

Cox's 1st Brigade, starting from the West Bank, forded the river at Umm es Shert and marched on Es Salt by the shortest route, via Arseniyet. They took the town without firing a shot. The 20th Indian Infantry Brigade joined them via Shunet Nimrin and the main road. One of the Jewish battalions, exhausted by their advance upriver through the mud hills, followed slowly and took no further part in operations.

The New Zealand Brigade crossed the Damieh bridge and also made for Es Salt. They were checked by a machine-gun post at the foothills, but overcame this and reached the town at 7 pm. Those Turks and Germans overtaken by the horsemen, 312 in all, laid down their arms. The West Indians followed close behind on foot.

Day Five: 23–24 September

Of the routes up the Moab mountains, Ryrie's was still rough and narrow enough to delay his arrival at Ain es Sir and Chaytor did not have all his force on the plateau until noon on the 24th. Then, based at Es Salt, he set about preparations for taking Amman. Some retreating Turks had swelled its garrison.

The New Zealanders and Cox's brigade went forward to Suweile, the halfway point to Es Salt. At night, 100 Aucklands, riding the best horses of their regiment, swept round Amman, cut the railway line five miles north of it and returned to Suweile within eleven hours, having covered twenty miles in darkness — a feat to match any of the whole cavalry campaign.

With these preparations the ANZACs were ready, but Chaytor, conscious of the excellent natural defences of the town and the ground contours favouring the enemy, was not inclined to risk an all-out assault. He ordered the mounted brigades to probe the objective, and if it proved to be strongly held to await the arrival of the Indian and West Indies battalions.

Day Six: 24–25 September

As Moltke said of plans, none survives contact with the enemy. However, the proviso, unless the plans were Allenby's, could now be added. In Chaytor's case, his probing of the Turkish defences was done so well by the young troop leaders, and the Turks were so demoralised, that it grew seamlessly into the main attack.

The ANZACs came in from the north and west, the New Zealand Brigade just above the Es Salt Road, Ryrie's brigade just below it, while Cox's brigade was poised in the north, closest to the objective, as reserve and left flank guard. The first encounter was with 200 enemy riflemen, whom the New Zealanders dispersed with shell fire.

The clearing of enemy outposts fell to the leading troops of the 5th and 7th Regiments, deployed on the Aucklands' right and astride the Ain es Sir road. The 6th Regiment was in reserve. Lieutenant B.R. Byrnes of the 5th, with fewer than 20 men, charged half a mile to the enemy's prepared ground, jumped from their horses and rushed the Turks with the bayonet. They shot poorly and at sight of the steel, surrendered. Lieutenant J.T. Currie's troop of the 5th advanced dismounted on exposed ground until less than 100 yards from a small redoubt, when the Turks raised a white flag. But as Currie's men came forward again, the Turks resumed fire, killing Currie and wounding all but two of those with him. This fuelled a blind rage in the survivors and Sergeant Kelly and two men, one already wounded, hurled themselves at the position and in a bloody encounter emerged the victors with 37 prisoners.

The 7th Regiment's screen under Lieutenant G.G. Finlay, working round the enemy's flank, drove in an outpost, taking 50 prisoners and a mountain gun.

Although the ANZACs were invigorated by the clean, crisp and dust-free air of the uplands, the sudden change brought on a drastic recurrence of malaria and the 7th's officers were so badly hit that Colonel Richardson was the only one of field rank left. But the junior officers, far from indulging qualms about this, saw only opportunities and reached out for the extra scope and responsibility.

Captain H.O.C. Maddrell took A Squadron east, right around the enemy's rear, but unfortunately too wide to be effective.

Lieutenant C.C. Stanley of B Squadron made a daring reconnaissance, on which he discovered some dead ground leading to within 80 yards of the enemy lines. He and Captain L.L. Williams led 35 men along this and rushed the Turkish trenches. The Turks were too stunned to resist and 100 of them surrendered. The Australians were unscathed.

This turned out to be the key to the battle, for it eased the pressure on the 5th Regiment immediately to the 7th's left, and they were able to strike out directly for the town.

At the same time, the New Zealanders with two regiments of Cox's brigade (1st and 3rd) were closing in from the north-west. Enemy machine-guns sited in the near-impregnable Roman citadel ruin that almost alone had won the day for the Turks in the first battle were still shooting, but the Canterburys managed to keep the guns' fire down with their own, from a hill just in front of it.

With the 7th Regiment on their right and the New Zealanders on their left engaging the Turks, the leading squadron of the 5th Light Horse galloped through between them, into the streets of Amman, and Turkish resistance there collapsed. It was almost a point of honour for the New Zealanders then to take Hill 3039, having been repulsed in the attempt in the first battle, and this time, with the help of Lieutenant Byrnes' troop of the 5th, they took it decisively. Pointedly. More New Zealanders and the 3rd Regiment occupied Amman railway station, while the 1st, extending across the Turks' line of retreat, cut it off, taking 2360 Turkish, German and Austrian prisoners with their artillery and machine-guns.

The capitulation of an enemy with all the advantages of numbers, guns and, especially, ground was due to the dispiriting and irrefutable conviction that their cause was lost. In the next few days, another 2500 prisoners were taken in and around the town, either voluntarily surrendering or trying to get away northwards.

My father was still in hospital for this battle. His AIF Statement of Service is cryptic and hard to read, being handwritten in part, but it appears he rejoined the 7th Regiment at Wady Hanein, their favourite Jewish village among the orange groves, wineries and dark-eyed girls on the west coast, on 19 October. But not for long. 'Met with a slight accident and am in hospital again,' he wrote. 'I was riding along one dark night by a prickly pear hedge and a projecting piece of the cactus struck me in the left eye, filling it with numerous small, hairy spicules. Had a pretty bad time of it, but it is just about right now. A lady eye specialist in Cairo has saved the situation very well and I expect to be discharged from hospital in a day or two.'

But not all the the spicules had worked their way out and he was in and out of hospitals in Gaza, Kantara and Moascar until mid-December 1918, when the eye healed and full vision was restored. Armistice Day came and went and he remained detached from the regiment.

I desire to convey to all ranks and all arms of the Force under my command, my admiration and thanks for their great deeds of the past week, and my appreciation of their gallantry and determination, which have resulted in the total destruction of the VIIth and VIIIth Turkish Armies opposed to us.

Such a complete victory has seldom been known in all the history of war.

26th September, 1918.

Allenby's general message on day seven of the Sleepless Fortnight. 2ND/14TH L.H.REGT
[QMI] MUSEUM ENOGGERA

TWENTY-FIVE

The Sleepless Fortnight: 'what about Damascus?'

The 4th and 5th Cavalry Divisions and the Australian Mounted Division had by now been stationary, in the sense of having gained no more ground, for two days; and the chapter title claiming none of them slept for a whole fourteen had better be defended. As an expression it was current, deriving from Sir Henry Gullett who ought to have known, having ridden with the Australians from Sharon to Aleppo as the official war correspondent. Other names for the offensive were The Great Ride, The Wonderful Fortnight, The Great Drive and so on, all triumphal and proof against criticism. But I like 'sleepless' for its whiff of human sweat and strain and hard yakka.

The price the mounted soldier paid for being carried was to keep in working order a being more fragile and susceptible to breakdown than himself. The quest for water and forage was eternal. Cleaning, grooming, feeding, stabling, inspecting (those frail legs) and picketing night and day, never ceased. If a spare hour happened between manhandling wagonloads of tibbin (Egyptian horse fodder) or setting up the horse lines and filling the water troughs, troops and squadrons would take their horses on grazing details.

That was routine at any time. But the troops at Beisan, Megiddo, El Afule, and now Gilead, had acquired huge front lines to police through standing and ad hoc patrols, they manned strong points and outposts round the clock, and they moved huge numbers of prisoners many miles. If they were not literally sleepless, it was because they had learned to anticipate and to snatch a spare twenty minutes when it came along. The title's slight overstatement stands.

A famously reported meeting between Allenby and Chauvel at Megiddo on 22 September has them marvelling at their success. Instead of the considerable casualties allowed for, there had been almost none. Instead of a Turko-German counterattack slicing through the line anywhere from Acre to Beisan, splitting the British in two, it hadn't happened. Chauvel tells the Chief he has 15,000 prisoners. The Chief growls jocosely: 'No bloody good to me! I want 30,000 before you've done.'

There was really not much work to do, not much to discuss. There had been no delays, no setbacks, no administrative or supply difficulties. Nothing to put right. The Chief says he would never have believed that a mounted brigade could accomplish what Wilson's 3rd Light Horse had at Jenin.

Then, perhaps turning his back to look out over the Plain of Esdraelon, he murmurs: 'What about Damascus?'

Chauvel, at his desk, makes some slight movement. His trim cavalryman's figure is poised, his expression is alert. 'Rather,' he says.

Carpe diem. The great make history without strings.

The idea itself would hardly have burst like a thunderclap on Chauvel, and of course Allenby had been mulling it over with the rest of his agenda for ending the war, but his actual plans stopped with this first phase. Even the advance from El Afule to Beisan had been contingent, a matter of opportunity. There was nothing on paper about Damascus. What appeared to have revealed itself was that this next step, obvious enough, could be taken so quickly. Without losing momentum, if they got on with it.

The occupation of Haifa and Acre on the coast had furthered this aim and the next preparatory moves would be to Semakh, a mean little mud village at the southernmost tip of Lake Tiberias, or the Sea of Galilee, eighteen miles north of Beisan: then to Tiberias town, eight miles further around the lake's western shore. These advances would give Allenby the line Tiberias–Nazareth–Acre. Chauvel was directed to proceed and he gave the job to Hodgson's Australian Mounted Division.

Hodgson's brigades had spent the two days manning the El Afule–Beisan front and were ready for fresh pastures. On the 24th, Grant was ordered to move with the 4th Brigade from El Afule to Semakh, via Beisan. The brigade cleared Beisan that afternoon and marched north, stopping at a point a few miles south-east of Semakh at nightfall, intending to attack the place at daylight. The brigade was drastically under strength, deploying only the 11th Regiment, one squadron of the 12th and Grant's machine-gun squadron, but had been promised reinforcements from Onslow's 5th Brigade.

Day Seven: 25–26 September

Grant decided not to wait for Onslow's men, and launched the dawn attack. The alternative would have meant withdrawal, discovery and courting attacks on his own weak force. What may also have influenced him was that, after taking Semakh, he was to cooperate with Wilson's 3rd Brigade, which was advancing on Tiberias independently and directly, from Nazareth.

To von Sanders, the bridge over the Jordan near Lake Huleh, fifteen miles north of Lake Tiberias, was essential to his troops' movements — the German still dreamed of a counter-offensive according to A.J. Hill — and he had appointed a German officer in command of the Semakh garrison with orders to resist any attack 'to the last man'.

Grant's men went forward before first light. The 11th Regiment was at once fired on by both rifles and machine-guns at close range. E.W. Hammond, in his history of the 11th Light Horse Regiment, recalled that 'the bullets whistled low over our heads, like the rustle of an immense flight of swallows and in the distance we saw pin-points of light dancing along the muzzles of the guns like the flicker of lightning'.

Major E. Costello, the leading squadron commander, called to Colonel H.M. Parsons just ahead of him, 'What orders, Colonel?' and Parsons replied instantly, 'Form line and charge the guns!'

Trooper Fowler, who was in the 12th's accompanying squadron, told Ian Jones that suddenly the air was filled with the rattle of rifle and machine-gun fire. The squadron stopped and were told that the 11th Regiment would form up on their left flank ready to charge, while they acted as moving targets to draw the fire of the enemy gunners. 'We rode over and back again, with a stream of bullets flying around, mostly overhead: we must have been closer to the enemy than they thought, to our great benefit. Our horses knew what those bullets meant and we had to work to control them. My pony stood on his hind legs many times and tried to gallop away.'

Two squadrons of the 11th formed up quickly in two lines and, writes Hammond, 'the thin blades of the swords sang as they leapt from the scabbards, the horses jumped to the touch of the spurs' and they were away, galloping hard in the darkness at German machine-gun nests.

One of these was quickly overrun, but fire could then be seen from Semakh's railway station, a two-storeyed stone building, Semakh's gesture to architecture, conspicuous in the moonlight a mile away on the right. The two squadrons wheeled straight for it at the gallop. Cavalry pits in the ground brought down some horses, and at 800 yards bullets brought down more. The riders urged them forward into that contorting, eye-bulging, mouth-gaping extension of their fastest gait.

The fire caused the two squadrons to diverge: Major J. Loynes, a South African war veteran of nearly 60, bore left for the little town, while Costello went round the railway building to the right. By moonlight their horses showed up like black counters on a draughts board and the machine-gunners kept felling them. Gaining the streets, Loynes' men reined up behind some mud huts and went for the railway station building dismounted. From its top-storey narrow windows, the defenders shot them point blank. The enemy had the ascendency: Loynes found cover in a drain with a slab fence along it and the squadron tumbled in, twenty yards from the station.

Costello's squadron galloped in from the east to raking fire from the enemy flank guard and dismounted 200 yards from the station. A hot fight developed at revolver range, but for more than an hour the struggle was stationary.

Grant ordered the Australian machine-gunners forward and they arrived from the south-east, together with the squadron of the 12th. The machine-gun fire at once reduced the enemy fire from the windows, and as dawn broke Loynes' and Costello's squadrons charged on foot from their cover. The fighting was now hand-to-hand and bloody. The garrison troops had two to one superiority in numbers, hand grenades and, according to Gullett, 'an abundance of rum' to sustain their resistance.

Costello's men made short rushes amongst the earthworks and railway stock, while Loynes' charged from cover right up to the doors of the station building. They battered one door open sufficiently to enter one by one and inside, in darkness, forced their way from room to room and floor to floor, driving the Turks and Germans back with their bayonets. Three Australian officers and six other ranks were killed in this building, but the fight raged until every enemy was accounted for, killed or captured. It was one of the most vicious hand-to-hand encounters of the campaign.

What tipped the balance for the Australians was the intervention of the machine-gunners, whose assault drove the defenders away from their firing positions at upstairs windows. Towards the end, some enemy tried to escape by boat, but they were caught by Hotchkiss fire and the boat was burnt. The Hotchkiss gunners also cut down fugitives fleeing along the railway.

Australian losses were 14 killed and 29 wounded, but the moonlit shooting accounted for 61 dead and 27 wounded horses — half the animals engaged. The enemy lost 98 killed and 364 captured, of whom 150 were German. Grant's Mob — this time, the regiment that had missed Beersheba through being on outpost and too far away — had done it again. And, says Cyril Falls, the garrison commander Hauptmann von Keyserling had lived up to the finest traditions of the German Army.

The Christian and Moslem dead were buried side by side on the lake's shore, in what was described as the one of the most impressive makeshift cemeteries of the war.

The operations of Wilson's 3rd Light Horse Brigade against Tiberias also commenced on this day, with the advance of a squadron of the 8th Regiment under Major Macpherson down the main road from Nazareth. Another party of the 10th Regiment were ordered to the top of Mount Tabor, from where they could observe the 8th squadron's progress and keep Wilson informed by heliograph.

The squadron's route followed that of the British 700 years earlier, where on a parched summer's day Saladin's cavalry had wiped out King Richard's force with a scrub fire, as well as their swords. The knights cooked in their armour. Macpherson rode in the tracks of the Crusaders, between two big hills called the Horns of Hattin, where the fighting took place.

When they reached high ground, the Australians were observed and the enemy sent patrols out to investigate. The Light Horsemen quickly cut these Turks off and captured them, while in Tiberias they remained unaware. Macpherson sent a troop with a Hotchkiss gun to the lake shore north of the town, where they blocked the escape of a convoy. Four British armoured cars working with the Light Horse engaged six enemy machine-guns in this area.

At 1130, a squadron of the 12th Regiment came up from Semakh to within reach of the town's outskirts and Macpherson, now holding all the approaches to the place except the one over water, decided to attack without waiting for the rest of his brigade.

It was a comparatively perfunctory action. The 12th's squadron advanced from the south-west, the armoured cars closed from the west and the 8th came in from the north-west. The 12th took an enemy machine-gun post at the gallop, one troop penetrated into the town and the Tiberias garrison of 200 capitulated without further resistance at 3 pm. The place was infested with cholera, so Wilson's brigade camped clear of it on the shore and all hands and horses had a couple of days swimming.

Day Eight: 27–28 September

An extraordinary and farcical twist to the war suddenly diverted the attention of the ANZACs on the Moab uplands from the north to the south.

They knew there was yet another Turkish force of about 6000 on the Mecca railway at Maan, 120 miles south of Amman. These troops had been fending off attacks from the Beni Sakr tribe of Arabs for some months, but the railway being cut, the Turks could not replenish supplies and were surely being forced northwards before the increasingly aggressive tribesmen. The ANZACs routinely alerted all forces east of the Jordan to the possibility of them coming and saw that the water supplies along their presumed routes could be denied them.

On the 27th, a squadron of the 3rd Light Horse Regiment mopped up over 400 Turks at Kalaat Ez Zerka, north of Amman, and incidentally sealed off that route to the Maan force. On the same day, a detachment of the 7th Regiment took Turkish prisoners near Leban, ten miles south of Amman, some of whom said their Maan compatriots were marching north and intending to stage at a point four miles south of the 7th's position.

Next morning, a British airman sighted them at the village of Ziza: just where the prisoners had said. A pilot dropped a message to them saying Amman and all water to the north were in British hands, resistance was useless and they should surrender, on penalty of being bombed that evening. There was no reply and Lieutenant Colonel D.C. Cameron commanding the 5th Regiment (not to be confused with another Lieutenant Colonel D. Cameron commanding the 12th) took two squadrons south to investigate.

Half a mile from Ziza, Turkish emissaries came up the line on a rail trolley with a letter from their commander, Colonel Ali Bey Wahaby, requesting a meeting. Then another letter arrived overtaking the first, saying Ali Bey wanted to surrender but his troops would be slaughtered by the Arabs if he did so and a single Australian regiment could not afford him sufficient protection. The Arabs, he said, numbered 10,000.

Cameron, seeing the huge host of Arabs crowding the flanks of the enemy, had to agree. Gullet describes these 'picturesque tribesmen, burning to strike and plunder, but fearful of risk, prowling like jackals around them. Riding their mean-looking but spirited horses, they galloped in wide circles about the fugitive force, uttering wild shouts, firing their rifles in the air, and threatening each hapless straggler with pillage and murder.'

Foremost of Cameron's priorities was to stop the RAF bombing raid, scheduled for that evening. His signallers had repaired the telegraph lines as he went and he was able to explain the situation to Colonel Browne, Chaytor's chief staff officer. He asked that the raid be stopped and reinforcements be sent. Browne said it would take some time to do both things: hang on. Cameron sent riders into the Turks' centre to lay out a panel of ground sheets, normally for marking the point where aircraft should drop messages and, to appearances, a friendly spot. Ali Bey conveyed his appreciation and added that if the raid could not be stopped, 'it would be the will of Allah'. At 8.30 pm Cameron was advised that the air attack had been called off.

But he had assessed that his reinforcements would not arrive by nightfall and ordered the Turks to retain their arms and man their trenches all night. By this time, the enemy troops appeared to be approaching collapse through fatigue and anxiety. They could not have marched back to Maan and every man was terror-stricken lest he should fall into Arab

272

hands: groups of stragglers were being caught and dragged off shrieking, to be robbed, tortured or killed.

Even so, Cameron was looked on as an ally by the Arabs and they insisted on their right, as allies, to seize the arms of the common enemy.

Cameron retorted angrily that if they committed any more attacks, he would open fire.

Major General Chaytor arrived just as Ali Bey made his entrance from his tent under a flag of truce. Chaytor confirmed the Australian reinforcements would probably not arrive before dark and Colonel Cameron's orders stood. He then added Ali Bey would be held hostage by himself: a reasonable concession to the Arabs.

The Turk didn't like it. Like any responsible commander, he said he should not desert his troops — and be seen to desert to safety. The consequences could be unpredictable. Could not the Australians stand off in the guise of his powerful allies, while he beat the Arabs into submission?

General Chaytor was known as much for his respect of the Turks as his contempt for the Arabs, but he could not sanction this. After more pondering and arguing, this most sagacious divisional commander confessed himself stumped and withdrew, leaving the problem for Brigadier General Ryrie to deal with when he arrived with the reinforcements. Turk, Arab, Australian or Briton, there was no better man for the job.

Ryrie was encamped fifteen miles away when he received orders to join Cameron. He had only the 7th Regiment available and led it out 35 minutes later. On the urging of Cameron that the dangerous situation could become unmanageable unless he could deploy his troops in daylight, he extended the 7th, alternately trotting and cantering, then dropping the pack horses off and covering the last five miles at a full gallop. They arrived just before dark.

According to Richardson: 'The 5th Regiment was concentrated, waiting, whilst the Turks in their trenches were ... holding off the Arabs with shell and machine-gun fire. The vulture-like appearance of these latter, who had spoilt our operations at an earlier date and were now willing that the British should do the fighting and they the looting, will not readily be forgotten.'

The Arab chiefs crowded round Ryrie, urging him to join them in their assault. The brigadier had already decided he must align himself with the

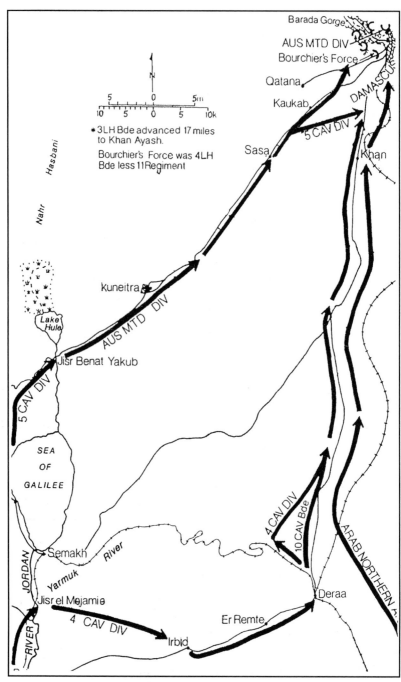

Pursuit to Damascus, September–October, 1918.

Turks that night. He let the Turks know of his intention, then ordering two of the most prominent sheikhs to come with him, galloped his two regiments through the Arab circle and into the Turkish lines. Dismounting, he told the unsuspecting sheikhs that if their followers attacked they would be instantly shot. Speedily the two hostages sent word to this effect and the Arabs, though never quiet, showed no further disposition to decide the issue. Richardson continues:

> It was getting dark as orders were received to gallop in and take the [Turks'] surrender, the 5th Regiment being on the left and the 7th on the right. Moving fast by squadrons and brushing the Arabs well out of the way, the Turkish positions, with the Turks kneeling with their caps [headgear] on their fixed bayonets, were quickly gained and [some elements] were taken charge of and brought into the Brigade concentration point near the railway station. C Squadron was placed on outpost and several times during the night had to use Hotchkiss rifles to prevent Arabs breaking through. [Otherwise] the Turks were sandwiched with various units of the Brigade and held the line ... using their machine-guns freely.

That Ryrie's threat to the sheikhs was a bluff was proven by Richardson's account of fresh Arab aggression and the two hostages remaining unharmed, though there were no more serious attacks. This boldest of strokes worked, like so many Ryrie pulled off as soldier and politician, with characteristic confidence and flair. If something had gone wrong, such as a partial break-out by the Turks, necessitating the Australians turning on them with loss of more lives, which might in turn have given the Arabs fresh impetus, and then spawned an out of control free-for-all imbroglio ... the only consequence to bear thinking about was Ryrie's certain dismissal and he must have known it.

What a night! These two regiments had seen each other through countless nights of shot and shell in every engagement since Gallipoli, and neither Queensland's finest of the 5th nor the New South Welshmen of the 7th had ever failed the other with timely help in a tight corner. Now, they broke bread with Turks, and, Richardson wrote, 'all enmities forgiven ... boiled their quarts and made chupatties over the same fires'. They didn't know it then, but for them, the shooting stopped with Ziza and it was as if the fates had laid on an end-of-war party. The Light Horsemen cheered this comic stunt and roared with laughter and yelled their appreciation of the Turks' gunfire at the perimeter. 'Go on Jacko! Keep 'em hopping! Give it to the bastards!' they shouted.

But all parties have to end and at 5.30 am on the 29th, Chaytor sent the New Zealand Brigade to relieve them. The Turkish prisoners-of-war were concentrated at the railway station and gave up their rifle bolts with no regrets. Then Ryrie made a final gesture. He ordered two of the best Anatolian regiments to keep their rifle bolts and full bandoliers in case of an attack on the march to Amman. The Arabs, furious but impotent, had started drifting away in their immemorial fashion and there was no attack: if there had been, the ANZACs could have interposed again and saved the day. 'But the sight of two fine Turkish units marching proudly into Amman, fully armed, created a brief sensation,' writes Cyril Falls; and perhaps that was what this generous soldier/politician of undoubted theatrical susceptibilities had wanted.

So ended the Trans-Jordan operations of Chaytor's Force. In nine days they had taken 10,300 prisoners and huge quantities of war material. Twenty-seven ANZACs had been killed in action, 105 wounded and seven were missing. Ziza was a dramatic close to the Great War for his regiment, which Richardson notes 'never fired a shot after this, in Palestine or Syria'.

The force withdrew from Moab, the mounted men escorting prisoners to Jericho and beyond. From then until repatriation, the ANZAC Mounted Division were out of the front line. The truth was, they were broken in health after the Jordan Valley summer and still succumbing in hundreds to malignant malaria and other illnesses. Soon, the worst scourge of all would kill more than all the battles: pneumonic influenza (Spanish flu) that spread all over the world in 1918–19. Of the British forces, the pioneer 1st and 2nd Brigades of ANZACs suffered most from it while the Turkish prisoners died like flies. A new operational factor introduced itself into Allenby's war: whether his troops could finish it while they were still on their feet.

TWENTY-SIX

The Sleepless Fortnight: roads to Damascus

A llenby called his corps commanders — Chauvel, Bulfin and Chetwode — to Jenin on 25 September, and a simple plan for taking Damascus was made. The infantry was by then able to occupy the cavalry's ground and free them for the next phase of operations.

The Turkish 7th and 8th Armies had been destroyed, but the 4th Army, badly mauled and retreating up the Hejaz railway, could pose a threat if it made a stand with the help of the garrison of Deraa. Lawrence reported that between 20,000 and 30,000 troops were marching on Deraa and Emir Feisal's Arabs, in their way of committing themselves when they could see a win, were harrying them and keeping in touch. The 4th Army was a tempting cavalry target.

General Barrow's 4th Cavalry Division was to march 30 miles further east from Beisan to Deraa and, cooperating with the Arabs, intercept and destroy this last enemy. Barrow was then to continue north by the rather ill-defined Old Pilgrim's Road to join with Chauvel's other two mounted divisions in the assault on Damascus.

Barrow needed to move from Beisan a day earlier than the other divisions, who would proceed north-easterly and directly for Damascus,

277

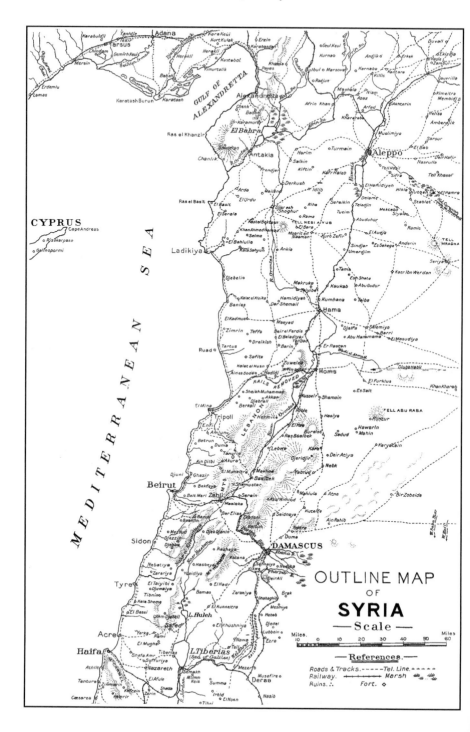

from Chauvel's new headquarters at Tiberias. They were to cross the Jordan River a few miles south of Lake Huleh over a three-span stone bridge called Jisr Benat Yakub (Bridge of the Daughters of Jacob).

The resumption of the offensive in this way held no surprises, but speed and coordination were just as essential for success. Faultless staff work and support would again be needed and problems for the supply trains could be foreseen, owing to rougher country. However, where these occurred the men and horses were able to live off the land.

On 26 September, Macandrew's division left Acre and Haifa for Nazareth, Barrow struck east across the hills for Deraa, and on the next day Hodgson's Australians, with Macandrew's Yeomanry and Indians following, rode north for the bridge at Benat Yakub.

They knew it had been blown by the enemy and Wilson's 3rd Brigade reconnoitred north and south of it for fords. There was immediate resistance: Captain von Keyserling of Semakh now defended Benat Yakub. Artillery, machine-gun and rifle fire from a rearguard on the east bank stopped Wilson until the 4th and 5th Brigades came up. Then, spread along the banks, more regiments were able to probe for crossings, though still under fire at close range. But the Royal Horse Artillery batteries were unable to pinpoint the opposing field guns and machine-guns and the advance was checked.

Then Colonel Bourchier with the 4th Light Horse Regiment, supported by the 14th, found a ford about two miles south of the bridge and were able to wear down the enemy's fire while they worked their way across it in single file. However, the opposite bank was so steep and broken with boulders that men and horses were unable to get clear of it until 7 pm. Further progress was impossible in darkness and Bourchier halted for the night.

In the meantime, northwards, the 10th Regiment had also crossed the river half a mile from Lake Huleh. The 8th followed and these two regiments struck out in the dark for Deir es Saras, the first locality worthy of a name five miles on from the bridge. Horses and riders groped and felt their way through long grass and around boulders. Suddenly, they blundered into point-blank machine-gun and rifle fire. The men slipped from their saddles and rushed the gun flashes with their bayonets. The enemy stood and fought well, but the Australians bore them back, not without casualties, until the post, along with 40 Turks, 12 Germans, a field gun and machine-guns, was theirs.

In the night, the enemy withdrew his whole rearguard in motor transport. It seemed his strategy was to delay Chauvel long enough for the 4th Army to reach Damascus and defend it: and a withdrawal was in order if a more advantageous place to stand offered later.

Day Nine: 28–29 September

Wilson's brigade joined the 8th and 10th Light Horse at dawn and, except for an air raid by three enemy aircraft — the first sighted since breaking out onto the Plain of Sharon — no enemy were seen and the Australians had advanced to the 'hungry little bluestone village' of Kuneitra by 10 am. The guns and all transport were still on the bank of the river behind them, but parties of Light Horsemen were digging out boulders to improve the stream bed and some crossings were made. Then in another three hours, Hodgson's engineers had improvised repairs to the bridge and it was ready for wheeled traffic.

Hodgson concentrated his division about Kuneitra that evening and Macandrew's 5th Cavalry Division in rear, camped a few miles further back. They spent a cold and blustery night without food, having outrun the supply wagons, but had good water.

Feisal's Arabs, now called the Northern Arab Army, were officially on strength as part of Allenby's command, with Lawrence acting as the liaison channel. Feisal's men operated against the Turks south of Deraa, while Barrow's closed on the town from the west. They were intended to meet and cooperate, and they did, but with some side effects that clouded Anglo-Arab relations briefly.

As much has been written about, and by, Lieutenant Colonel T.E. Lawrence as Allenby himself. Lawrence wrote frankly self-serving accounts of his part in the turbulent politics of the region and how they became a climactic maelstrom with the capture of Damascus. To some, he was little short of a poseur. Chauvel was to have major difficulties on his occupation of the place, firstly through lack of a political adviser. According to A.J. Hill, Allenby just told him to 'do what we did at Jerusalem. Send for the Turkish Vali [civil governor] and tell him to carry on, giving him what extra police he requires'. Chauvel's second difficulty was brought about through the thrusting, Machiavellian dealings of Lawrence in his efforts to gain Syria for the Arabs at the expense of the French, whose claims had been recognised by the British in the Sykes–Picot Agreement of 1916, and his third difficulty was caused by the instant collapse of the Turkish administration, which saw Turks brawling with Germans in the streets.

The Australians' relations with Lawrence were not so vital, but are part of the story. Neither liked the other. Lawrence wrote that Australians were 'thin-tempered, hollow, instinctive and ... had put off half civilisation with their civil clothes'. Some Arab guerillas were trained in the use of Lewis guns by Light Horse Sergeant Charles Yells, who Lawrence described as 'long, thin and sinuous, his supple body lounging in unmilitary curves. His hard face, arched eyebrows and predatory nose set off the peculiarly Australian air of reckless willingness to do something very soon'. Ian Jones, from whom these notes are borrowed, adds that Lawrence could not have given a better description of a Light Horse 'Billjim', as the soldiers were popularly known back in Australia.

For their part, the Australians angrily repudiated Lawrence's claim that his Arabs captured Damascus when in fact the 10th Light Horse Regiment did so, and they looked on the Arab Northern Army and its works with disgust.

Barrow's progress towards Deraa had been slower than anticipated. For over twenty miles, the route was over sharp stones, on which horses were at risk of injury to fetlocks and pasterns in their faster paces and the troops had to negotiate narrow defiles in the ranges. There was also stiff enemy resistance at the halfway point of Irbid, and again, seven miles short of the town.

When he reached Deraa, Barrow was preparing to take the place, unaware that the 4th Army had come and gone from it and the Arabs were in occupation. They had spent the night of 27 September in celebratory slaughter, arson and looting. Barrow's first contact with Lawrence was on the next day.

Lawrence shaved and put on fresh robes for the occasion. He was, says Cyril Falls, 'eager to prove that his irregular Arab troops could restore and maintain discipline as well as regulars'. Lawrence, who said he was determined to behave with 'histrionic nonchalance', thought Barrow was nonplussed at having been beaten to the goal. The lordly Lawrence announced that Barrow's men would be guests of the Arabs: furthermore, there was no need to post sentries, because that had been done.

The picture from Lawrence's own account is of a gifted eastern potentate condescending to a dull and plodding soldier. Barrow was nothing of the sort: he was of attractive humour, convivial, and sharp enough on this occasion to salute the pennant of one of Feisal's most notable lieutenants, to the delight of the watching Arabs. But he was to claim that in all his service in the war, he never saw such appalling misery as confronted him in Deraa. The British official history records:

> ... the sight of Deraa Station and its encampments ... was ghastly beyond aught that any man had yet witnessed. Everywhere there were dead Turks, but they were the fortunate ones; for the wounded lay scattered about, despoiled and in agony, amid a litter of packages, half looted, half burnt, of torn documents and smashed machinery. A Turkish hospital train stood at the station; the driver and fireman were still in their cab, still alive but mortally wounded; the sick and wounded in the train had been stripped of every rag of clothing.

That Lawrence had apparently not intervened in this carnage enraged Barrow and he issued furious orders that it be stopped. Too late: he did not know that there had been even more frightful butchery, by both Arabs and Turks, the day before.

Lawrence was in pursuit of a Turkish column approaching Deraa when he came to the Arab settlement of Tafas, the home of a leading Arab named Talal, riding with him. The Turks had just passed through Tafas and left it a charnel house.

Gullett wrote that the stoical, enduring Turkish fighter and docile, unresentful prisoner-of-war had another side: '"he" reverts swiftly to the qualities of his wild, marauding forebears ... and he will burn, ravish, and mutilate ... The same Turkish soldiery ... who almost invariably respected the Red Cross, excelled, when turned loose with license to do their worst [to the Armenians] in every conceivable act of unchivalry, cowardice, and indescribable violence ... The Turkish soldiers revelled in this horrible work because they enjoyed it, because it sated their desires ... The Armenians and their possessions were systematically fed to the Moslem soldiery as a stimulant'.

The film *Lawrence of Arabia* reconstructed what the Turks did at Tafas and what the Arabs did to them. Censored they may have been, but the scenes do not lack for horror. The Arabs usually left women and children alone but the Turks, when their blood was up, slaughtered whatever being was to hand, man, woman or child. A little child ran from Lawrence in terror, crying out 'Don't hit me, Baba!', then fell with blood pumping from a mortal wound. Lawrence wrote: 'I looked close and saw the body of a woman folded across it [a sheep hurdle] bottom upwards, nailed by a saw bayonet the hilt of which stuck hideously in the air between her naked legs'. The film showed this all but completely.

The Turkish column was overhauled, trudging along exhausted without a backward look, to the monotonous tinkling of a camel bell. Talal pulled the hood of his burnous over his head and charged at the Turks. He was shot dead at once. Auda, another senior Arab, called on Allah for mercy on Talal's soul and swore that the Turks would pay.

Lawrence struck at the tail of the column until it split into three groups. The Arabs destroyed two of them but the third were Germans who saved themselves with systematic, cool defence. Lawrence described them 'sheering through the wrack of Turk and Arab like armoured ships, high-faced and silent'. Otherwise, every enemy prisoner taken was killed and the heads of all the wounded were bashed in.

The falling out between Barrow and Lawrence lasted well into peacetime and reverted to print in Barrow's book *Fire of Life* and Lawrence's *The Seven Pillars of Wisdom*. Their detractors and supporters took sides and neither of the principals ever said a good word for the other. But the advance on Damascus continued after Deraa, with Barrow marching for Kiswe on the Old Pilgrim's Road and the Arabs taking the easterly route, more or less in parallel, up the Hejaz Railway.

Day Ten: 29–30 September

Hodgson intended to move on from Kuneitra by night on the 29th. Other voices, including Brigadier General Wilson's, whose 3rd Brigade were advance guard, suggested a daylight attack — the enemy were known to hold a strong position astride the road, four miles south of Sasa. But their counsel did not prevail and the 3rd Brigade led off at 3 pm.

This country, now known as the Golan Heights, is extremely difficult: wide areas of lava rocks and rubble, and fissures over which man and horse could only struggle, even in daylight. At night, there would have been little prospect of outflanking an enemy in such country. But darkness offered concealment.

It was already dark when the 9th Regiment's leading squadron were detected, sustained casualties from artillery fire and were halted. Wilson brought the rest of the brigade forward, but all attempts to move by road were checked by six well-sited and registered machine-guns. Mounted movement off the road being impossible, two squadrons of the 9th dismounted and tried to probe and outflank the enemy from the left, while the third squadron moved off-road to the right.

For hours the Light Horsemen floundered over rocks. The 10th Regiment joined them and 1400 men now struggled in the infernal lava. The advance did make slight progress, and Hodgson, fretting over the clock, called for another effort. At 2 am, the men on the flanks experienced a trace of give in the resistance: the 8th Regiment then moved off the road and, locating the machine-guns by their flashes, crept forward and seized all six of them without losing a man. The Germans and Turks again took to their waiting motor transport and hastily retreated, pursued by the 10th.

The enemy attempted to make another stand a mile short of Sasa, but the 10th dismounted, and with the bayonet, dislodged them quickly.

By now Wilson's brigade was widely scattered and two regiments of Grant's 4th Brigade, the 4th and 12th, took the lead. Grant himself had been kept at Kuneitra with the 11th Regiment as a communications rearguard.

Damascus now lay only 40 miles away and Bourchier's Force eagerly took up the running. After a hard night, relief and excitement seized all ranks and they revelled in a sense of destiny and in their chance to be first to take the great prize.

After they cleared Sasa village, the lava rocks were behind them and they were on a great brown plain, level and clear. The squadrons gave themselves room and the lead squadron went up to a spanking pace. They rode through small bands of unresisting Turkish and German fugitives not worth drawing rein for. This was the day, they knew, when they had the chance to virtually end the campaign. 'Caution went to the winds,' wrote Gullett. 'With swords flashing in the early sunrise, little parties of three and four raced shouting on bodies of Turks ten and twenty times their number. [A troop] on a flank, chopped boldly across the rear of a strong column, and compelled the surrender of 180 men, a field gun, and several machine-

284

guns. Bourchier, still following the road with Cameron of the 12th Regiment, had to ride hard to keep touch with his exuberant horsemen.'

At the Barbar River, with which the Barada River makes up 'the Waters of Damascus', they reined up, watered horses and ate breakfast. Here the 3rd and 5th Light Horse Brigades caught up with them and the division was nearly at full concentration again; and in a metaphorical salute to the last campaign of mounted troops, Falls says the formation of Hodgson's 'whole division now deployed, each brigade in columns of squadrons in line of troop columns … has never been repeated.'

Away to the east, they saw the billowing dust of Barrow's division still advancing, still on the heels of the Turkish 4th Army. Hodgson did not know at this stage whether the 4th Army had reached Damascus, or what state it was in.

His brigades moved on. From the right, a large enemy force appeared and headed across the Australians' front. Then they set up a strong line of machine-gun posts. This called for tactics and a more orthodox approach than the early headlong ride. Bourchier's Force of the 4th and 12th Regiments were still advance guard. Stony ridges and ravines, with the enemy behind them near the village of Kaukab, traversed their line of advance. Bourchier moved to a ridge a mile away and, concealed behind it, made ready for a mounted assault.

This enemy force lacked any artillery, which gave the Royal Horse Artillery batteries attached to the Australians a free hand. They could deploy on top of a ridge out of range, and fire over open sights. Hodgson ordered Brigadier General Onslow's 5th Brigade to move clear, to the west of the coming engagement, then to take his troops past the Turks to their right rear. Onslow's French Colonials on their grey horses made good time past the Turks' right flank and duly menaced their rear. The RHA batteries opened fire.

The victors of Beersheba, the 4th and 12th Regiments, with swords drawn, waited with their memories. Beersheba had been glorious — afterwards. But there had been terror in the whining bullets and near-impossible odds, then trauma: the crashing horses and tumbling men and the bestial kill-or-be-killed bayonet fighting would haunt them until they died. What would they have thought of this coming charge?

Hodgson gave the order. Two squadrons of each regiment went, leaving two squadrons in reserve. The lines of horsemen raced for the crest of the ridge, went over, and keeping to their spaced artillery formation, galloped at the facing slope. They knew what was in store. Now, they might have thought, or Come on, or Let's have you. Trooper Fowler told Ian Jones: 'We expected to go into heavy machine-gun fire. I heard someone yell as we galloped along, "Why don't you fire, you bastards?" it was hard on the nerves, waiting for that blizzard of bullets.'

It didn't come. For the first time, the German gunners, evidently unnerved by charging horses and waving swords, the French Chasseurs and Spahis to their right rear and the accurate RHA bombardment falling around them, broke and fled. The Light Horsemen beheld a veritable exodus of 2500 Turks and Germans sprinting for cover in all directions.

The Barada Gorge, outside Damascus. The massacre here blocked the road, railway and river. AWM B01112

The last charge of the Australian Light Horse was bloodless. The captured machine-guns had not fired a shot. Bourchier told the elated squadron commanders it was like a drill manoeuvre.

Onslow's brigade went on, past Daraya, four miles from Damascus. The 14th Regiment reached the edge of the great garden area of the city, where the enemy made another stand, soon dealt with by a mounted flanking movement through the gardens themselves.

All enemy were spent. As the Australians progressed, 5000 or 6000 of them fell back and started along the road to Beirut, which led from the Barada Gorge. The road and railway wound through this gorge, and the river tumbled into the city. Its sides were high desert cliffs.

The French regiment swung into these heights above the route and shot down the head of the escaping column. Shattered and distraught, the Turks surged back. However, a small party of the 14th Regiment had got across the entrance into a house, and from its apertures poured fire at a few yards' range into their front. Turning again, the enemy was confronted by more of the 14th, who had deployed at ground level. Four thousand of them threw down their arms.

But it was only a portent of the carnage to come in this place.

TWENTY-SEVEN

The Sleepless Fortnight: Damascus falls

Day Eleven: 30 September–October 1

With darkness on 30 September, the Australian Mounted Division were halted on the southern and western approaches to Damascus. On the British (UK) side, Chauvel had sent a brigade of Macandrew's across the few miles eastwards to join Barrow's pursuit of the Turkish 4th Army and these Indians and Yeomanry routed a column of 2000 enemy moving from Kiswe to Damascus, by which time the brigade gained the last ridge south of the city.

Barrow's advance, slowed up on the ill-defined and in places absent Old Pilgrim's Road and the old Roman road, had reached a point thirteen miles south of the city late on the 30th. Dead and dying enemy troops and abandoned equipment marked the 4th Cavalry's passage, the stench of death filled the air, and as the hours passed it seemed to matter less whether the Turkish 4th Army reached Damascus or not: the signs were that they were in no condition to defend it.

The Arab Northern Army still advanced on Barrow's right, about five miles distant and twelve south of the city but on better ground, and they

288

spurred through the night. Their ambition to be first into Damascus carried all of Lawrence's hopes and aspirations for their destiny. The culmination of all his work lay in the seizure of the city and he was acutely conscious that the Arab cause must be advanced powerfully if history could show that they had liberated this great prize.

The Australians spent another ware and wakeful, freezing night. They were not encamped, just halted on impassable ground. Chauvel's plan was for them to isolate Damascus by occupying the Barada Gorge and blocking the roads to both Beirut and Homs, the first going through the gorge from the city and the second leading north directly from the city.

Even as Bourchier's Force made their charge at Kaukab, Hodgson had ordered Wilson to follow Onslow's French advance guard when they outflanked the Kaukab action and continued north.

While Onslow's men secured the Barada Gorge, Wilson tried to cross it near the settlement of Dumar, five miles out of Damascus. Lieutenant Colonel Scott's 9th Regiment with six machine-guns made the attempt on the right of the French regiment, but as he tried to descend into the gorge he found both stiff opposition and most treacherous footing.

Brigadier General L.C. Wilson (seated left) and staff, 3rd Brigade, Australian Mounted Division. AWM B00776

Wilson came to the view that if he stuck to the original planned route around Damascus, his brigade would become scattered in these ragged foothills and would probably not succeed in cutting the road to Homs and Aleppo in time to prevent an exodus of 4th Army and/or Turkish garrison troops. An alternative was to ride northwards through Damascus itself. Via urban and suburban streets, he could seal off the Homs road almost effortlessly. The city's garrison was strong, but whether it was still organised and disciplined enough to block such an attempt was the judgment he had to make.

This Brisbane solicitor had won Jenin and stormed the ancient, crooked streets of Es Salt with galloping horsemen because he had intercepted a message from General Hodgson saying the town must be taken by nightfall. Now, with the 10th Light Horse Regiment, Wilson would add another military masterstroke to his name.

Meanwhile, as Scott and the men of the 9th peered down from their eyries on the gaunt red rocks above the gorge, they saw movement below. Another immense column of Turkish troops, transport, railway trains and vehicles of all kinds was attempting to get through, from the Damascus end. There were horses, cattle, camels, civilians including women — and presumably therefore children — all mixed with troops out of formation but still armed. Some rode in buggies, some walked. The gorge was only 100 yards wide and the twisting, rapid river, the railway and the road took up much room; the humanity and animals were crammed into a doomed, slowly-moving mass. Even the river was full of men and horses. There are many accounts of what happened in this gorge, and all use words such as 'bloodbath', 'shambles', 'butchery', 'massacre'.

Brigadier General Onslow said he never gave an order with greater reluctance and abhorrence. 'I turned eight machine-guns and every available rifle onto this mass of humanity. It was awful.'

The French Colonials and Australians raked them with fire, then as night came and the light faded, shot at any movement. The fugitives were caught between the 5th Brigade in front and the 3rd Brigade in rear. German machine-gunners, in their robust tradition, returned fire from the tops of motor vehicles, but while they did so, ruled out the possibility of surrender. An unofficial count of the dead was 375. Ian Jones says it took 300 German prisoners two weeks to clear the debris.

Also on this night, Wilson concentrated his brigade near Dumar, at the western end of the gorge, in preparation for his hazardous sally into the heart of the city next morning.

Light Horse Captain Hector W Dinning Wrote *Nile to Aleppo*, a travel book post-war, and as 'H.W.D.' contributed an extract describing Damascus at that time, to *Australia in Palestine, 1919*.

H.W.D. said the main attraction of the place was in its plant variety and greenery. Lush gardens and orchards throve, watered by the Barada and Abana Rivers. This was in most marked contrast to the lank, brown and seer country on all its sides. Compared to Cairo, it had few minarets, but they were dotted around in pleasing relief to the flat roofs. The ubiquitous and accursed cactus hedge was present, but in competition with other green things and not as obtrusive as in the rest of the region. 'When we came to Damascus it was drought-stricken. Soon afterwards, it rained torrentially for a day. Then the sun shone and drew from the city such colour as we never dreamed was there.'

But it stank mightily. The alleyways surpassed even Cairo's for foulness. Offal, refuse and nameless rot lay around in every street. The Abana River was curdled with sludge. It was here that Allenby's army contracted the diseases that killed them, just as the bullets stopped. The place was neglected in all ways: the ruts and potholes broke the springs of military transport and the warped and buckled tramlines rose out of their beds.

Yet, H.W.D. wrote, 'Foul as this city may be, there is beauty in every foot of it'. This lay, he said, in small vistas and small things: the space of a marketplace, a mosque, a tiny piece of architecture. 'It is a beauty in colour rather than in form. Form in Cairo counts for much — in Damascus for almost nothing.' He thought the beauty in Damascus came from its extreme age, a mellowness. 'You feel the age of it as you pace every yard of its alleys. Cairo is comparatively modern, and comparatively garish. There is a fine, if filthy, harmony in Damascus.'

Wilson's men were preoccupied only with its defences at this stage. They assessed their chances in the light of obvious turmoil in the city and what must have been ineffective government.

It was better than that. After 400 years of Turkish misrule, overnight there was no government. Soldiers and refugees continued to struggle in from the south and some still fit and strong enough went out through the north. Other refugee columns encroached on the city's eastern limits. Jubilant, menacing Arabs ran through the streets with the green flag of the Hejaz, discharging their rifles and threatening the timid Christians and Jews. Djemal Pasha, the Turkish Commander-in-Chief, chivvied and prayed for his last remaining army, but along with his hatred of the Germans was the knowledge that only they, in particular the valorous machine-gunners, could make any difference: Djemal's tempestuous passions and irreconcilable prejudices took over and he would not plead for help. On 30 September, he left all to their fate and fled Damascus. The antagonistic alliance had anyway fallen apart, with Turks and Germans fighting bloody battles in the streets over transport to escape in.

Like some comic Iago, a certain Ali Riza Pasha el Rikabi, a Baghdad Arab whose attainments included graduation from the Turkish Military Academy, a career in the Ottoman Army concluding with the rank of general and one-time command of a corps in Mesopotamia, now commanded the city's garrison as its military governor. The possibility had been recognised that his ultimate loyalties might waver and in an earlier, quieter time, Djemal Pasha himself had appointed him to this backwater.

He entered on his duties apparently with zeal, and on the fateful 30th he vanished. He reappeared to the British, however, galloping with his body-guard straight for the headquarters of the 4th Cavalry Division. At 2 am on 1 October, he breakfasted with General Barrow and laughed so heartily over how he had placed the heavy batteries in positions where they could not be served that he kicked over the breakfast table.

Day Twelve: 1–2 October

At 5 am on 1 October, Wilson commenced his move through Damascus. From Dumar, it was necessary to pass through the reeking Barada Gorge from end to end. The brigade were the first Australians to do so. One squadron had to clear the way for nearly an hour before the advance could start. The men were restricted to a walk by the wrecked vehicles, dead and wounded Turks and Germans, cattle and horses. Great numbers of wounded, not yet attended to, moaned and cried out. A flock of sheep driven by one of the columns were all dead and even the dogs had not escaped the fire. The brigade secured a troop train on the line with 480 live prisoners.

Lieutenant Colonel Todd's 10th Regiment led, with Major L.C. Timperley's squadron as advance guard, accompanied by Major A.C. Olden, second-in-command of the regiment. The terrible gorge could not dash their spirits for long on a morning of such promise. Gullett remarks that: 'The train at Dumar had contained, beside great wealth in gold and silver coin, a store of German cigars; and as the troops passed out of the gorge, and the sun-touched minarets of the city rose above the beautiful tangle of green gardens splashed with ripening fruit and gay with flowers, they blew forth clouds of smoke and seemed to have no thought beyond their keen relish of the moment'.

They followed the swift and swirling Barada River out of the gorge and along a dusty road on the left bank that seemed to lead into the city. A mud wall to their left gave way to high, sloping gardens that enclosed some of the richest homes in Damascus. There was a sudden burst of ragged fire — soon identified as no cause for alarm. A few shots came from some Turkish sniper, but the rest were exuberant greetings from Arabs.

Now committed to the entry, the squadron drew swords and kept them at the carry. Olden stepped up to a gallop, and in a dense cloud of dust they dashed for the city centre.

The road still ran beside the river and on the opposite bank, less than 200 yards away, they passed a three-storeyed fortress-like Turkish military barracks, and hospital, said to contain 12,000 men. The soldiers were just stirring. One or two scattered shots were heard: a troop of the 10th swerved to make a feint charge in their direction and the shooters lay low, allowing the galloping squadron to pass on.

At the Victoria Hotel they came to a bridge over the stream, and on the other side Olden and Timperley saw a great throng of people outside what seemed to be the building they were looking for: the Hall of Government or Town Hall, also called the Serai. Over the bridge they clattered, then through the shouting and gesturing crowd. People pointed the way, many eager hands seized their bridles and through the babble of welcoming voices they understood that they had come to the right place. The two majors dismounted and with drawn revolvers walked briskly up the marble steps.

They entered an ornate, imposing chamber. Olden later wrote in *Westralian Cavalry During the War* that 'a large gathering, clad in the glittering garb of eastern officialdom, stood formed up in rows. Their general demeanour was quiet and dignified. Behind a table, in a high-backed gold and plush chair, sat a small man of distinguished appearance wearing European clothes and a tarboosh.' This was Emir Said. He told Olden that he had been installed as governor when the Turkish civil governor fled the city the previous day, with Djemal Pasha.

Olden told him what he must have concluded himself: that Damascus was surrounded by many thousands of Chauvel's troops and resistance would be futile. Then he demanded safe conduct onwards for his troops and stated in return that the citizens of Damascus and their property would not be harmed.

The Emir replied, 'in the name of the civil population of Damascus, I welcome the British Army' and wrote out a formal document containing the assurances Olden required.

How sensible, orderly and dignified it had been, and how right Wilson was. Now, the brigade could get on with their other job of blocking the road to Homs and Aleppo.

They left the Serai before 7 am, with an Armenian colonel as guide to the onward march. Now more people were about and more were coming, as the good news spread. The Armenian could not be persuaded that the brigade wanted to get clear of the city and encouraged a triumphal progress, for the crowd's gratification. They were hysterical with delight and deliverance, for it was rumoured that the Germans, who had fired ammunition dumps overnight, intended to burn the whole city.

Olden said the people clung to the horses' necks, kissed the men's stirrups, showered confetti and rosewater over them, shouted, laughed, cried, sang and clapped. From windows, Moslem women raised their veils and called 'Meit allo wesahla! Meit allo wesahla!' (a hundred welcomes). The dusty troops in their big and battered hats, still with drawn swords, accepted the grapes and suffered the flowers and confetti, but showed no elation or excitement, rather patience and resignation as they guided their equally patient horses through. When the brigade finally cleared the city they at once deployed on the Homs road and rode hard after the enemy, it may be assumed with some relief.

Lawrence, dressed in gold and white robes and riding in a blue Rolls-Royce, arrived in Damascus two hours after Wilson had gone, but he maintained all his life that he had got there first. Some of his Arab irregulars did get into the city at night on the 30th, but vastly fewer than the 4000 they claimed and these were clandestine infiltrators, carrying no imprimatur, making no proclamation. On the other hand, Wilson thought so little of what he had done, merely a means to an end in his eyes, that he neither advised any superior of his intention nor sent any message of its execution. He was ordered to pursue the enemy, and going through Damascus was how he did it: he left no 'occupation' troops but spurred after the Turks with every man he had. The city was no longer of strategic importance since the 4th Turkish army remnant had fled.

Many underlying issues of the campaign and region came to a head in the tumultuous days after Damascus fell. The city was convulsed with international, racial and factional politics.

Chauvel was hurrying from Kaukab to take over the new domain. This, he recognised, would be less a fruit of victory and more an unmanageable political maelstrom. He would need above all political advice and was entitled to rely on Lawrence to deliver it in British best interests. His first reverse was that, having reached Barrow's HQ just south of the city limits, he learned that Lawrence, who had spent the last three days with Barrow, had departed early that morning without a word and, Barrow believed, made his entrance into the city.

A.J. Hill quotes Chauvel's notes on this time for an address he made to the Romani Dinner in 1923. He says he had to 'go after' Lawrence, and 'see what he was up to'. He found him at the door of the Serai 'in a magnificent Arab costume, which I believe cost him £250. With him was another magnificent person, whom he introduced as Shukri Pasha. Lawrence's excuse for his unceremonious departure from Barrow was that he thought I would like him to come at once and find out what the situation was, and that he had intended to come out immediately and tell me.'

He next told Chauvel that Shukri was the Civil Governor of Damascus. Shukri was obviously an Arab. Chauvel said, 'I want to see the Turkish Vali [governor]. Will you send for him at once?' Lawrence told him that the Vali had fled the day before and Shukri had been elected by a majority of the people.

There may have been two governors operating at the same time, then: Shukri and Emir Said, who had surrendered the city to Major Olden. Chauvel was unaware of this, but if Lawrence did not know he soon found out. Cyril Falls gives an account of seething Arab politics during this charged time: briefly, Lawrence declared Said's governorship dissolved, owing to the latter's hostility to Feisal. However, Shukri resigned within a few days — to be succeeded by the wily Ali Riza Pasha el Ribaki.

Chauvel now agreed to Shukri's appointment on behalf of the Commander-in-Chief. Lawrence then suggested to him that he should establish himself in the British Consulate. Chauvel opted for a clean orchard where he could pitch his camp. The next day, 'a bronzed, bearded individual in an Arab head-dress and a khaki uniform' appeared. He was the British supply officer to the Hejaz Forces, Captain (later Sir) Hubert Young. 'Before discussing supply matters, however, he proceeded to tell me of the mistakes I had made.'

Young said that Shukri Pasha had not been elected by a majority of the people, but only by a small faction — the Hejaz supporters. By endorsing him, Chauvel had virtually admitted the rule of King Hussein over Syria. The Arabs were minimising the British part in the conquest, in order to persuade the populace that it was they who had driven out the Turks. 'That is why,' Young said, 'Lawrence asked you to keep your men out of the city. And they have no intention of asking you for any police.' Chauvel had agreed to minimise the British forces' presence.

'They are getting the British Consulate ready for you. If you go there, you are not defining yourself as the conqueror of this country, but rather as a contributory ally. You should take possession of Djemel Pasha's house, which is the best one in the place and which they are reserving for Feisal.'

Young said there was absolute chaos in the city, as Chauvel observed on his drive in, on streets strewn with dead humans, camels and horses, with Arabs galloping about shooting indiscriminately, drunk with conquest and plunder. The bazaars were closed and all the more responsible and moderate people were terrified of the 'Hejaz crowd' being in charge. Young advised a show of military force as soon as possible.

Chauvel's notes continued: 'On that, I decided to have a march through the city on the following day ... and I took possession of Djemal's house.'

BOURCHIER, STILL LEADING THE 4TH AND 12TH LIGHT HORSE REGIMENTS, SPENT the night of the 30th near some gardens to the south-west of the city. At daylight, Hodgson had ordered him to probe forward. A squadron of the 4th came upon the huge Hamidieh Barracks, also now serving as a hospital: unknown to the squadron, Wilson's brigade must have passed it a

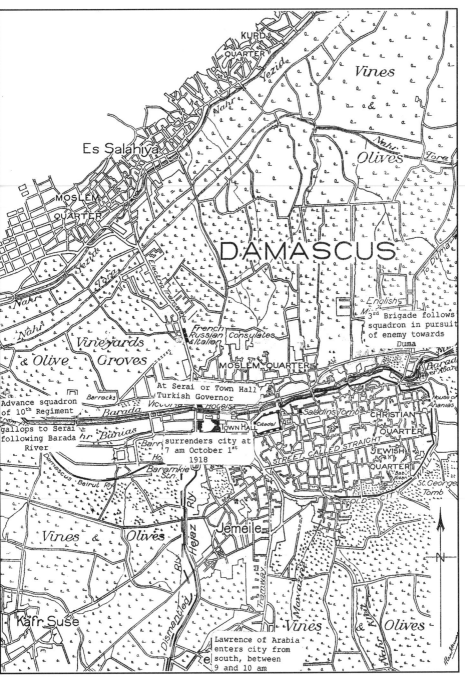

Capture of Damascus by 10th Australian Light Horse Regiment, 1 October 1918.

short time earlier, going into the city on the other river bank. Thousands of armed Turks were assembled, but although they showed no disposition to fight, the Australian squadron waited for the rest of the regiment to arrive before issuing a challenge. When the regiment appeared, about 12,000 Turks surrendered.

These fellows were in a dreadful state. Driven by Barrow's men and harassed by Feisal's, they had marched for ten days on short rations and most were ill with something: dysentery, malaria or typhus. The converted hospital was crammed and overflowing. When the 4th's troopers entered it, they found hundreds of rooms and thousands of beds, each one containing a dead Turk. Most of these had died from pneumonic influenza, which was now about to rampage through the Desert Mounted Corps. It seemed as if Damascus, taken with no battle casualties at all, would have its revenge on the victors with disease.

Major Jack Davies, apparently having left his liaison job with Barrow's division and returned to the 12th Regiment, writes again to his darling Mill:

As I write, the sun rises over Damascus and the Gardens this side, the place fell yesterday, or rather we got what looked like 10,000 prisoners out of it yesterday. There was no fight in them, these poor chaps are just on their last legs. They have been fairly run off their feet. I am quite OK now [he had contracted an illness]. They evacuated me to Tiberias but I got out again and managed to hang on for a day and got to the Jordan next morning, was better and by the time we got here yesterday, quite well again. I was most anxious to be in this show, and it was a great march if nothing else.

Chauvel wrote home: 'I wrote you last from Megiddo. Since then we've marched about 120 miles and I am now writing this on Djemal Pasha's desk in his own house in Damascus. We have had a glorious time, and the Chief, who motored from Tiberias to see us, has just told me that our performance is the greatest cavalry feat the world has ever known.' (Elyne Mitchell)

Starting at midday on 2 October, Chauvel led his divisions through the city. They stretched from end to end. Nearly every part of the Desert Mounted Corps was represented, including New Zealanders, who were not deployed there but must have been on detached duty from their ANZAC brigade. Twenty thousand mounted troops from so many parts of empires were indeed an impressive sight: the Indian Lancers, French Spahis, the British armoured cars, Horse Artillery and Yeomanry and the solid phalanx of hard-bitten Australians conveyed nothing so much as power. The Damascenes and Arabs watched them pass with awe and fear, and there was an immediate improvement in law and order. 'Damascus went back to work,' says Gullett. However, great difficulties still lay ahead for the troubled town.

Emir Feisal (left) and aide. DAVIES FAMILY ARCHIVE

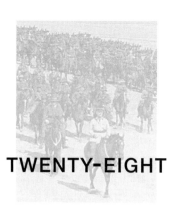

TWENTY-EIGHT

The Sleepless Fortnight:
the unheralded end

Wilson's 3rd Brigade had caught up with the enemy rearguard ten
miles from Damascus, near the village of Duma on the Homs road.
This ran through vineyards and olive groves, kinder country than the
hinterland they had come through, but it gave good cover to German
machine-gunners. However, the Australians quickly cleared the first nest
of two that offered resistance. Then a squadron of the 9th Regiment left
the road on a wide outflanking movement and closed on Duma from the
north-west. The enemy here were strong numerically but demoralised,
and a determined mounted advance disconcerted the German backbone
of resistance: after a brief exchange of fire they either surrendered or fled.
Five hundred prisoners including 40 Germans and 37 machine-guns
were captured.

The enemy made a stand again at Kusseir Khan, two miles further on.
This was secured by street fighting, some with the bayonet, and resulted in
another 160 prisoners and more of the inexhaustible machine-guns.

Next, a Turkish column 2000 strong could be seen seven miles away,
making for a pass in the hills near Khan Ayash. A squadron of the 9th

Regiment attempted to head them on their left, but were held up by machine-gun fire. The Australians then matched them with their own machine-guns and pressed closer.

Wilson was trying to work round this force when he was advised of enemy cavalry, 3000 strong, four miles away and closing from the northeast. His machine-gunners were on their last belts of ammunition and, as he was operating in isolation, no replenishment was possible. He called off the regiment from this attack but sent a squadron of the 8th forward to reconnoitre the new force. It was of no concern: a huge procession of camels was taking Arabs southward on their annual pilgrimage to Mecca.

Wilson's force had eaten their last rations and forage at dawn before entering the Barada Gorge, and were now compelled to fall back on Duma and bivouac, taking pot luck supplies from the locals. The fare was inadequate, but cold and hungry that night under bivvy sheets, they could have reflected on a historic and lively day that had yielded Damascus, seventeen more miles of territory, 750 prisoners and 80 machine-guns.

Day Thirteen: 2–3 October

At 6 am on the 2nd, the brigade marched on. A large number of enemy infantry were seen to the north, making briskly for a pass through the hills at Khan Ayash. Trotting through vineyards, Major Daly, temporarily in command of the 9th Regiment, came up on the left of this column, with the road to their right.

Against machine-gun fire, Daly rode on until the regiment was abreast of the column's centre. Then he sent forward two of his squadrons, one to seize the pass at Khan Ayash and the other to get astride the Homs road. He dismounted his remaining squadron and opened Hotchkiss and rifle fire at the column.

The advancing squadrons quickly secured their objectives. The Turks, seeing their retreat cut off, halted and appeared to have a debate around the head of their column. Daly remounted his squadron and charged. Shouting and brandishing their swords, the Australians influenced the debate decisively. All 2000 enemy threw down their arms. This was a tactically clever and dashing victory, taking less than an hour from first to last, but it was due mainly to the Turks' woeful conditions and hopeless prospects. In their brief parley, they had apparently opted for security, care and food from a benevolent enemy, rather than more hardships, dangers and forced marching to no avail.

Supplies for Wilson's brigade were now precarious, and with the prospects of improvement further on unlikely, his brigade was withdrawn to Kaukab. No-one knew it then, but the Australian Light Horse had fought their last action of the war.

It was not their last act of war, however: after the surrender, Light Horse signallers J.N. Smyth and N.C. Halliday of the 9th Regiment were riding back to regimental HQ when they stumbled on a party of three Germans and 85 Turks. A German officer was loading a machine-gun for action. The two signallers charged him on their horses: bombs were thrown at them but they overpowered the German and one turned the man's revolver on the Turks while the other trained the machine-gun on them. The whole party, cowed and despairing, surrendered.

Allenby had no thought of stopping the advance. The way was now clear right to Aleppo and he was determined to reach it while his men and horses could still travel. But it was a race against debilitation and sickness: every day now the Desert Mounted Corps numbers fell by scores as the men succumbed to disease and their effectiveness was diminishing so rapidly that a temporary halt to operations was imperative.

Damascus itself, however, was on the way to rehabilitation, largely through the work of Colonel Nuri Bey, Feisal's Chief-of-Staff. He organised restoration of the water supply, and as the days went by established control over the looters and rioters by his own strong-arm methods, largely freeing Chauvel's troops from routine policing. The streets were cleared of filth, electric lighting and telegraph lines were restored. New bank notes were printed in an attempt to put a brake on inflation. Fires were put out.

But already there was looming political unrest among the Arab leaders. On 3 October, Allenby came up from Tiberias to set the scene for resumption of the advance northwards and to settle a matter with Feisal and, incidentally, Lawrence.

The Arab leader's adherents had become politically active in the west and north of Syria, which the French and British governments had agreed was 'of special interest' to France. It was no part of the Allies' arrangements that the Hejaz movement should extend to here, but evidence was now coming in of Feisal's secret Arab committees in Beirut, Tripoli and other centres, of having seized governing bodies and raised the Hejaz flag. This irked the French, causing tension with the British, and Allenby was required to restore the status quo.

Chauvel was present at Allenby's meeting with Feisal at the Victoria Hotel, as were Lawrence, Nuri Bey and the other Chiefs-of-Staff of the principals. Chauvel's family made his notes on the occasion available to A.J. Hill and to posterity.

The Chief told Feisal that France was to be the protecting or mandatory power over Syria. Feisal, representing his father King Hussein, was to have the administration of Syria, less Palestine and the Lebanon province, under French guidance and financial backing.

The Arab sphere would include Syria only and Feisal would have nothing to do with Lebanon, which would extend from the northern boundary of Palestine (about Tyre) to the head of the Gulf of Alexandretta.

Feisal would forthwith have a French liaison officer who would for the present work with Lawrence and would give Feisal every assistance.

Feisal objected 'very strongly'. He said he knew nothing of France in the matter, that he understood from the adviser Allenby had given him (i.e., Lawrence) that the Arabs were to have the whole of Syria, including Lebanon but excluding Palestine, that a country without a port was no good to him and that he declined to have a French liaison officer or to recognise French guidance in any way.

The Chief turned to Lawrence. 'But did you not tell him the French were to have the protectorate over Syria?'

'No sir, I knew nothing about it,' said Lawrence.

'But you knew, definitely, that he, Feisal, was to have nothing to do with the Lebanon.'

'No sir, I did not.'

Addressing Feisal, Allenby told him that, as a lieutenant general under his command, he must obey orders. He must accept the situation as it had been explained and the matter would be finalised at the end of the war. Feisal then said he accepted it and left. Lawrence stayed behind.

Temporary Lieutenant Colonel Lawrence then told Field Marshall Viscount Allenby that he would not work with a French liaison officer either. He added that he was due for leave to England and thought he had better take it now.

According to Chauvel, the Chief said, 'Yes! I think you had!' and Lawrence left the room.

If these bewildering ambiguities, disjunctions and lies were representative of current political factors, then the acquisition of territory by the British had got so far ahead of how to deal with it that it courted disaster.

Chauvel's apparent position of ignorance is the most excusable. Allenby prescribed the breakneck advance of his corps commander without political advice, apparently heedless that he might act contrary to British policy in complex or delicate matters. Lawrence, as demonstrated under the press of events, could not be relied on to advise Chauvel properly and the Chief must have known it.

Allenby's muted reaction to Feisal's, and especially Lawrence's, mutinous rejection of French advisers is puzzling. Where was the famous explosion of temper?

Every record says that both Feisal and Lawrence were lying about future plans for Syria. To cite one authority, Cyril Falls' *Armageddon 1918* says the division of Syria proposed by Britain and France under the Sykes–Picot Agreement of 1916 'was already known to King Hussein and his sons' (Feisal and three others). If Feisal knew, Lawrence knew, and it was absurd to entertain their denials: how could they have planned or discussed the future with anyone in isolation of this agreement? Though eventually discarded, it was the future, then.

Lawrence's veneration of the Arabs came from mysticism, scholarship and study pre-war, and when this expertise was required, first in a junior military intelligence capacity and then as an emissary to and recruiter of Arab tribes at the age of 26, he was of great value. Miraculously, the man for the job fell into British laps. But he brought with him, or let himself assume, a political brief as well as a military one. He was a total convert to Arab causes and when these did not coincide with British causes he put himself in disloyal opposition. It worked out that way: no-one foresaw it.

But it was only in the last years of World War II that British Liaison Officers with anti-Japanese guerillas were schooled to have nothing to do with the political aspirations of their movements. They turned their backs and kept their distance. The common purpose started and ended with winning the war.

Lawrence left the Middle East and lobbied the British government at the highest levels. He found sympathetic ears, including Churchill's, but how could Britain repudiate her principal wartime ally? He took Feisal to the Conference at Versailles in 1919, but his detestation of the French was ill-concealed and the pair's ideas for improving their terms of Feisal's administration of Syria were dismissed. In conciliatory mood, Allenby arranged an audience for Lawrence with George V and, vainglorious to the last, he attended in flamboyant Arab costume. His Majesty demanded whether he considered it fitting to come into his presence wearing 'foreign uniform'.

No sooner had the occupation troops begun to rest and recuperate in Damascus than the full force of the malignant malaria and pneumonic influenza epidemics hit them. Cyril Falls records that hospital admissions for influenza in the Desert Mounted Corps were 1246 for the week ending 5 October and 3109 for the next week. In many regiments, more than half the men were laid low. Those who had contracted malaria in the Jordan Valley suffered relapses, while others who had merely passed along the river on their advance and been bitten by mosquitoes also succumbed. Beisan was the most virulent source of infection. On their final ride into Damascus, some men reeled in their saddles in high fever. All hands were run down by their blitzkrieg campaign and their natural resistance was gone. The British and Australian medical officers worked as they had never worked before, but were ravaged themselves. Of the six doctors in the 3rd Australian Light Horse Field Ambulance, only two were fit for duty, or rather, stayed on their feet: one was ill himself, but carried on.

Every army headquarters from corps down to squadron was, perforce, a hospital where the lucky ones lay on stretchers and the rest lay on the floor or under trees. Survivors of all the shot and shell from Gallipoli onwards died miserably in these places.

As well as the two main diseases, typhus was also rife, but its more pernicious twin, cholera, was checked by the herculean efforts of German medical officers with the Turkish Army who isolated any Turkish unit with a case. Only one British soldier caught it and, geographically, it was confined to cases in Tiberias.

The Turks having been defeated, Damascus was under Arab administration. The Turkish authorities may have suffered by comparison with Western nations' ideas of civic responsibility, but the Arabs, with rare exceptions such as Nuri Bey and a few Turkish-trained dragomans, simply had no concept of them. Their experience had been just of their own small, scattered settlements in the desert. The ways of a city of 250,000 people were beyond their ken. They were also indifferent to human suffering — especially of Turks — so Chauvel, with the agreement of Feisal, appointed Lieutenant Colonel E.M. Williams to control all Damascus hospitals. Williams had commanded the ANZAC mounted troops in France in 1916–17. (These were the 13th Light Horse Regiment, a squadron of the 4th Regiment and one of Otago Mounted Rifles. They served as Corps Mounted Troops to General Monash.)

The Turkish captives were dying at a rate of 170 a day. They had lost everything, including the will to live. Only the will of Allah mattered. Kismet, fatalism, turned their faces towards the Mohammedan Paradise of the next world.

They had to be got out of Damascus. There were 20,000 of them and 16,000 could still walk. These were marched down to Kaukab, where they were put in the care of Lieutenant Colonel Todd, who commanded the 10th Light Horse Regiment. When this phase of the offensive began, Todd himself was in hospital in Port Said, recovering from severe wounds, but he got out, found a friendly pilot to fly him to Jenin and resumed his command. His health remained indifferent, but after his regiment was withdrawn with Wilson's brigade from the Duma area to Kaukab, he set about succouring the Turks as commandant of their camp.

Brigadier General Wilson wrote: 'When we took the Turks over they were in a mob under some scattered palm trees near Kaukab on the bank of a creek. They had no cover for even the sick. There were a large number of officers with them, but they were also in a dazed condition and would not make the slightest effort to organise or ameliorate the condition of the men. Few of the men had blankets; they had no medical organisation. There were no drugs, bandages or food fit for sick men; no sanitation. Food for the prisoners was scarce.' He quoted the 170 per day death rate and continued:

> Lieutenant-Colonel Todd took the control of the compound in hand, and soon put a different complexion on the matter. Very little assistance could be obtained from the local Arab authorities of Damascus, who had taken possession of the Turkish army stores. They demurred from doing anything unless paid exorbitant rates in gold. However, by bluff and threats, blankets for the men were got

out of them; sheep were requisitioned from the surrounding country. Prisoners were organised into companies of 100 each under their own N.C.O.'s; arrangements were made for the daily cleaning of the area; three Syrian doctors were obtained from amongst the prisoners; the worst of the sick were removed under cover in a neighbouring village, and the daily death rate was reduced from 170 to fifteen. About 1,500 died during the period that we controlled that camp.

With Williams running the hospitals, Todd running the Turks' camp and an increasing flow of British medical supplies, slowly the tide turned.

Poor Todd died of illness himself, in Egypt in 1919, aged 46. Like many, he never recovered full fitness, but refused to give up the strenuous front-line service that sapped his strength to the point of no return.

TWENTY-NINE

The last post

The campaign's end came almost as a formality, but it was accomplished 'with rare ambition and resolution' on the part of Allenby, Gullett says.

It was the 5th Cavalry Division's turn to lead, and on 5 October, Macandrew took the main rail and road route from Damascus, via Baalbek and Homs towards Aleppo, 200 miles away. Having been in reserve, the 5th was less jaded and was suffering least of the three divisions through illness. Barrow's 4th Division followed Macandrew, while the Australian Mounted Division remained in occupation of Damascus. The only Australian element of Macandrew's force was the No. 1 Light Car Patrol. The Arabs, striking out on the right of the cavalry, were to join up with the advance at Homs.

The leaders were aware that the supply difficulties experienced by Wilson's 3rd Light Horse Brigade north of Damascus would also be critical for them, and Allenby's 'rare ambition' was to seize a port on the coast, from which the men and horses could be sustained. Beirut was chosen: it lay only 30 miles from Baalbek on a main road and was nearly halfway to Homs.

All went well. Two days before Macandrew set out, General Bulfin's 7th (Meerut) Infantry Division marched for Beirut and Haifa. Progress of the cavalry was rapid, with the enemy estimated to be 20,000 strong, but of unknown fighting strength, withdrawing before Macandrew all the way to Homs, which was reached on 15 October. An armoured car reconnaissance to Beirut found the enemy had already abandoned the port and French

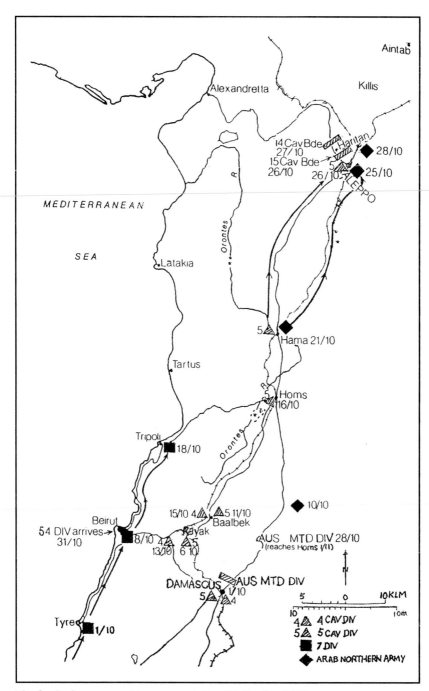

The final advances: positions at armistice, 30 October 1918.

warships were in it. The Indian infantry had also arrived, with subsequent relief of transport and supply problems for the cavalry divisions.

Aleppo was still 100 miles away. With an anxious eye on the fitness of his mounted troops, Allenby ordered a rapid resumption of the march. He was almost too late. Both cavalry divisions were suffering, but Barrow's 4th were in dire straits. They could not keep up and by 20 October, when Macandrew left Homs, they were still at Baalbek, with not enough fit men to attend even the horse lines and a fighting strength of 1200, against 2500 of the 5th. When the 4th did move, the riderless horses had to be driven, not led.

Further offensive action by the collapsing division was impossible. Chauvel withdrew them to Damascus and ordered the Australian Mounted forward. Hodgson force-marched from Damascus on 27 October. On the eve of reaching Homs on the 31st, news came that an armistice had been concluded with the Turks.

The word travelled head-to-tail down the hurrying squadrons and there was an almost imperceptible relaxation; a slackening of reins, an easing of shoulders, a slight slump. The hoofbeats momentarily slowed. Then attention returned to the day and the hour and to reaching Homs before daylight and they picked up the rate again. Their armistice march covered 50 miles.

Indians, British and French took it similarly, with only a moment's pause. All were too wrung out to celebrate and too unnerved by tragedy. In Damascus, they had been shaken by the thousands of non-combat deaths and left depressed and weary beyond expression. Only at the next halt, and in quiet moments of the next weeks and months, did they allow themselves to dwell on the fact with utter thankfulness. It was over.

The expression of it in letters was in the same vein. My father wrote from hospital, 'Well, the job is finished at last, it has been a long and hard one, but I was always sure of victory. I only hope we won't be too lenient in the winding up'.

General Sir Phillip Chetwode to his friend Chauvel:

I do congratulate you on your ably conducted and historic ride to Damascus and on all the rest of the performance of your cavalry in this epoch-making victory ... We did our part with the infantry, but it was the cavalry who put the lid on the Turks' aspirations forever.

Heaven send that now the Germans are talking peace, we shall show them no mercy.

Macandrew, and the Arabs, had appeared before Aleppo on the 22nd. He had been ordered to wait for the Australian Mounted, but protested that he should push on, and Allenby agreed. Under a flag of truce, he sent a note to the Turkish commander demanding his surrender. The reply said, 'The Turkish Commander of the Garrison of Aleppo does not find it necessary to reply to your note'. Macandrew had only a brigade and some armoured cars with him and was now obliged to wait, for the garrison appeared to be strong. The armistice intervened.

All the conquered lands from the Suez Canal to Aleppo and beyond were now British mandated territory and it was recognised that the Australians and New Zealanders, volunteers from other countries, need have no part in its policing. This was to be the task of British forces, whose service in the region was anyway comparatively brief.

The Australian Mounted Division marched west to a well-found camp in Tripoli, to await passage home. The ANZAC Mounted Division joined them from Richon le Zion and Wady Hanein. The ANZACs had suffered even more severely from influenza and malaria. The 1st and 2nd Light Horse Brigades and the New Zealand Brigade had alone borne all the privations since crossing the Suez Canal and were the least robust of all troops.

The months at Tripoli passed in organised time-killing: training, lectures and classes, guided tours to the Cedars of Lebanon. The men were patient. Officers and men were still dying of disease, yet so far as pneumonic influenza, or Spanish flu, was concerned, so were many people around the world.

At the end of November, the Dardanelles and Constantinople were occupied and the Australians and New Zealanders were requested to provide two token regiments for the Gallipoli occupation force. Jaded as they were, all regiments bid for the honour of revisiting the sacred ground: the 7th Light Horse and the Canterbury Mounted Rifles were chosen. Colonel Richardson of the 7th wrote that it was 'a great honour indeed to be the one regiment of the A.I.F. to represent Australia in revisiting the graves of fallen comrades at Anzac'. Every endeavour was made to smarten up the regiment and many expedients were resorted to to acquire new uniforms, hats and equipment. Colonel J.M. Arnott, a former CO of the regiment, made available £20 from the Cinema Fund for 'boot polish and metal polish to brighten up the service-worn gear'.

The two regiments spent three winter months, including Christmas, camped on Gallipoli and, predictably, influenza hit them again. My father followed the fortunes of his old regiment from Moascar in Egypt: 'We don't get much news of the Regiment, but they are still on Gallipoli. A good many of them have been taken ill and some have died of pneumonia. One of our best officers who was never sick for a day while the war was on, died almost as soon as they got there. It was a sad mistake to take worn-out men there in such a season.' The deceased officer was Lieutenant J. Dalton. Coincidentally, Colonel Richardson, who was wounded three times but suffered no illnesses throughout the war, caught pneumonia on Gallipoli.

However, the letter-writer was apparently fit again and waiting to go home:

> I am carrying on here as squadron sergeant major, we have many men in camp and they are all champing at the bit and heartily sick and tired of parades, drills etc. However, all things come to those who wait.
>
> We had a pretty lively Christmas and a remarkably fine dinner, there are a good many sergeants here and we have a good mess, of which I have recently been appointed president.

This was my father's last letter from the army. He seemed to be enjoying his recovered health and his status as a pioneer old hand and senior NCO. How rosy life's prospects must have seemed.

The two ANZAC regiments returned to Palestine and a camp at Rafa in mid-January 1919. Revisiting old sites, tending graves and (at last) seeing Constantinople had broken up their long wait to go home.

On a November night of the old year, in the Desert Mounted Corps camp then near Ludd, a New Zealand trooper was awakened by the snatching of a bag he was using as a pillow from under his head. He sprang up and saw an Arab running from the tent with it. He gave chase, shouting to the pickets on the horse lines as he went. He gained on the thief and was about to tackle him when the man turned, shot him in the chest with a pistol and made good his escape. The trooper died just as the pickets reached him.

The camp was immediately aroused. Grim and purposeful, the New Zealanders followed the Arab's footsteps in the soft sand to the village of Surafend, a notorious nest of brazen thieves: the stolen item was one of many. But this was murder. Some ANZACs were shot by Arabs before and after the armistice. Over three years, the troops' frustration and resentment had mounted and now it would erupt.

British policy to native peoples of invaded territory was a model of enlightenment. The army paid its way. Native custom, habit and, especially, religion — those of Moslim persuasion were always presumed to be devout — were to be respected and resolution of issues tended to favour those imposed on. It was fiercely resented by troops being robbed blind, having their wounded killed and their dead dug up for the clothes they wore, being reported on by enemy spies and having artillery fire directed on them by de facto forward observers. They could not but chafe under orders that appeared to give greater consideration to hostile Bedouins than to themselves. The rarefied political approach of the authorities could never be reconciled with the private soldier's lot.

The New Zealanders threw a strong cordon around Surafend and guarded it all night. No Arab was allowed to leave. At daylight, they summoned the village chiefs and demanded the surrender of the murderer. The chiefs pleaded ignorance and innocence.

General Chaytor sent a senior staff officer to GHQ to impress upon Allenby's staff the strength of the men's resolve, and he ordered another senior officer to 'take charge' of the cordon rather than court outright disobedience of an order to break it up. However, GHQ ordered it broken up. Chaytor went to GHQ himself to elaborate on the inflamed passions of his troops and the necessity to apprehend the murderer immediately. His view was that it was a job for the military police, backed up by troops if necessary. GHQ repeated their order. Chaytor could only obey.

At least he must have been relieved to see his own order obeyed. The men walked away from the cordon. Then a stream of Arabs who no doubt included the quarry poured from the village and the troops' bitter temper hardened once more: they would have retribution, no matter what.

All day, the New Zealanders, now aided and abetted by the Australians, quietly prepared for Operation Surafend and that night, with Australians in support, marched 'many hundreds strong' into the village. Stony-faced, they passed out the women and children, then armed mainly with heavy batons and pieces of wood, fell on the men. Some 30 Arabs were clubbed to death and few escaped injury. The village was razed, then fired. Gullett records that 'The flames from the wretched houses lit up the countryside, and Allenby and his staff could not fail to see the conflagration and hear the shouts of the

313

troops and the cries of their victims'. Having disposed of Surafend, the ANZACs fired a neighbouring Bedouin camp, then went back to their lines.

'In the morning,' continues Gullett, 'all the disciplinary machinery of the army was as active as hitherto it had been tardy.' Presumably the machinery included the military police: none had put in an appearance. GHQ demanded the names of those who had attacked the village and done the killing. The ANZACs said nothing. Not a single individual could be identified and charged.

Allenby wasted no more time. The division was assembled dismounted in a hollow square and the Commander-in-Chief lived up to his reputation by letting them know what he thought of them. He called them murderers, which they were, and cowards, which they were not. It was argued that his formidable tongue made things worse, piling insult on injury: the men would have accepted strong disciplinary action, but they rejected abuse. A.J. Hill quotes officers who were present and the correspondence of a soldier. Allenby said the killing of the natives was a worse atrocity than any the Turks committed and their good name was gone. He was 'no longer proud' of them, 'at which the boys laughed', wrote the soldier, 'and he immediately rode away … We had to march in full order over a mile either way for this affair and the boys would have counted him out if he had not galloped away.'

The division were marched to a camp at Rafa where they were to be confined until repatriation, but that was countermanded when the Light Horse were needed to quell an Egyptian rebellion in March 1919. The Chief's encomiums about his troops now pointedly avoided the name of ANZAC and he withdrew all outstanding recommendations for decorations in the division. Chauvel kept pressing for these awards to be made as late as 1921.

In mid-1919, the 2nd Light Horse Brigade and the New Zealand Brigade were on the eve of departure, but no word of farewell or recognition had come from Allenby. Gullett says Allenby 'was visited by an Australian who pointed out to him the unsatisfactory position which existed. He expressed surprise at the feeling engendered by his speech' though he did not resile from any word of it. The Australian was Sir Henry Gullett himself and his approach resulted in a 'glowing and appreciative farewell order to the Australians'. It said:

I knew the New South Wales Lancers and the Australian Horse well in the Boer War, and I was glad to meet some of my old friends of those days when the light horse came under my command just two years ago.

When I took over command of the Egyptian Expeditionary Force in July, 1917, the light horse were already veterans, tried and proved in many a fight. Since then, they have shared in the campaigns which achieved the destruction of the Turkish army and the conquest of Palestine and Syria, and throughout they have been in the thick of the fighting. I have found them eager in advance and staunch in defence. At Beersheba, a mounted charge by a light horse regiment armed only with rifles, swept across Turkish trenches and decided the day. Later, some of the regiments were armed with swords, which they used with great effect in the pursuit of last autumn.

On foot, too, they have equally distinguished themselves as stubborn fighters. They have shown in dismounted action the dash and enterprise of the best type of light infantry.

The Australian light Horseman combines with a splendid physique a restless activity of mind. This mental quality renders him somewhat impatient of rigid and formal discipline, but it confers upon him the gift of adaptability, and this is the secret of much of his success mounted or on foot. In this dual role, on every variety of ground — mountain, plain, desert, swamp or jungle — the Australian light horseman has proved himself equal to the best.

He has earned the gratitude of the Empire and the admiration of the world.

There was no mention of New Zealanders.

Soon after the Armistice, General Hodgson handed over the Australian Mounted Division to the newly promoted Major General Ryrie. Hodgson had commanded the division since it was formed in 1917 of half Yeomanry and half Light Horse as the Imperial Mounted Division, and thus confounded those (mostly politicians) who would insist that Australian officers lead Australian men. Chauvel's view was that mixed nationals learned from each other and said the men didn't care where their commander came from, as long as he knew his job. Hodgson was proof of that.

Ryrie had chafed at both Hodgson's and Chaytor's preferment to himself. Chauvel thought he was too much the politician at times — notably when he had taken leave in England to attend a parliamentary conference, leaving Galloping Jack Royston to handle both his own and Ryrie's brigade at the Battle of Romani. Chaytor was a regular soldier and more suited by training and experience for greater responsibility, and as a New Zealander it was fitting for him to have a 'turn' commanding the ANZACs. Ryrie simply had to wait until one of them moved; and Hodgson's return to England created the vacancy.

Chauvel compensated his gifted, shrewd and popular new commander for his long wait with a recommendation for a knighthood along with the promotion.

Ryrie had an opportunity to deploy his division on active service, after all. Just as the Light Horse handed in their equipment and were concentrating at Kantara for passage home, an Egyptian seditious movement, that would now be called an independence movement, broke out in open revolt. The rebels were saboteurs and threatened to paralyse Egypt's roads, railways and telegraphic communications.

There was little fighting to do, but because of the spread of the rebels country-wide, large numbers of troops were needed to contain them and the remaining British units were too few. The men had no great heart for it, but re-armed and saddled up again without complaint. The revolt was soon put down, Wilson's famous 3rd Brigade distinguishing itself again for its work around Zagazig.

This spell of peace-making delayed their embarkation for two months, but before the 1919 summer ended the Australian force was on its way. The long journey of the 2nd Brigade of ANZACs ended on 3 August, when HMT *Madras* entered Sydney Heads on what Colonel Richardson described as 'a beautiful, bright morning': 'The 6th and 7th Regiments were disembarked at 2.30 pm and our good old comrades of the 5th proceeded by train to Brisbane next day. The officers and men of the Regiment were driven in motor-cars to the ANZAC Buffet, where friends and relatives were met.'

The last word is reserved for Richardson. Writing in 1923, he says:

> One's memory goes back to the varied scenes and battles and pictures arise that even the years will not efface. The long, hot marches of the desert, the attempted surprise at Bir el Abd, or Salmana in the grey dawn, the fog-enshrouded wadis and the gallop which captured the

Turkish Divisional Commander at the first Battle of Gaza ...
Beersheba and the gallop for the Hebron Road ... the Jordan and the
long toiling up the goat tracks to the uplands of Moab to fight bloody
battles; Ziza, with its Gilbertian setting of friends and enemies in a
common defence.

Weighing up his concluding lines, he might have pondered the sadness of
things passing and the legends of the brave unceremoniously stowed away
by time. An unmanageable disquiet could have seized him that they had
ventured too much for too little: one of his statistics was that to keep the
regiment going with between 400 and 500 fit men, 4000 had had to pass
through its ranks.

But he would not end on that note:

And now, alas, the Regiment is no more; officers and men are
scattered all over Australia — old friends — none more truer than
those who have stood the test in battle — in many cases, to meet no
more. Yet it is something, and always will be something, to have lived
those years and to have been a soldier in the most efficient body of
mounted troops the world has ever known — the Desert Mounted
Corps.

He lays down his pen. It is unwise, and unsoldierly, to indulge grief,
whatever the heart says.

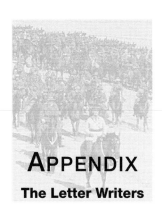

Appendix

The Letter Writers

Major Nathaniel Dunbar Barton, MiD, CBE, was born in 1894. He interrupted medical studies to join the 7th Light Horse Regiment in 1914 as a second lieutenant and served on Gallipoli and in Sinai and Palestine. Promoted to major in command of C Squadron at 23, he was severely wounded at the Battle of Amman 1918 and repatriated to Australia.

Barton graduated in medicine, married Mary Mort, and commenced practice in Lithgow. He preserved his army links as citizen-soldier, commanding 6th Light Horse Regiment, 1935–40. In 1937 he was second-in-command of the Coronation Contingent for the coronation of King George VI and rode in the Sovereign's Mounted Escort.

From 1940 to '46 Barton was a lieutenant colonel in the Army Medical Corps and served in Darwin, New Guinea and Borneo. He was promoted to colonel, became Assistant Director, Medical Services, of the 11th Division, and was later awarded the CBE. On discharge, he resumed practice in Wellington, NSW, where he died, aged 91, leaving four children.

MAJOR JACK RUPERT CYRIL DAVIES, MC, WAS BORN in 1883. A grazier in the Scone district, in 1915 he embarked for Egypt as a captain with the 12th Light Horse Regiment. To his disappointment, he remained in Egypt on residual duties while the 12th went to Gallipoli. Subsequently, his mounted service in Sinai, Palestine and Syria was uninterrupted by wounds or sickness.

Awarded the Military Cross for leading the left front of the Beersheba charge, Davies was the first Australian into the town. Promoted to major, he commanded B Squadron until hostilities ceased.

Davies had married Mildred Traill before the war, by which time they had three children. The family moved to Cairo during the war and Mildred, with other English and Australian wives, helped nurse wounded troops. Under this scheme, serving husbands could see their families when they got leave to Cairo. Mildred filled positions as liaison officer between Red Cross and Australian army hospitals and was in charge of medical supplies for military hospitals in Egypt. In 1919 she was awarded the MBE for this work.

As Lieutenant Colonel (Militia), Jack Davies commanded the 12/16 Light Horse Regiment, 1927–32. In World War II he served full time again as second-in-charge of recruitment in NSW, then as liaison officer for troops with the ship's complement on board the troopship *Queen Mary*. He made three voyages, two to the Middle East and one to Singapore with the ill-fated 8th Division.

Davies retired from the army in 1943 and died aged 73, leaving Mildred and four children.

SERGEANT BYRON (JACK) BALY, MM, WAS BORN IN 1887. On the outbreak of war he returned to Australia from Argentina and joined the Light Horse in April 1915. He sailed to Egypt as a reinforcement for the 7th Light Horse Regiment and went to Gallipoli in October.

Baly's regiment pioneered the Sinai front as part of the 2nd Brigade, ANZAC Mounted Division. He served in Major Barton's C Squadron, and while neither correspondent mentions the other their accounts are complementary, notably on the Battle of Amman 1918. Barton and other squadron officers were wounded and Baly was awarded a Military Medal. The citation reads in part: 'owing to the loss of three squadron officers, it looked as if the line would fall back. Sergeant Baly did very excellent work rallying the men under heavy fire and induced them by his example to hold on. His conduct was most gallant throughout the operations.'

One of many ANZAC troops evacuated from the Jordan Valley with malaria in the 1918 summer, Baly was recommended for a commission, but on return to active duty was immediately hospitalised again after an eye accident and the end of the war overtook this promotion.

On return home, he married Kate Deuchar and they had three children. In his last years, Baly was striving to make his way in various enterprises, but all were unsuccessful and he took his life aged 47. War experiences and the Depression are likely contributory causes.

ACKNOWLEDGMENTS

Initiation came very early. Sprawled on the floor with Sir Henry Gullett's Official History, I would say: 'Did your regiment capture a Turkish *General*, Dad?'

'Yes, it did. That was at Gaza. The Light Horse were surrounding it and these four fellows …'

It was always 'the Light Horse' or 'the brigade' or 'the regiment,' never 'I' or 'we'. Pressed repeatedly on the Military Medal, he affected a sort of Amos 'n' Andy patois and said it was for 'climbin' up a tree and fallin' down and scratchin' ma nose'.

I found some .303 bullets in the sandy butts of a disused rifle range. He hefted them in his hand, exclaiming softly.

Mother said, 'I don't know how you could be so interested in those frightful things'.

He drawled, 'If you'd had 'em whistlin' past your ears and diggin' in the ground at your feet, you'd be interested in 'em, too'.

'Well, I suppose so.'

He and I had to get around her resistance to 'filling the child's head with war stories'. She and my sister went to see a film called *Magnificent Obsession*, about a woman's undying sacrificial love for a blind man, while we settled down with Gullett and the 5th and 7th Regiments' gallop for the Hebron road. He got the rounds of the kitchen for that, too, and told me to tone down my somewhat pointed appreciation. We didn't really have such a terrific time as I was making out, did we?

So the seed was planted. Seven decades later, it has had this unlikely flowering in competition with the overshadowing, irrepressible — but still beautiful — Gallipoli flower.

Mine would never have bloomed without help.

I am grateful to the Department of Veterans' Affairs for financial assistance towards the work, under the 'Their Service – Our Heritage'

programme for 2000. At the Light Horse Association Federation Camp in
Toowoomba in 2002, I was able to thank personally the then Minister for
Veterans' Affairs, Bruce Scott, for the grant.

A disproportionate number of Light Horse leaders, and good regiments,
came from Queensland. It is no wonder the Light Horse Association is
headquartered there and I owe another debt of gratitude to a member,
Captain Adele Catts, who as curator of the (now armoured) 2nd/14th Light
Horse Regiment's Museum allowed me to select photographs from this
archive for publication.

My old friend Admiral John Stevens, through academic work since his
retirement, has come to enjoy a reputation for critical acumen, and
consented to read my manuscript. He is responsible for a better book.

Of great value has been the work of two other modern writers on the
Light Horse. Ian Jones, the Victorian journalist, knew and talked to the
'gentle' old soldiers of the Victorian regiments, accumulating a store of oral
history and practical knowledge about how a mounted force works and
fights, which he published in *The Australian Light Horse* in 1987. The other
writer is the soldier and scholar Alec (A.J.) Hill, who wrote Chauvel's
biography and who personally guided me on aspects of my book. If they
had not written their books, mine would be the poorer.

I am grateful for permission to quote Patsy Adam-Smith's *The Anzacs*
and to the Richardson family, through Mrs J.T. Richardson of Raymond
Terrace, for licence to use Major General J.D. Richardson's history of the
7th Light Horse.

The estate of Chauvel's daughter, Elyne Mitchell, has allowed me to
quote from her book, *Light Horse: The Story of Australia's Mounted Troops*.
Excerpts from *The Desert Column* by Ion Idriess are included with
permission of publishers ETT Imprint of Sydney.

Cyril Falls' *Armageddon 1918* (Weidenfeld and Nicolson 1964)
provided the broad background for the story of the British Middle East
campaign. Attempts to trace the copyright holder of this book, including
enquiries by the Orion Publishing Group Ltd in UK, have been
unsuccessful.

The bound collected letters of Major Jack Davies and Major Nat Barton
are recent additions to the Australian War Memorial archive. Along with
my father's letters, they tell the story of the Light Horse from three
individual perspectives. Mrs Elsie Ritchie (née Davies) of Ermington,

together with Mrs Sue Hawker of Grafton and Robyn Barclay of Narromine (both née Barton), joined forces with me to set these stories against family and personal backgrounds and enhance them. To these collaborators go my thanks.

My sister-in-law Marjorie traced some of my father's letters in the Mitchell Library and made copies. They were quoted by Professor Bill Gammage in *The Broken Years*.

The maps are based on those in A. J. Hill's *Chauvel of the Light Horse*, drawn by Wendy Gorton. Simplified versions, with contemporary spelling to conform to the text, were adapted for *Horseman, Pass By*, by artist Pat Hollis: another voluntary, demanding task.

In the same spirit, Peter Dalkin offered help when the IT dimension failed me. Without him, all, and I mean the whole MS, would have been lost.

In the Australian War Memorial, the terse brevity of Light Horse Regiments' War Diaries, such as the 12th Regiment's, quoted on the most desperate fighting of the failed Es Salt raid, evoked the immediacy and pressures under which they were written.

I wrote and read at leisure, however, and consulted much: Lord Birdwood's manuscripts, Chandler's letters, Gullett's notes and, in the National Library, the letters to his wife of Sir Granville Ryrie — surely the most colourful of all those BIG men, individualists all, who led the force.

Geoff Brewster's staff in the Research Centre lived up to the War Memorial's reputation for ready and intelligent help. I mention specially those who handle the online data bases: my needs in the photographic area were well catered for and I thank particularly Curator Ian Afflick for releasing to me the cover photograph, since it was at the time withdrawn for reprocessing.

One of the Memorial's subtleties now seems to be an emergent patina of age. After all, it signposts our history since before the last century — we can talk of centuries now. A little of our raw Australian newness fades.

The visitor walks the corridors and halls with pride and pity and with a sense that *they* are close by, seeing us as we see what ghastliness befell *them*. C.E.W. Bean wrote nothing more prescient than his inscription at the entrance: 'Here are their spirits …'

Every effort has been made to gain permission to quote from *Westralian Cavalry During the War: The Story of the 10th Light Horse Regiment* by A.C.N. Olden, but without success. The publishers would be pleased to hear from the copyright holder of this work.

Lindsay Baly,
Byron Bay, NSW,
December 2002

SELECT BIBLIOGRAPHY

Adam-Smith, Patsy, *The Anzacs*, Thomas Nelson, 1978.

Barclay, Robyn, ed., *Nat D. Barton's Letters Home, 1914–1918*, self-published, 1999.

Bean, C.E.W., *The Story of Anzac*, Vol. II, *Official History of Australia in the War of 1914–18*, Angus & Robertson, 1940.

Bennett, Jack, *Gallipoli*, Angus & Robertson, 1981.

Carlyon, Les, *Gallipoli*, Pan Macmillan, 2001.

Conway, Ronald, *The End of Stupor*, Sun Books, 1984.

Denton, Kit, *Gallipoli Illustrated*, Rigby, 1981.

Falls, Cyril, *Armageddon 1918*, Weidenfeld & Nicolson, 1964.

Frame, Tom, *The Shores of Gallipoli: Naval Aspects of the Anzac Campaign*, Hale & Iremonger, 2000.

Gammage, Bill, *The Broken Years*, Penguin, 1975.

Gullett, H.S., *Sinai and Palestine*, Vol. VII, *Official History of Australia in the War of 1914–18,* Angus & Robertson, 1923.

Gullett, H.S., and Barrett, Charles, eds, *Australia in Palestine*, Angus & Robertson, 1919.

Hammond, Ernest, *History of the 11th Light Horse Regiment*, William Brooks & Co., 1942.

Hill, Alec, *Chauvel of the Light Horse*, Melbourne University Press, 1978.

Idriess, Ion, *The Desert Column*, Angus & Robertson, 1932.

Jones, Ian, *The Australian Light Horse*, Time Life Books, 1987.

Lawrence, T.E., *The Seven Pillars of Wisdom*, Jonathan Cape, 1976.

Mitchell, Elyne, *Light Horse: The Story of Australia's Mounted Troops*, Macmillan, 1978.

Olden, A.C.N., *Westralian Cavalry During the War: The Story of the 10th Light Horse Regiment*, Alexander McCubbin, 1921.

Preston, the Hon. R.M.P., *The Desert Mounted Corps*, Constable, 1921.

Richie, Elsie, *Crusaders of the Southern Cross*, self-published, 1999.

War Diaries at the Australian War Museum, Canberra.

INDEX

Ranks shown after surnames of officers and men are the highest known rank attained by the individual.

Index